The Pack of Autolycus

THE PACK OF AUTOLYCUS

OR

Strange and Terrible News

Of Ghosts, Apparitions, Monstrous Births, Showers of
Wheat, Judgments of God, and other Prodigious
and Fearful Happenings as told in
Broadside Ballads of the Years
1624–1693

EDITED BY

HYDER EDWARD ROLLINS

Cambridge, Massachusetts
HARVARD UNIVERSITY PRESS

DISTRIBUTED IN GREAT BRITAIN BY OXFORD UNIVERSITY PRESS, LONDON

PUBLICATION OF THIS BOOK HAS BEEN AIDED
BY A GRANT FROM THE HYDER EDWARD ROLLINS FUND

LIBRARY OF CONGRESS CATALOG CARD NUMBER 27-4308

SBN 674-65125-1

PRINTED IN THE UNITED STATES OF AMERICA

Who makes a ballad for an ale-house door,
Shall live in future times for evermore!

THE RETURN FROM PARNASSUS.

PREFACE

THE ballad-collection of Anthony Wood, the celebrated Oxford antiquarian, is preserved in Bodley's Library, and (according to his biographer's statement) consists at the present time of only 279 separate broadsides. These are scattered through eight volumes, and are, on the whole, poorly arranged and poorly preserved. For the poor arrangement Wood himself is to blame, as the broadsides have remained unchanged since he pasted them on the pages haphazardly and carelessly. Far different was the care with which Pepys arranged and bound his volumes. But Wood was a prince of collectors. Ballads interested him immensely, and as soon as he had bought a new specimen he customarily jotted down some note on it, and pasted it in any volume that happened to be at hand; whereas the evidence goes to show that Pepys bound his ballads only after his collection was almost complete.

Wood's 279 ballads seem almost pitiful when compared to the some 1800 that make up the five volumes once owned by Pepys. But the difference in these figures is altogether misleading. And although numbers alone have caused Pepys generally to be regarded as the most notable of collectors, he should at least share that distinction with Wood.

For one reason, Pepys based his collection upon that of John Selden, which he either bought or "borrowed." He claims to have added many older pieces to Selden's nucleus. The title-page of his first volume reads: "My Collection of Ballads. . . . Begun by Mr Selden; Improved by ye addition of many Pieces elder thereto in Time; and the whole continued to the year 1700. . . ." But this statement is misleading. The collection falls into two definite groups: in the main, the first volume contains only ballads printed before 1640, the last four volumes only ballads that date from 1675 to 1700. The gap between 1640 and 1675 gives away Pepys's secret. Selden died in 1654, so that clearly he was responsible for all, or nearly all, the printed ballads in volume I: Pepys himself apparently took little interest in ballads (as the almost complete silence of his diary indicates) until about 1675. From 1680 to the end of his life he collected assiduously, and for the reigns of James II and William and Mary his collection is matchless.

Wood, on the contrary, throughout his life was a persistent collector. He began when he was a boy, amusing himself by filling the margins of his broadsides with imitations of the woodcut pictures and with scribbled reproductions of lines that struck his fancy. His books and manuscripts, too, are full of jottings about ballads, which he continued to buy until his death in 1695. Though fate has scattered his collection widely, the fact is that at his death it was very large — possibly the largest in existence and certainly a worthy rival in every particular to that of Pepys.

In *The Shirburn Ballads* (1907) Mr. Andrew Clark, Wood's biographer, has produced evidence tending to prove that the greater part of the Roxburghe collection in the British Museum and all of Rawlinson's 217 ballads in the Bodleian came by theft from Wood. He thinks it probable, furthermore, that the three volumes of John Bagford's collection in the British Museum were stolen from Wood, pointing out that one entire volume of Wood's ballads which was in the Ashmole Museum when the catalogue was made in 1710 had disappeared when the collection was recatalogued in 1837.

Even as it stands, Wood's collection, though small in bulk, is one of the most valuable and most interesting of all. About 210 of the ballads are unique, and the thieves did their work so

PREFACE

ignorantly that what remains in the collection is not matched elsewhere. Thanks only to it we may know of what is in some respects the most picturesque period in the history of the ballad — the period between 1660 and 1675.

Wood's taste seems to have run particularly to ballads of strange and marvelous news. To turn his pages is to get a vivid impression of the horrors, the marvels, the superstitions that made the wares of Autolycus so fascinating to Dorcas and Mopsa. A number of Wood's ballads (five are reprinted in my *Pepysian Garland*, 1922) deal with marvels that occurred, or were supposed to have occurred, before 1640. It is peculiar that John Selden failed to get copies of them, for his inclination, also, was toward rhymes in which marvels and criminals were featured. Sir Charles Firth once remarked to me that perhaps Selden remained unmarried because he was so deeply impressed by the many ballads he found about murderous women! Possibly the same explanation might account for Wood's celibacy — though he was an extremely crusty and disagreeable man long before the age at which the adjective "old" could appropriately have described him as a bachelor.

Comparatively few Commonwealth ballads are in Wood's collection, but more than are in Pepys's. During the years that immediately followed the Restoration, however, Wood bought a large number of ballads, and it is chiefly these that enable one to know what type of subject was most esteemed after 1660. From 1660 to 1675 Wood's collection is especially noteworthy. Nowhere else is there such a delightful assortment of strange and wonderful news. It is curious that Pepys, a Londoner, failed to secure copies of these ballads, while Wood, an Oxford man, bought them. But Wood no doubt had stationers in London to act as agents for him, while Pepys had not yet begun actively to collect.

PREFACE

For the benefit of the common people Wood's ballads discuss in popular form exactly the same subjects as those to which learned men like Glanvill were devoting themselves — the same subjects as those to which the newly founded Royal Society lent an attentive and oftentimes credulous ear. That Society listened to and published accounts of human and animal monstrosities, of wheat that rained from the sky, of ghosts and witchcraft, of enchantment, earthquakes, and judgments of God. In tuneful rhyme the common people heard narratives of these same prodigies and accepted them as absolute truth, especially when they were vouched for by lists of witnesses. Wood's collection features ballads of the unusual or marvelous, and twenty-two of the most interesting are reprinted below. Of special interest are those that deal with the Campden Wonder, the punishment of Dorothy Matley, the "Tedworth Demon," the ghost of Mr. Powel, the spirit that 267 years after death appeared to Richard Clark, the fire that destroyed the De Laun family, and the shower of wheat that fell at Shrewsbury in 1681.

Pepys's collection, as my *Pepysian Garland* proves, abounds in terrors and marvels earlier than 1640, but has almost none for the years between 1640 and 1680. Frcm 1680 onwards it has many sensational news-ballads that Wood ought to have known. He would heartily have enjoyed the five Pepysian ballads I reprint, especially those dealing with Thomas Cox and Dorothy Winterbottom — two frail mortals who had personal and disastrous conflicts with Satan.

I have drawn also upon the Rawlinson and Douce collections in the Bodleian Library, the Euing collection in the University of Glasgow Library, and the unnamed collection in the Manchester Free Reference Library. From the last, five ballads

PREFACE

have been chosen. Rawlinson's ballads furnish two accounts of monstrous births, Douce's a description of an unusual fish and the stunning ghost-story of Edward Avon. From the Euing collection come four ballads: a report of a monstrous birth; a warning against sleeping in the grass by the melancholy example of Mary Dudson, who swallowed an adder; a tale of Margery Perry, who for perjuring herself had her soul carried away by the Devil in person; and an equally terrible story of the punishment inflicted by an angel and the Devil on Gabriel Harding.

Surely it *is* a good deed to make these forty ballads accessible, for there must be many people who, like Mopsa, "love a ballad in print o' life," for then they can be sure the news is true! When Dorcas inquires about a particular ballad, "Is it true too, think you?" Autolycus quickly replies, "Five justices' hands at it, and witnesses more than my pack will hold." The same answer might well be made for most of the ballads in this volume.

It remains to add that in every essential particular the texts of the ballads are reproduced exactly. Thus the antiquated spelling and punctuation are followed, except that in some few cases the points at the end of lines are changed (as from a comma to a period) and that unmistakable misprints (like inverted or transposed letters) are corrected without notice. When, however, the misprints are at all out of the ordinary, they are indicated in foot-notes. Titles have been uniformly printed in black letter, and tunes in italics, in order to retain something of the flavor of the original broadsides; but long *f* is always printed *s*.

I am indebted to the officials of the Bodleian, Pepysian,

PREFACE

Glasgow University, and Manchester Free Reference libraries for permission to reprint the ballads and for other courtesies; to Professor Albert S. Borgman for various helpful suggestions; and, most of all, to my friend Miss Addie F. Rowe for her kindness in reading the proof-sheets during my absence from America.

H. E. R.

LONDON
June 23, 1926

CONTENTS

CONTENTS

CONTENTS

CONTENTS

ILLUSTRATIONS

FROM THE ORIGINAL BROADSIDE BALLADS

The Pack of Autolycus

I

A godly new ballad

Manchester, I, 4, black letter, two columns. Apparently this ballad formed only half of a broadside, but the second part of the sheet has been torn off. What remains is badly mutilated, as the inserted square brackets indicate.

Here is presented strange and dreadful news of the condition, as a puritanical writer saw it, of Elizabethan society. The ballad was registered by Edward White on August 1, 1586, under the title of "Thabuses of the wicked world &c," and was reëntered in the Stationers' Registers on December 14, 1624, as "Good Lord, what a wicked world" (Rollins, *Analytical Index*, Nos. 7, 1021). The printer of this ballad, R. E., is not named by Arber in the list of printers prefixed to the fifth volume of his *Transcript*. For the tune see Chappell's *Popular Music*, I, 227.

𝔄 most excellent 𝔊odly new 𝔅allad:
[𝔖hew]ing the manifold abuses of this wicked world, the
intolerable pride of people, the wantonnesse [of] women,
the dissimulation of flatterers, the subtilty of deceiuers, the
beastlines of drunkards, the filthinesse of 𝔚horedome,
the vnthriftines of 𝔊amesters, the cruelty of 𝔏andlords,
with a number of other inconueniences.

To the tune of *Greene-sleeues.*

1 GOod[1] Lord what a wicked world is this,
   [when] euery man doth liue amisse,
  [And n]o regard of conscience is,
   [and su]rely the more is the pittie.
  [Amend,] therefore, good people all,
   [d]o speedily for mercie call,
  [Th]at God may blesse both great and small,
   in euery Towne and Citty.

[1] *Text* Ood (*torn*).

[3]

THE PACK OF AUTOLYCUS

2 Few men do feare the Lord of might,
    and who regards his word aright,
  They come to Church but for a sight,
    and surely the more is the pitty.
       Amend, &c.

3 Pride doth beare so great a swaie,
    no man but monsters goe by the way,
  Dressing themselues in foolish array,
    and surely the more is the pittie.
       Amend, &c.

4 Wantonnesse walkes in euerie place,
    that modesty dares not shew his face:
  Discretion counted a foole in this case,
    and surely the more is the pitty.
       Amend, &c.

5 Flattery is friended gallantly,
    and beares his countenance verie hie,
  VVhose lips are taught to cog and lie,
    and surely the more is the pitty.
       Amend, &c.

6 Plaine truth is driuen out of towne,
    and flattery florisheth in renowne
  Deceit doth walke in a garded gowne,
    and surely the more is the pitty.
       Amend, &c.

7 Cruelty creepes in euery place,
    hatred beares a friendly face,
  And slander seeks his neighbours disgrace,
    and surely the more is the pitty.
       Amend, &c.

8 Idlenes walks in euery coast,
    yet flaunts it in brauery with the most
  Which keepeth Tiborne as hot as a toast:
    and surely the more is the pittie.
       Amend, &c.

9 [Corre]ction lieth sicke in a sweat,
    [and w]anton children must not be beate,
  [They will be] wilfull when they be great
  [and surely the more is the] pitty.
        [Amend, &c.]

10 Whoredome is counted a youthfull sport,
     greatly pleasing the letcherous sort,
   Not caring whither their soules shall resort,
     and surely the more is the pitty.
        Amend, &c.

11 The gaming houses who will shun,
     where tripping dice do daily run,
   Till all their wealth from them be won?
     and surely the more is the pittie.
        Amend, &c.

12 And few will learne in reasons schoole,
     which way they may their vices coole,
   But cals good counsell doting foole
     and surely the more is the pittie.
        Amend, &c.

13 Vsury weares a veluet coate,
     by cutting of his brothers throate,
   Which without gaines will not lend a groat,
     and surely the more is the pittie.
        Amend, &c.

14 The Land-lord with his incomes great,
     doth set his house in such a heat,
   The Tenant is driuen to lie in the street,
     and surely the more is the pittie.
        Amend, &c.

15 Couetousnesse hath taken such root,
     to call and crie there is no boote:
   Although the needy dy at their foote
     and surely the more is the pittie.
        Amend, &c.

[5]

16 Charity now is choaked with care,
      pittie is caught in cruelties snare,
    And mercy exilde both naked and bare,
      and surely the more is the pitty,
          Amend, &c.

17 The Father being of greedy kinde,
      doth force his daughter against her mind
    To marry where she may substance find,
      and surely the more is the pitty.
          Amend, &c.

18 What life is led betweene them twaine,
      when one the other doth disdaine?
    Their end must needs be griefe and pa[ine,]
      and surely the more is [1] the pittie.
          Amend, &c.

19 But laying all these things awaie,
      remember well your dying day,
    And how you shall consume to clay,
      if you be wise and wittie,
          Amend, &c.

FINIS.

At London printed by R. E.

[1] *Text apparently* morels.

2

The two inseparable brothers

Manchester, II, 46, black letter, four columns, three woodcuts, slightly mutilated. The gaps are filled in from the copy, itself sorely mutilated, that was reprinted from the Roxburghe collection by Ebsworth in the *Roxburghe Ballads*, VIII, 23 ff., 876.

That the wonderful twins John Baptist and Lazarus Colloretti (Pudd'n-head Wilson and Mark Twain should have known them!) actually existed admits of no doubt. Parker's description of them was probably made from personal observation, and may have been designed as an advertisement. Ebsworth points out that a picture and a discussion of the twins are included in Gerardus Blasius's *Fortunius Licetus de Monstris*, Amsterdam, 1665, pp. 114, 274. The date of the strange birth is there said to have been March 19, 1617. A broadside, dated 1815, in the British Museum (2188 [3]) informs us that

Dr. Green of Lichfield, makes mention of a Genoese, of the name of LAZARUS COLO REDO, who had suspended from him a perfect twin: he was seen in Basle in Switzerland, when of the age of 28 years. Bartholine, an accurate and judicious naturalist, also notices this horrid error of nature, in the first volume of his Historiarum Anatomicarum rariorum Centuria I and II. In the Gentleman's Magazine, there is a Portrait of Coloredo, in the dress of the times, with a cloak and band, boots, spurs and swords; both his breasts open, with the twin hanging from him.

The portrait referred to occurs in the *Gentleman's Magazine* for December, 1777 (XLVII, 572),[1] and is copied from the copperplate engraving in Bartholin's *Historiarum Anatomicarum Rariorum Centuria I et II* (1654), p. 117. It differs considerably from the woodcut that accompanies the ballad and that is reproduced below and in the *Roxburghe Ballads*, VIII, 23.

Bartholin's account (pp. 116–117) of the twins (it is summarized in Nathaniel Wanley's *Wonders of the Little World*, 1678, p. 6, and in William Turner's *Compleat History of the Most Remarkable Providences*, 1697, pt. II, p. 8, and is translated in the *Gentleman's Magazine*, XLVII, 482–483) runs thus:

Frater pectori fratris connatus:

Lazarum Colloredo Genuensem Hafniae primum vidi, deinde Basileae 28. annos natum, sed utrobiq; cum stupore. Fraterculus huic Lazaro in pectore erat adnatus, si rectè conjeci, osse xyphoide utriusq; cohaerente. Pes sinister solus illi dependebat, duo brachia, tres in manibus singulis tantum digiti. Vestigia pudendarum partium

The correspondent (pp. 375, 572) points out that Joseph Shaw (*Letters to a Nobleman*, 1709) saw in Amsterdam "an Italian youth, that had a live child growing out of his side."

[7]

THE PACK OF AUTOLYCUS

comparebant. Manus, aures, labia movebat, In thorace pulsus. Excrementa nulla minor frater excernit nisi per os, nares, & aures, nutriturq; eo qvod major assumit. Unde partes animales & vitales distinctas habebit, qvum & dormiat, sudet, moveatur, qvando major vel vigilet, vel qviescat, vel siccus est. Uterq; etiam suo nomine ad baptismatis fontem insignitus fuit, major Lazari, minor Joh. Baptistae. Naturalia verò viscera, ut hepar, lien &c. utriq; communiaerunt. Oculi clausi ferè Joh. Baptistae, respiratio minor, admotâ enim plumâ parum movebatur, admota verò manu exilem halitum calente deprehendimus. Patulum ferè illi & hians os, dentibus prominulis, saliva perpetuo ferè madens. Caput videbatur solum omne alimentis in sui augmentum absumere. Praegrande enim & majus qvam Lazaro, sed deforme, capillis supino situ dependentibus. Barba utriq; crevit, sed Baptistae neglecta, Lazaro compta. Erat autem Lazarus justae staturae, corpore decenti, moribus humanis, & ad aulae morem ornatus. Inducto pallio fratris tegebat corpus, fovebatq;, nec monstrum intus condi primo alloqvio diceres. Animo ubiq; praesenti videbatur, nisi qvod de fato subinde sollicitus, mortem fratris timebat, qvod se faetore & putredine exstingvendum qvoq; praesagiret, hinc magis in curando fratre qvam se laborabat. Rarissimi Monstri effigiem à vero haud abludentem lectorum oculis sisto.

Robert Milbourne registered on November 23, 1637, "a Picture of the Italian yong man with his brother growing out of his side with some verses therevnto" (Rollins, *Analytical Index*, No. 2083), possibly Parker's own ballad; on December 12, 1637 (*ibid.*, No. 1268), John Wright, Jr., secured a license for a ballad called "The Italian Mountebancke," which may have dealt with Lazarus. Earlier than these was the license that on November 4, 1637, Sir Henry Herbert, Master of the Revels, granted "for six months . . . to Lazaras, an Italian, to shew his brother Baptista, that grows out of his navell, and carryes him at his syde. In confirmation of his Majesty's warrant, granted unto him to make publique shewe" (Malone's *Variorum Shakespeare*, XIV [1821], 368).

Lazarus was still exhibiting himself and his twin in London late in 1639, when *A certaine Relation of the Hog-faced Gentlewoman* (1640) was written. That pamphlet remarks (sig. A4):

I will onely remember unto you a very handsome young man, late (if not now) in Towne, whose picture hath bin publickely set out to the common view, and himselfe to bee seene for money; who from one of his sides hath a twin brother growing, which was borne with him, and living still; though having sence and feeling, yet destitute of reason and understanding: whence me thinkes a disputable question might arise, whether as they have distinct lives, so they are possessed of two soules; or have but one imparted betwixt them both: but of this let the Philosophers, or rather the Divines argue and Define, bein I must ingeniously confesse an Argument much above my element.

The *Relation* was registered at Stationers' Hall on December 5, 1639 (cf. Rollins, *Analytical Index*, No. 1638). Shortly after that date Lazarus was showing himself at Norwich, as is proved by this record in the Mayors' Court Books for December 21, 1639 (J. T. Murray's *English Dramatic Companies*, II, 359): "This daie Larzeus Colleretto have leave to shewe a

THE TWO INSEPARABLE BROTHERS

monnster vntil the day after twelfe, he shewing to the Court a lycense signed with his Maties owne hand." Probably he went on a tour of exhibition through other provincial towns, though the breaking out of the civil war must have injured his business. Nevertheless in April, 1642, he was showing himself for money to Scottish audiences. Witness this picturesque entry in John Spalding's *Memorialls of the Trubles in Scotland and in England, A.D. 1624–A.D. 1645* (1792, Spalding Club *Publications*, No. 22, 1851, II, 125–126; cf. Robb Lawson's *Story of the Scots Stage*, 1917, p. 93):

> Thair cam to Abirdene ane Italian man monster, of about 24 yeires of aige, haueing from his birth growing fra the breist vpward, face to face, as it war ane creature haueing heid and syd hair, lyk the cullor of the man's hair; the heid still drovping bakuardis and dounward. He had eies, bot cloissit, not opnit. He had eires, tuo armes, tuo handis, thrie fingeris on ilk hand, ane body, ane leg, ane fot with six taes; the vther leg within the flesche inclyning to the left syde. It had the prik of ane man, bot no balcod. It had a kynd of lyf, and feilling, bot void of all vther sences, fed by the manis owne noorishment and evacuat that way as his wes. This gryte wark of God wes admired of be many in Abirdene and throw the countreis as he trauellit; yit suche was the goodness of oure God that he wold go and walk quhair he listit, carying this birth without ony pane, yea or on-espyit when his clothes wes on. When he cam to the toune he had tuo seruandis avaiting vpone him, who with him self were weill clad. He had his portraiture with the monster drawin, and hung out at his lodging, to the view of the people. The one seruand had ane trumpettour who soundit at suche tyme as the people sould cum and sie this monster, who flocked aboundantlie into his lodging. The vther seruand receaved the moneyis fra ilk persone for his sight, sum less sum mair. And efter there wes so muche collectit as culd be gottin, he, with his seruandis, schortlie left the toun, and went southuard agane.

Very interesting references to Lazarus and John Baptist are made (as I pointed out in *Modern Philology*, XVI [1919], 121) by John Cleveland (*Poems*, ed. Berdan, p. 123) and Alexander Brome (*Poems*, 2d ed., p. 244).

The tune comes from the ballad of "The Wandering Jew's Chronicle... To the Tune of, *Our Prince is welcome out of Spain*" (*Roxburghe Ballads*, VI, 695).

THE PACK OF AUTOLYCUS

The two inseparable brothers.

OR

A true and strange description of a Gentleman (an Italian by birth) about seventeene yeeres of age, who hath an imperfect (yet living) Brother, growing out of his side, having a head, two armes, and one leg, all perfectly to be seen. They were both baptized together; the imperfect is called *Iohn Baptist,* **and the other** *Lazarus.* **Admire the Creator in his Creatures.**

To the tune of *The wandring Iewes Chronicle.*

1　TO England lately newes is come,
　　　Which many parts of Christendome
　　　　haue by experience found
　　To be the strangest and most rare,
　　That fame did to the world declare,
　　　　since man first walkt o'th ground.

THE TWO INSEPARABLE BROTHERS

2 I many Prodigies haue seene,
   Creatures that haue preposterous beene,
       to nature in their birth,
   But such a thing as this my theame,
   Makes all the rest seeme but a dreame,
       the like was nere on earth.

3 A Gentleman well qualifide,
   Doth beare his brother at his side,
       inseparably knit,
   As in this figure you may see,
   And both together liuing be,
       the world admires at it.

4 In *Italy* this youth was borne,
   Whom nature freely did adorne
       with shape and Pulchritude,
   Like other men in each respect,
   And not with common intelect,
       he's inwardly indude.

5 This yong-man doth compleatly walke,
   He can both read, write, sing, or talke,
       without paine or detraction,
   And when he speakes the other head,
   Doth moue the lips both Ruby red,
       not speaking but in action.

6 This head and face is rightly fram'd,
   With euery part that can be nam'd,
       eares, eyes, lips, nose, and chin,
   His vpperlip hath some beard on't,
   Which he who beares him yet doth want,
       this may much wonder win.

7 One arme's about his brother cast,
   That doth embrace his body fast,
       the other hangeth by,
   These armes haue hands with fingers all,
   Yet as a childs they are but small,
       pinch any part hee'l cry.

8   Onely one legge with foot and toes
    Is to be seene, and some suppose,
        the other is contain'd
    Within his brothers body, yet
    Nature hath vs'd him so to it
        [he never thus is pain'd.]

The second part, To the same tune.

9   YEt nothing doth the lesser eate,
    He's only nourish'd with the meate
        wherewith the other feeds,
    By which it seemes though outward parts
    They haue for two, yet not two hearts,
        this admiration breeds.

10   For sicknesse and infirmities,
    I meane Quotidian maladies,
        which man by nature hath,
    Sometimes one's sicke, the other wel
    This is a story strange to tell,
        but he himselfe thus saith.

11 Th'imperfect once the small poxe had,
Which made the perfect brother sad,
　　but he had neuer any,
And if you nip it by the arme,
Or doe it any little harme,
　　(this hath beene tride by many,)

12 It like an infant (with voyce weake)
Will cry out though it cannot speake,
　　as sensible of paine,
Which yet the other feeleth not,
But if the one be cold or hot,
　　that's common to both twaine.

13 Some seauenteene yeares of age they be,
A perfect proper youth is he
　　to which the lesse doth cleaue,
They were baptized being young,
Few then did think they'd liue so long,
　　as few would now beleeue.

14 But that to ratifie this truth,
Now in the *Strand* this wondrous youth
　　is present to be seene,
And he with his strange burden, hath
Bin shewne (with maruaile) as he saith
　　to our good King a[nd Queen.]

15 *Iohn Baptist* is th'imperfect nam'd,
Who through the christian world is fam'd,
　　his Brother which him beares
Was called *Lazarus* at the Font,
And if we well consider on't
　　a mystery in't appeares.

16 From *Italy* their natiue place,
They haue some certaine late yeares space,
　　gone one still with another,
Indeed they cannot otherwise doe,
He that see's one must needs see two,
　　the brother beares the brother.

17   Through *Germany*, through *Spain* & *France*,
   (Deuoyd of danger or mischance)
     and other Christian Lands
   They trauell'd haue, nay rather one
   For both, so many miles hath gone,
     to shew th' work of Gods hands.

18   And now in England they haue beene
   About a moneth although vnseene,
     till now obtaining leaue,
   In seeing this or such strange things,
   Let vs admire the King of Kings,
     and of his power conceaue,

19   That just opinion which is due,
   To him who is all good all true,
     whose works we can't find out,
   Let admiration then suffice,
   Sith theres no man that is so wise,
     but of 's owne wit may doubt.
                  And so doe I.

𝔉𝔦𝔫𝔦𝔰.
                         Martin Parker.

Printed at London for *Thomas Lambert*, at the signe
of the Hors-shooe [in Smithfield.]

3

A marvelous murther

Manchester, II, 1, black letter, four columns, two woodcuts. The sheet is slightly mutilated, the first and last columns being torn.

My search for information about the murder of George Drawnefield, of Brampton, has been unsuccessful. Possibly — this is a mere guess — the date of the murder was about 1638; for I have found (S. Glover's *Derby* [1829], I, ii, 265) that at the assizes held at Chesterfield on March 15 and 16, 1638, five men and one woman were hanged. They may or they may not have been connected with the crime narrated in this ballad.

The tune of *My bleeding heart* is equivalent to *In summer time* or *Maying time* (cf. my *Pepysian Garland*, pp. 161 f.). For the last see Chappell's *Popular Music*, I, 377. See also the notes to No. 22.

𝔄 𝔐𝔞𝔯𝔲𝔢𝔩𝔩𝔬𝔲𝔰 𝔐𝔲𝔯𝔱𝔥𝔢𝔯,

𝔠𝔬𝔪𝔪𝔦𝔱𝔱𝔢𝔡 𝔲𝔭𝔬𝔫 𝔱𝔥𝔢 𝔅𝔬𝔡𝔶 𝔬𝔣 𝔬𝔫𝔢 *George Drawnefield* 𝔬𝔣 *Brempton*, 𝔗𝔴𝔬 𝔪𝔦𝔩𝔢𝔰 𝔣𝔯𝔬𝔪 *Chesterfield*, 𝔦𝔫 *Darby-shire*, 𝔴𝔥𝔬 (𝔣𝔬𝔯 𝔏𝔲𝔠𝔯𝔢 𝔬𝔣 𝔥𝔦𝔰 𝔴𝔢𝔞𝔩𝔱𝔥) 𝔴𝔞𝔰 𝔪𝔬𝔰𝔱 𝔠𝔯𝔲𝔢𝔩𝔩𝔶 𝔪𝔲𝔯𝔱𝔥𝔢𝔯𝔢𝔡 𝔦𝔫 𝔥𝔦𝔰 𝔟𝔢𝔡, 𝔬𝔫 *Whitsunday* 𝔞𝔱 𝔫𝔦𝔤𝔥𝔱, 𝔟𝔶 𝔠𝔢𝔯=𝔱𝔞𝔦𝔫𝔢 𝔟𝔩𝔬𝔬𝔡𝔶 𝔙𝔦𝔩𝔩𝔞𝔦𝔫𝔢𝔰 𝔴𝔥𝔢𝔯𝔢𝔬𝔣 𝔗𝔥𝔯𝔢𝔢 𝔞𝔯𝔢 𝔦𝔫 *Darby* 𝔍𝔞𝔶𝔩𝔢, 𝔒𝔫𝔢 𝔣𝔩𝔢𝔡, 𝔞𝔫𝔡 𝔱𝔥𝔢 𝔯𝔢𝔰𝔱 𝔟𝔬𝔲𝔫𝔡 𝔬𝔲𝔢𝔯 𝔱𝔬 𝔱𝔥𝔢 𝔄𝔰𝔦𝔷𝔢𝔰.

To the tune of *My bleeding heart*.

1 IN sorrow and compassion great,
   I of a story sad will treate
   A story full of wonderous woe,
   As by the sequell you may know.

2 Neere *Chesterfield* in *Darbysheire*,
   In *Brampton* parish (as I heare)
   A murder was (in barbarous sort)
   Done there as now I shall report.

3 *George Drawnefield* was this lucklesse wretch,
   'Bout whom the deuells imps did stretch
   Their damb'd, inuention how they might,
   Kill him and take his goods by night.

4 Hee was a man that labour'd hard,
   To get his liuing with regard,
   Hee liued a priuate single life,
   With neither man, mayd, child, nor wife.

5 Through his Industry, Care and paines,
   (Which euery day increst his gaynes)
   A competent estate got he,
   Passing most men of his degree.

A MARVELOUS MURTHER

6 [But] 'twas to him vnfortunate,
   And caus'd him to expyre his date,
   [B]efore that nature claimd his breath,
   [So 't]wa[s] his wealth that wrought his death.

7 [And now on] *Whitsunday* it befell,
   [The m]an did droope and was not well,
   [But yet of de]ath there was no signe.
   [But still some w]retches did combine,

8 That seeing now this small defect,
   Men would the deed much lesse suspect,
   Then if he had beene perfect sound,
   On this ocasion did they ground.

9 *Whitsunday* after euening prayer,
   Some certaine neighbours did repayre,
   To visit him and with him staide,
   Till time for sleepe prouision made.

10 And then theire leaues of him they tooke,
   In friendly maner hands were shooke,
   None thought to find what accident,
   Next morning did to them present.

11 The bloody Homicides i'th night,
   Broake in to th' house and killed him quite
   But with such deuelish subtilty,
   As show'd the Authors policy.

12 The manner how I must defer,
   Least in the story I should ere,
   And tell you how they did by stealth,
   Out of the house conuey his wealth.

13 Some boyes that saw them had for feese,
   (To hold their peace) some bread and cheese
   Thus they his money, bondes and goods,
   Hid vnder ground and in the woods.

14   Next morning newes abroad was spreade,
How that *George Drawnefield* he was dead.
His passing peals was Rung likewise,
And all was past as they surmise.

The second part To the same tune.[1]

15   THe neighbours who were their last night,
And saw his wealth in open sight,
Which was in money bills and bondes,
To th' valew of three hundred pounds,

16   To see the house of all bereft,
And onely two Six-pences left,
Beside a little houshould trash,
It with amazement them did dash.

17   Yet 'twas past ore, and hee to soone,
Was buryed in the afternoone,
And no suspition of the thing,
Unlesse some priuate murmuring.

18   The news of this was quickly carryed,
Unto his Sister that was marryed.
Twentie miles of and she made hast,
To see how matters all had past.

19   His goods weare her's by proper right,
Which being gone (as well she might)
Shee did mistruste that some foule play,
Had tane both life and goods away.

20   This Ielousie tooke such effect,
That quickly as she did direct,
The corps were taken vp anon,
The Coroners quest was set thereon.

---

[1] The original broadside has here the same cut as that shown on page 90, below,—evidently a misfit in this ballad.

21   But they so cunningly had wrought,
The Iurors could that time see nought.
So he againe was put i'th ground,
Nothing at all amisse was found.

22   Yet did their consciences them sting,
And they i'th night brought euery thing,
Which from the house they had conueyde,
And neere without the dore them laid.

23   His Sisters husband beeing one,
Approu'd of great discretion,
Caus'd the dead corps to be once more,
Tane vp and washed cleane all ore.

24   Besides the Iury chosen then,
All vpright, and judicious men,
Hee brought a Surgeon who well skild,
Found by his Art the man was kild.

25   In such a sort it makes me wonder,
For they had broke his necke in sunder,
And also in his head and side,
Some signes of deadly blowes were spide.

26   With Dough they stopt his nose and eares,
His mouth and throate to shunne all feares,
That might insue through bloods effusion,
As was found out in the conclusion.

27   O noate the Deuills pollicy,
Withall the power of God on hie,
Though Sathan and his imps be cunning,
Yet from Gods Iustice ther's no running.

28   Diuers for this foule fact were tane,
Three now in *Darby* Iayle remayne,
One's fled away the other Foure,
To the asises are bound ore.

29 Take heede you bloody minded m[en,]
For blood still asks for blood agen.
You see what plots these villaines did
Yet murther can no way bee hid.

30 Beware lest Sathan you possesse
With the roote of euill couetou[sness.]
For money *Iudas* sould his friend,
And money brought this man to's [end.]

𝔉𝔦𝔫𝔦𝔰.

Printed at London for *Francis Coules* and are to be
sould at his shop in the Old [Bailey.]

4

A lamentable list of hideous signs

Wood 402 (67), black letter, four columns, one woodcut. Nearly all of the fourth column (ten stanzas) is torn away. The fragmentary stanzas are here omitted.

The ballad seems to have been registered for printing by John Okes on August 20, 1638 (Rollins, *Analytical Index*, No. 1411), as "A Lamentable List of certaine hidious signes seene in the Ayre in Germany &c." The present copy was published by Thomas Lambert, who on February 7, 1638 (*ibid.*, No. 361), had secured a license for "The Complaint of Germany." A long poem by Martin Parker on the same doleful subject is described in J. P. Collier's *Bibliographical and Critical Account of the Rarest Books in the English Language*, II, 98–99.

The "Lamentable List" is summarized from Captain L. Brinckmair's *The Warnings Of Germany. By Wonderfull Signes, and strange Prodigies seene in divers parts of that Country of Germany, betweene the Yeare 1618. and 1638* (Wood 211). On the fly-leaf of his copy Anthony Wood wrote, "Many egregious lyes in this book." The book (which is accepted at its face value and elaborately summarized in R. Burton's — that is, Nathaniel Crouch's — *Surprizing Miracles of Nature and Art*, 1685, pp. 97 ff.) and the ballad supply an almost unexampled collection of terrible prodigies. According to the popular belief, many of them were, sooner or later, repeated in England, as the other ballads in the present collection show.

Apparitions in general no doubt owe a good deal of their popularity to those which, in the pages of Josephus, figured so noticeably before the fall of Jerusalem. England seems to have been especially favored with warnings in the form of blazing stars. Abraham Fleming's translation (1577, 1618) of a treatise on blazing stars by F. Nausea, Bishop of Vienna, interprets these heavenly bodies in a manner more doleful than is customary in ballads. Fleming's influence is felt in Richard Shanne's comment (Additional MS. 38,599, fol. 49) that the death of Queen Anne, James I's consort, and terrible wars in Bohemia followed shortly after blazing stars were seen over London.

For the tune see Chappell's *Popular Music*, I, 162–167.

THE PACK OF AUTOLYCUS

𝕬 Lamentable List, of certaine Hidious, Frightfull, and Prodigious Signes, which have bin seene in the Aire, Earth, and Waters, at severall times for these 18. yeares last past, to this present: that is to say, *Anno*. 1618. untill this instant. *Anno*. 1638. In *Germany*, and other Kingdomes and Provinces adjacent; which ought to be so many severall warnings to our Kingdome, as to the said Empire.

To the tune of *Aime not to high.*

1   YOu who would be inform'd of forraine newes,
     Attend to this which presently insues,
    And you shall heare such marvels here exprest,
    In eighteene yeares last past made manifest.

2   In *Germany* that famous Empire faire,
    Strange sights were seene i'th water earth & aire,
    Which from good testimonies hither brought,
    That we may know w^t wonders God hath wrought.

[22]

A LIST OF HIDEOUS SIGNS

3   In Anno sixteene hundred and eighteene,
     A blazing Starre was o're *Bohemia* seene,
     Which for the space of seven and twenty dayes,
     Within the sky most fearefully did blaze.

4   And in *Hungaria* (as 'tis understood,)
     Water was Metamorphos'd into bloud.
     In *Brunswick-land* (within an evening faire,)
     Were seene two armies fighting in the aire.

5   Three *Raine-bowes* and three *Suns* (all in one day)
     Were at *Vienna* seene in *Austria:*
     And over *Lints* in *Austria* (nam'd before,)
     A noyse like Ordinance in the aire did roare.

6   At *Darmsted* bloud did drop from leaues of trees,
     And what at *Tursin* hapt with this agrees,
     Where chaires, stooles, wals, and other things did sweat,
     An oyle resembling bloud by iust conceite.

7   I'th Dukedome of *Wirtemberg* it raigned gore,
     (As it hath bin in *England* heretofore.)
     Over *Bohemia* fiery beames did oppose
     The Sun, and crackt like Rockets in our shoes.

8   A dreadfull tempest haild at *Ratisbone*,
     Strange fruit neere *Frankendal* yᵉ like ne're known.
     Crowes in *Silesia* fought a mortall battle,
     Lightning and thunder in the sky did rattle.

9   The Sun in monstious forme i'th aire was showne
     With a strange Raine-bow over *Hamborow* towne:
     Great bands with horse-men in aray did stand,
     With Ordnance in the aire o're *Pomerland*.

10   Neere *Strausburg* was brought forth a monstrous birth,
     Such as was seldome seene upon yᵉ earth.
     A sword, and rod within the Heavens were,
     At *Saxon* in (*Sylesia*) seene to appeare.

THE PACK OF AUTOLYCUS

𝕿𝖍𝖊 𝕾𝖊𝖈𝖔𝖓𝖉 𝕻𝖆𝖗𝖙 𝖙𝖔 𝖙𝖍𝖊 𝖘𝖆𝖒𝖊 𝕿𝖚𝖓𝖊.

11 STrang fire ran through the towne of *Coburg*, and
   No hurt it did (that men could understand.)
   In *Saxony* water to bloud did turne,
   At *Magdenburg* a child in armour borne.

12 O're *Lutzin* was a beautious Virgin seene,
   A Candle, and a Hand-kercheife betweene
   Her hands she held, (in open view of all:)
   Water turn'd bloud in *Saxony* at *Hall*.

13 Bloud issued from a loafe of Bread, (firme dry,)
   At *Frowensteine* a Towne in *Saxony:*
   A monster borne at *Kempton* in *Swabland*,
   And likewise bloud did spring out of a Pond.

14 In *Brandenburg* (at *Berlin*) heaven sent
   Both bloud, and brimstone, from the firmament:
   A fiery Scepter was i'th aire beheld,
   Great flocks of Birds fought, & each other kild.

15 Bloud perfect from a water Conduit ran,
   A Worme was found i'th' full shape of a man.
   At *Weimer* water did to bloud convert,
   These wonderous Signes may move a Christian heart.

16 At *Vienna* a Woman strange appear'd,
   (Whereat some of the people were affeard:)
   And at St. *Stephens* Church, the Bels did ring
   Without the helpe of man.   (A wonderous thing.

17 Now what events these progidies [1] have wrought,
   (And what effects have since to passe bin brought,)
   England (and all the Christian world) hath had,
   Sufficient notes and motives to be sad.

18 Intestine warre, contagious pestilence,
   And other miseries deduc'd from thence;
   As pinching Famine (which hath caus'd) of late,
   A desolation of that firtile State.

[1] *Sic.*

19 Such wonderous signes, & tokens Heaven sent,
That faire *Ierusalem* might in time repent:
Prodigious sights, and fearefull blazing starres,
As learn'd *Iosephus* speakes in's Iewish warres.

20 But all these tokens served to no end,
For the rebellious Iewes did still offend;
And slighted these Celestiall warnings still:
The Viols of Gods wrath their sins did fill.[1]

Printed at *London* for *Tho. Lambert,* and are to
be sold at the Sign [of the Horse-Shoe in
Smithfield.]

[1] Ten fragmentary stanzas are omitted.

5

A famous sea-fight

Manchester, II, 36, black letter, four columns, four woodcuts. The title is mutilated, and a stanza and a half are torn away.

On John Looks (or Lookes) himself see the notes in my *Cavalier and Puritan* (1923), p. 126. A ballad by him is a rarity, and the finder of it may well congratulate himself. The battle with which Looks deals and its sequel (of October 11) which he predicted in stanza 11 were enormously popular subjects. Martin Parker, for example, described both in "A Lamentable Relation of a Fearful Fight at Sea, upon our English Coast, Between the Spaniard and the Hollander," which is reprinted in *Ballads from the Collections of Sir James Balfour* (ed. J. Maidment, 1834), pp. 8–12. Laurence Price's contribution, "A New Spanish Tragedy," is reprinted in my *Pepysian Garland*, p. 455, where are listed other ballads on the same subject.

On September 6, 1639, the Dutch fleet under Admiral Tromp drove a Spanish fleet, which was carrying troops to Dunkirk, into the Downs. Sir John Pennington, English Admiral guarding the Narrow Seas, insisted that the neutrality of the roadstead be preserved. But on October 11, after receiving reinforcements from Holland, Tromp attacked and destroyed the Spanish fleet, while Pennington looked on helplessly. He had no instructions to do anything else, though apparently his sympathies were with the Spaniards. As the numerous ballads indicate, England received the news of the Dutch victory with joy, for it was popularly believed that the Spanish fleet had sailed, at the invitation of Charles I, to crush English liberty.

Looks's ballad was registered for publication as "The sea fight betweene Hollander and the Spaniard" on September 23, 1639 (Rollins, *Analytical Index*, No. 2383). For the tune see Chappell's *Popular Music*, I, 114.

A famous Sea-fight:

OR,

[A Bloo]dy Battell, which was fought between the *Spaniard* [and t]he *Hollander*, beginning on the sixth day of this present month of *September*, 163[9,] being Friday; and continued for the most part, till Sunday-noon fo[ll]owing; being neer 70 sail of the *Spaniards* when they begun, and [b]ut 15 of the *Hollanders*, till 12 sail more came to their ayd. The Rela-

A FAMOUS SEA–FIGHT

tion you sha[ll] habe in the insuing Ditp, with what
hapned on the [thr]ee dapes abobe=named.

To the Tune of *Brave Lord Willoughby.*

1   G Ive ¹ ear you lusty Gallants,
        my purpose is to tell
    [News of] the bloody Battell
        [whic]h late on Seas befell:
    [Near] our English coast it was,
        not far from *Dover* where
    The *Dutchman* with the *Spaniard* met,
        whose greetings bitter were.

2   [T]his present month *September,*
        [a] Fleet from *Spain* there went
    [With s]ouldiers then for *Dunkerck,*
        [which to the] King was sent: ²

3   And on the Friday morning
        they did begin to fight,
    Continuing the Battell
        untill that it was night:
    Discharging of their roaring Guns,
        the victory for to gain,
    Till two ships of the *Hollander*
        were sunk into the main.

¹ *Text . . .* e (*torn*).   ² Twelve lines are here torn away.

4 But yet the valiant *Hollander*,
    which scorns at Sea to fly,
The next day with the *Spaniard*
    another bout did try:
Where 12 sail more came to their ayd,
    and then in that same fight,
One of the *Spaniards* great Gallons,
    and two ships sunk e're night.

5 And then the next day following,
    being the Sabbath, they
At two o'th clock i'th morning,
    began a bloody fray:
And then with stinging Bullets
    they did each other vex,
Till blood into the Ocean
    run streaming from the Decks.

The second Part To the same tune.

A FAMOUS SEA–FIGHT

6 THe *Hollanders* great Admirall,
the *Spaniard* boarded thrice;
(Had not the *Dutch-man* quench'd the same)
it had been fired twice:
Three score and six great Ordnances
the Admirall did bear;
Her Souldiers and her Seamen then
above a thousand were.

7 Each side did their indeavour,
for conquest of the day;
And for eight hours together
there was a bloody fray:
Then slaughtred men on every side
they over ship-board cast,
Not possible to number them,
they threw them out so fast.

8 But in the *Spanish* Admirall,
it is for certain known,
A hundred men were slain therein,
and over ship-board thrown:
Abundance more in it besides,
which under cure lyes;
Some maim'd, and some dismembred
in lamentable wise.

9 And then the valiant *Hollander*,
in signe of victory they
Did take one of the *Spaniards* ships
and caried quite away.
At ten of the Clock i'th forenoon,
the battell ended were,
For then the King of Englands ships
towards them approched near.

10   But when the valiant *Dutchman*
      our English ships past by,
  They bowd there Sails unto them;
      the *Spaniards* did deny.
  But when as *Sir John Pennington*
      did see they were so proud,
  He threatned them with Canon shot
      and then the *Spaniards* bowd.

11   The *Spaniard* in our English Coast
      being forced for to fly,
  For harbour to the South foreland,
      where now at road they lye
  The *Hollander* not farre from thence
      doth wayt their comming out,
  Being resolved before they goe
      to have the other bout.

12   No certain Number their is known,
      how many their is kill'd;
  Though many hundreds on both sides
      their dearest bloud hath spild:
  The *Spaniard* hath no cause to boast,
      the *Dutchmen* queld their pride:
  And those that gained Credit most,
      was of the loosing side.

13   God blesse our gracious King and Queen
      and our brave English fleet,
  And give them victory on the seas,
      when they with foes do meet:
  Defend them from ill sands and rocks,
      and Lord their battell fight
  As thou didst for *Elisabeth*
      in the yeare *88*.

FINIS.

John Looks.

London, printed for *Fr. Grove*, neer the Sarazens
head, without Newgate.

6

A warning-piece for engrossers of corn

Wood 401 (162), black letter, four columns, four woodcuts. There is another copy in the Euing collection, No. 379.

From references to Charles I and (in stanza 21) to Queen Henrietta Maria's coming to land, it is evident that the date of the ballad is 1643. The Queen, who had left England early in 1642, returned in February, 1643, after her ship had been driven back to Holland by a storm. Though this is not an especially good ballad, it shows how street songs were used as effectively as the hell-and-brimstone sermons of more recent days. It is bare-faced propaganda directed at "profiteers." Dozens of ballads of this type are known. Often they cite the fate of Archbishop Walter Gray, of England, and the German Bishop Hatto. Compare also the calamity that befell John Russell (1631), in my *Pepysian Garland*, p. 370.

During the "generall dearth" of 1587 the price of wheat, says John Stow's *Annals*, varied from 8s. to 13s. a bushel. In the "wonderfull hard" times of 1648–1649, according to the *Diary of Ralph Josselin* (ed. Camden Society, pp. 69–70), wheat sold for over 9s. a bushel, rye for 7s. and more, and "all things very deare." In 1657, Josselin reports (p. 126), wheat rose to 11s. Eight shillings was the price asked by Goodman Inglebred and promised by the Devil. I have not traced Mr. Inglebred to his lair in Boughton, near Lynn; but one must follow the advice of Autolycus and believe in the ballad because there are three witnesses' "hands at it."

For the tune see Nos. 3 and 22.

THE PACK OF AUTOLYCUS

𝕬 𝖂arning-peice for 𝕴ngroosers of 𝕮orne;
𝕭𝕰𝕴𝕹𝕲

𝕬 true 𝕽elation how the *Divell* met with one 𝕲oodman *Jnglebred* of *Bowton*, within six miles of *Holgay* in *Norfolk*; as he was comming from *Linn* 𝕸arket, and 𝕭argain'd for a great quantity of 𝕭arly for eight shillings a 𝕭ushell and gabe earnest; and when he came to fetch it, brought 𝕮arts and 𝕳orses (to their thinking) and while 'twas measuring the *Divell* banished, and tore the 𝕭arne in pieces, and scattered all the 𝕮orne with such 𝖂indes and 𝕿empest, which hath done such great harme both by 𝕾ea and 𝕷and, the like was neber heard of before; the 𝕵armer now[1] lyeing destracted.

𝕾ent in a 𝕷etter to be 𝕻rinted, by *Christopher Emmerson, George Dixon*, & *Richard Higgins*.

To the Tune of, *In Summer time, &c.*

1   GOod People all pray lend an eare
    　to this my Song, that's strange and true,
    Wherein I breifly shall Declare,
    　the full Relation here to you.

2   If any Misers you do know,
    　that hoards up Corne, to starve ye Poore,
    If that these Lines you to them show
    　'twil make them sure bring out their Store.

3   In *Norfolk* did this chance befall,
    　at *Bowton* where this Man did dwell,
    And Goodman *Inglebred* they do him call,
    　who had great store of Corne to sell.

[1] *Text* new.

[32]

4　But he as many thousands more,
　　　without any remorse or pitty,
　　Was fully resolv'd to keep his Store,
　　　to bring a Dearth in Town and City.

5　He being at Market on a day,
　　　at *Linn* a place that's known full well:
　　And Riding home upon the way,
　　　He had a Customer from Hell.

6　The Devill did him over take,
　　　in Habbit being very brave,
　　Who did a bargaine with him make,
　　　and Halfe-a-crowne in earnest gave.

7　The price was very great they made,
　　　and Barly that must be the Graine,
　　Eight shillings a Bushell must be paid,
　　　being well contented with such gaine.

8　And thus the Devill and he agreed,
　　　likewise the time to fetch the same:
　　The Miser hy'd him home with speed,
　　　for to provide against he came.

9　When he came home he was full glad,
　　　and to his Wife he did unfold
　　What bargin, and what price he had,
　　　likewise what quantity he sold.

10　With that his Wife made this reply,
　　　as by his Servants it was told,
　　None but the Divell would give so high
　　　a price (quoth she) as you have sold.

The second Part, to the same Tune.[1]

11　TO Thrashing straight he set his Men,
　　　to make it ready against the day,
　　And the Divell was as ready then,
　　　against the time to fetch't away.

[1] *Text* to same the Tune.

12 The day being come, the Divell brought
   his Furniture, to take these stores,
 With Horse & Carts, as to their thought,
   the Man he straight threw ope yᵉ doores.

13 To measuring straight his Barly out,
   this Man began with all his speed;
 With that the Divell made a Rout,
   and of his Bargain soone was freed.

14 The Divel vanish'd straight away,
   such Storms and Winds nere heard before
 No People thereabouts durst stay;
   the Barne in peeces all he tore.

15 His Barne and Corne it all was spoil'd,
   and all the Country round likewise,
 Had all their Houses then Vntyl'd,
   such Winds they nere saw from yᵉ Skys.

16 This Farmer fell distracted straight,
   he cannot take no Rest nor Sleep,
 And cryes the Divil doth for him waight,
   his Bargaine he must with him keep.

17 All you that hoard, and buy up Corne,
   and keepe it up to make it deere,
 Although you long have been forborne,
   there's Rods in piss for you I heare.

18 Your Villainny now is brought about,
   and pay for't deare you will ere long,
 Your Stores you will be made bring out,
   you shall not doe the Poore such wrong.

19 The Lord I hope will heare the cryes,
   of thousands which are in distresse,
 Of gallant Hearts, that daily lyes
   still hoping, yet have no redresse.

20 The Lord preserve our King and blesse
    him from the trecherous hands of those,
That are his Enemies, yet professe
    they love Him yet prove secret Foes.

21 The Queen God send her safe to land,
    and all the Progeny preserve;
Likewise for those that faithfull stand
    and from him yet did never swerve.

22 My prayers shall daily be for those,
    with many thousands more beside.
But such I take his cheifest Foes,
    that's given to Covetuousness & Pride.

23 For you that deale in Corne and Graine,
    to whom these Lines in cheif belong,
Beware of such unlawfull gain,
    where none but Poore doth bear ye wrong.

24 So to Conclude and make an end,
    for Peace and Plenty, let vs pray,
That God may stand ye poore-mans freind,
    for ye Poore are now the rich-mans pray.

FINIS

London, printed for *William Gilbertson*, at the
Bible in *Giltspur-street*.

7

Strange news from Brotherton

Manchester, II, 39, black letter, four columns, two woodcuts.

From stanza 9 it is evident that the date of the ballad is about 1648. Unfortunately, the author gives only a few facts about the rain of wheat in Brotherton, and for those few he presumably follows some printed pamphlet which I cannot find. The prodigy that he relates, however, was far from unique: many such wheat-showers have been reported throughout England, as the introduction to No. 36 shows.

The German maid referred to in stanza 6 — the celebrated Eve Fliegen, of Moers — is said to have lived sixteen years on the smell of a rose. There is in the Bodleian Library (A 4° P 46) a 1611 pamphlet, translated from the Dutch by Thomas Wood, dealing with Miss Fliegen. It is reprinted in my "Notes on Some English Accounts of Miraculous Fasts" in the *Journal of American Folk-Lore*, XXXIV (1921), 364–368. Her picture and a ballad on her fasting are reproduced in Andrew Clark's *Shirburn Ballads*. For a general discussion of Eve Fliegen and other fasting maids see also George Hakewill's *An Apologie or Declaration of the Power and Providence of God*, 1635, IV, ch. vii, §9, pp. 439–441. Katerin Cooper, of Germany, who in 1589 had gone for some twelve years without food, and Jane Balan, who in 1603 had fasted for more than three years, are dealt with in pamphlets preserved in the British Museum (C.31.e.19 and Huth 86); and Veitken Johans's fast of four years is described in a booklet of 1597 in the Lambeth Palace Library.

But these were foreign wonders! In England itself numerous cases of miraculous fasts are recorded, often with authoritative names to vouch for them. Roger Bacon, for example, tells of a thirteenth-century Norwich woman who lived without food for twenty years (*Opera*, ed. J. S. Brewer, I, 373). Cecily de Rygeway, of Nottingham, fasted for forty days in 1357 (*Calendar of the Patent Rolls, Edward III*, X, 529). A Kendal (Westmorland) woman who took no food for fourteen years is described in Dr. John Worthington's *Diary* (ed. James Crossley, I, 340 ff.), June 24, 1661. In 1668 Martha Taylor, of Derbyshire, professed to have fasted fifty-three weeks, as is told in pamphlets written by Thomas Robins (1668), John Reynolds (1669),[1] and H. A. (1669). Other notorious fasts were those attributed to Jane Stretton, of Hertfordshire (1669), Rebecca Smith, of Ox-

---

[1] Reynolds's pamphlet is reprinted in the *Harleian Miscellany*, IV (1809), 43–58. In it he tells of persons who fasted three, four, seven, fifteen, eighteen, twenty-nine, thirty-six, forty, and seventy-seven years.

fordshire (1671), and Ann Moore, of Staffordshire (1810). For detailed discussions see my "Notes on Some English Accounts of Miraculous Fasts," *Journal of American Folk-Lore*, XXXIV (1921), 357–376; William A. Hammond's *Fasting Girls; Their Physiology and Pathology*, 1879 (for modern cases, like that of Mollier Fancher of Brooklyn, who in 1878 claimed to have lived fifteen years without food); F. G. Benedict, *A Study of Prolonged Fasting*, Carnegie Institute, 1915; and the findings of the Physiological Department of the University of Chicago as reported in the daily papers for October 11, 1923.

Huge hail-stones (cf. stanza 7) are almost too common to require notice. An early account of their falling at Chelmsford and Ipswich is given in Stow's *Annals* under the date of July 16, 1565 (reprinted in Arber's *Transcript*, I, 293). "Stupendous" hail-stones "above five inches about" fell at Norwich in 1656, and in many of them "there was to be seen the figure of an eye, resembling the eye of a man, and that so perfectly, as if it had been there engraved by the hand of some skilful artificer" (*Harleian Miscellany*, II [1808], 288 f.). The *Philosophical Transactions* (II, 481 f.) of the Royal Society reports that in Suffolk on July 17, 1666, hail-stones "full as bigg as Turkeys-Eggs" fell. Others eight inches around devastated London on May 18, 1680, as is described in a ballad (No. 35) reprinted below. Much more prodigious was the German hail-storm recounted in *Strange News from the West, Being a true and perfect Account of several Miraculous Sights seen in the Air Westward* (1661, p. 5):

It is confirmed likewise by Letters from Hambirdge of the same date, That there fell in *Egersteed* a wonderful great storm of Hayle, which was of an exttrordinary [*sic*] weight, and blood-red, this hail was so hard and durable that they could not make it melt in the fire, nor burn to Ashes; but at last being put into the water, did turn it into a blood-red colour; this likewise is reported for truth by several credible men.

Impressive also are certain modern instances. Thus a hail-storm on August 1, 1846, created havoc enough in London to bring it the honor of half a column in the *Athenaeum* (August 8)! The New York *Times* reported that on May 23, 1921, in Caroline County, Maryland, "stones as large as hen's eggs fell, doing great damage to growing crops and fruits of all kinds. Cattle were killed in the fields." An Associated Press dispatch on July 8, 1925, vouched for hail-stones "from three to six inches in diameter ... some of which weighed from four to five pounds," that fell in Minneapolis.

That blood rained from the sky (cf. stanza 7) at Poole in June, 1653, is certified by the *Moderate Intelligencer* (June 27–July 4, 1653, p. 70), by the *Weekly Intelligencer* (June 28–July 5, p. 905), and by other news-books. *Mirabilis Annus Secundus*, 1662, tells (pp. 13–14) of a sun in Leicester "red as blood," with drops of blood as big as cherries on the leaves of the trees; and (p. 23) of a storm in Staffordshire that rained great drops of blood on some of the door-posts. Books that told of blood raining upon "Strale

THE PACK OF AUTOLYCUS

Sonet" (?Stralsund) and Rome were registered for publication on September 26, 1597, and January 29, 1620 (Arber's *Transcript*, III, 91, 664; cf. also *Coryat's Crudities*, II [1905], 46, *Roxburghe Ballads*, I, 357–358, and the instances given in No. 4, above). That the same marvel happened at Monte Carlo in November, 1920, was printed in all the newspapers.

Three suns (cf. stanza 8) are reported to have been seen in Cheshire and Shropshire — they are "astrologically handled" in William Lilly's *World's Catastrophe* (1647) — on April 3, 1647, and again in Cumberland and Westmorland on April 11, 1650 (Thomason Tracts, E. 603 [3]). An earlier work of Lilly's, *The Starry Messenger*, treats of three suns that were visible in London on November 19, 1644; and a later one, *An Astrologicall Prediction of the Occurrances in England [in 1648–1650]*, discusses three that were seen in Lancashire on February 28, 1648. Four suns are said to have appeared over Edinburgh on June 15, 1626 (Arber's *Transcript*, IV, 163), and in France on April 9, 1666 (*Philosophical Transactions* of the Royal Society, I, 219 ff., following the narrative of *Le Journal des Scavans* for May 10, 1666). *Mirabilis Annus*, 1661 (pp. 36–38), speaks of seven suns that frightened Danzig on February 20, 1660, and adds that the observer might have seen nine suns if he had looked sooner, for he "could well discover the foot-steps of two more."

Armed men and various other apparitions visible in the air (cf. stanzas 8, 9) are reported from almost every corner of the globe. Examples too numerous to mention are given, say, in Stephen Batman's *Doome* (1581), in *Mirabilis Annus* (1661), and in *Mirabilis Annus Secundus* (1662). Among the Thomason Tracts are pamphlets about apparitions seen and heard in the air in Cambridgeshire and Norfolk on May 21, 1646 (E. 340 [3]), at the Hague on the same day (E. 340 [33]), at Bolton on February 25, 1650 (E. 594 [18]), in Cheshire on April 11, 1651 (E. 628 [16]), and so on. See further the titles listed in Arber's *Transcript*, II, 431, 655, III, 388, and the examples given in Nos. 4 and 14. Floods in which nearly every living thing perished except a young baby were not, it appears, uncommon. Many instances of this strange happening are brought together in Beard's *Theatre of God's Judgements*, pt. I (4th ed., 1648), pp. 442–444. Wanley (*The Wonders of the Little World*, 1678, p. 627) tells of a baby that was found on a hill in Holland (to which it had been carried by the great flood of 1568), sound asleep "in its Cradle with a Cart lying by it"; and of another that was protected (in an earthquake of 1627, at Apulia, which destroyed 10,000 persons in one city alone) by a church bell, which fell from the steeple and covered it. *A true report of certaine wonderfull ouerflowings of Waters*, 1607 (ed. E. E. Baker, 1884, p. 18; cf. *Harleian Miscellany*, III [1809], 383 f.), remarks that in Somerset "An infant likewise was found swimming in a Cradle, some mile or two fro' ye place where it was knowen to be kept, and so was preserved"; Richard Niccols, in the tragedy of "Richard III" which he contributed to the *Mirror for Magistrates*, 1610 (ed. Haslewood, III, 798), declares that

STRANGE NEWS FROM BROTHERTON

> Trees hid their heads, dumbe beasts on hilles were drown'd,
> Infants in cradles wandred to and fro;

while about 1675, in Laurence White's ballad (cf. No. 32) of "A True Relation of the Great Floods" (*Roxburghe Ballads*, VII, 690) we are informed that

> In many places people they were drown'd,
> Infants in cradles one the shore was found.

To conclude his marvels, the ballad-writer mentions the defeat of the Spanish Armada, the Gunpowder Plot, and the adventurous trip of Prince Charles in 1623 to arrange a Spanish marriage. Equally marvelous, he thinks, are the escapes this same Charles, now king of England, has had from the dangers of battle. The ballad ends with a statement that Charles I is invulnerable, and a prayer that the Lord will send him home in peace to a united land. Such a prayer could hardly have pleased the official licenser of printing.

For the tune see Chappell's *Popular Music*, I, 381. On the printer, John Hammond, see my *Cavalier and Puritan*, p. 45.

THE PACK OF AUTOLYCUS

Strange Newes from Brotherton in Yorke-shire, being a true Relation of the raining of Wheat on *Easter* day last, to the great amaizment of all the Inhabitants; It hath rained Wheate more or lesse every day since, witnessed by divers persons of good ranke and quality, as the Lady *Ramsden* who gethered some her selfe, some of it was sent to Judge *Green*, and M. *Hurst* dwelling at the *Fountaine* Taverne in Saint *Anns* Lane neere Aldersgate in *London*.

To the Tune of *The rich Merchant man*.

1 OH wretched *ENGLAND* mind!
  the wonders God doth show,
Obserue and lay it well to heart,
  before thine Overthrow:
It rained Wheat of late,
  as thousands witnesse can,
In *Brotherton* [1] in *Yorke-shire*,
  obseru'd by many a man.
The wonders of the LORD,
  let none forget therefore,
But carefully beare them in mind,
  both now and evermore.

2 It rained Wheat I say,
  a thing which we do want,
Our sinnes is cause [2] of our strife,
  our strife made all things scant,
By divers honest men,
  by some of good renowne,
Some of the wheat that fell that time,
  was brought to *London* Towne.
The wonders of the LORD, &c.

---

[1] Text *Brothertn*.   [2] *Perhaps read* causer *or* cause of all.

3   At *Oxford* to likewise,
     before these warres began,
   It rained wheat as it is known,
     and many witnesse can:
   But what it doth presage,
     there's none but God can tell,
   Or what shall happen unto us,
     who in this Island dwell.
   The wonders of the LORD.

4   To raine downe wheat on earth,
     the clouds in sunder breake,
   And we without offence to God,
     may this construction make;
   That when the Time of dearth,
     small foode to us is given,
   Those that do put their trust in God,
     they shall be fed from heaven.
   The wonders of the LORD, &c.

5   As GOD his people fed,
     within the Wildernesse,
   The self-same love he still doth beare,
     when his are in distresse,
   The Widows cruse of Oyle
     in times most perilous,
   Unwasted did continue still,
     a thing most strange to us.
   The wonders of the LORD,
     let none forget therefore,
   But carefully beare them in mind, &c.

6   THe *German* Maid likewise,
     to manifest Gods power,
   Her friends not able her to keepe,
     preseru'd was by a flower:

THE PACK OF AUTOLYCUS

A Dearth of things is now,
    and likely to be more,
Gods power hath bin lately showne,
    in helping of the poore.
The wonders of the LORD,
    let none forget therefore,
But carefully beare them in mind,
    both now and evermore.

7 Our Chronacles report,
    if it be understood,
A little before a civill warre,
    one day it rained blood,
Hailstones as big as Eggs,
    another time then fell,
Which did much hurt to countryfolks
    our Chronacles doth tell.
The wonders of the LORD.

8 Within the firmament,
    two suns hath often bin,
And armed men presaging warre,
    to scourge the world for sin:
The Sea did overflow,
    and man and beast did drowne,
A Child within a Cradle then
    a live the people found,
The wonders of the LORD, &c.

9 When th' *Scotcsh* and *English* iar'd,
    about eight yeares agoe,
The like did hap at *Knottingley,*
    as many people know:
Strange Apperitions too,
    of armed men did traine,
On *Barkestone Moore* not farre from thence
    as many will maintain.
The wonders of the LORD, &c.

10 Old eighty eight methinkes
    should never be forgot,
With many wonders of the Lord
    likewise the powder Plot:
A thing first hatcht in Hell,
    by Heaven brought to light,
God helped us as we may say,
    by his most powerfull might.
The wonders of the LORD.

11 Our King when he was Prince,
    and journed into *Spaine*,
It was a wonder that he did
    returne so safe againe:
In time of bloody warre,
    when thousands fell we know,
The Lord preseru'd our royall King
    where ever he did go.
The wonders of the LORD, &c.

12 And since there's none hath power,
    to do him any harme,
God him defend against his foes,
    with his out-streaching hand: [1]
And let it be the Prayer,
    of all that love his Grace,
To send him home unto his owne,
    and to his Royall Place.
The wonders of the LORD,
    let none forget therefore,
But carefully beare them in mind,
    both now and evermore.

Finis.

Printed by John Hammond, dwelling over-against
S. Andrews Church.

[1] The rhyme requires *arm.*

8

The poor man, the merchant, and the king

Wood 401 (51), black letter, four columns, no woodcuts.

According to the list of printers in Lord Crawford's *Catalogue of English Ballads*, Charles Tyus printed only during the years 1659–1664. H. R. Plomer's *Dictionary* (1641–1667) gives the dates as 1656–1664. The ballad, however, though printed about 1660, is at least as old as 1650, because another version of it occurs in *Bishop Percy's Folio Manuscript*, ed. Hales and Furnivall, III, 127–134. The language and the narrative-technique point to a still older date of composition, although the archaisms may be due to a process of oral tradition that led in one case to the Percy MS., in the other to Tyus's press. The MS. copy has two hundred lines, and is twenty-four lines, or six stanzas, longer than the ballad. The two versions have verbal differences in nearly every line, and some of them are striking. Evidently each was made independently from some common original (like the "history" mentioned in the second line) or from oral tradition.

The MS. copy is entitled "Marke more ffoole," and throughout the ballad Solomon's brother is called "Mark" or "Lord Mark." Dr. Furnivall, who knew only the MS. exemplar, believed "Mark More" to be a corruption of "Mark Morio," that is, "Mark Fool." Undoubtedly, however, the name is a corruption of Marcolf (possibly "Mark More Fool" represents "Marcolf Morolf"), and the connection between the ballad and the enormously popular mediaeval stories of King Solomon and Marcolphus is too obvious to require argument. For discussions of these stories see F. H. von der Hagen's *Narrenbuch*, 1811, pp. 215–268, 498–513; W. A. F. G. Schaumberg's *Untersuchungen über das deutsche Spruchgedicht Salomo und Morolf*, 1874; C. H. Herford's *Studies in the Literary Relations of England and Germany*, 1886, pp. 253–272; and *The Dialogue or Communing between the Wise King Salomon and Marcolphus*, edited by E. G. Duff, 1892.

The ballad deals with three incidents which, though common enough separately, are seldom found together, as here. Particularly widespread is the story of the lost purse. The following parallel versions (many of them pointed out to me by Professor Kittredge) may be noted: *Tales, and quicke answeres, very mery, and pleasant to rede*, ca.1530, No. 16 (*Shakspeare's Jest Book*, ed. S. W. Singer, pp. 12 f.); *Pasquils Jests*, 1604 (*Shakespeare Jest-Books*, ed. W. C. Hazlitt, III, 17–18, 2d pagination); *The Pleasant Conceits of Old Hobson*, 1607 (*ibid.*, 35–36, 3d pagination); H. L. de Prezel, *Diction-*

THE POOR MAN AND THE MERCHANT

naire d'anecdotes, 1767, II, 417–418; *Facecies, et motz subtilz . . . en françois & italien*, ed. Lodovico Domenichi, 1573, pp. 52 f.; Barbazan and Méon, *Fabliaux et contes*, 1808, II, 120, No. 15; Pierre J. B. Le Grand d'Aussy, *Fabliaux ou contes*, 3d ed., 1829, III, 66–70; *Histoires plaisantes et ingénieuses*, p. 323; *Nouveaux contes à rire et aventures plaisantes de ce tems*, 1709, p. 294; Giovanni B. Passano, *I novellieri italiani in verso*, 1868, p. 91; Giraldi Cinthio, *Hecatommithi*, 1565, 1st decade, 9th story; *Karls Recht*, 1493, reprinted by K. Müllenhoff in Haupt's *Zeitschrift für deutsches Alterthum*, XIV (1869), 525–530, and by Joseph Bergmann in *Das Ambraser Liederbuch* (Stuttgart Literarischen Verein, 1845), No. 138; Johannes Pauli, *Schimpf und Ernst*, ed. Hermann Österley, 1866, No. 115 (pp. 85, 485 f.). A few additional parallels to the incidents of the ballad are given in W. A. Clouston's *Popular Tales and Fictions*, II (1887), 367–371; and very many indeed are listed in Theodor Benfey's *Pantschatantra*, I (1859), 394–396, and the work of Österley cited above.

Almost an exact parallel to the three main episodes of the ballad and to the judgment of the Marquis occurs in novella 4, "De iusto iuditio," in the *Novelle di Giovanni Sercambi*, edited by Alessandro d'Ancona, 1871. In that story Sercambi (1348–1424) tells how Landrea found a wallet containing money, returned it, and was accused by its owner of theft, as was the poor man of the ballad. Next he helped a horse from a bog, but pulled out its tail in doing so. As the owners of purse and horse were dragging him to a judge, Landrea inadvertently frightened a horse on which a pregnant woman was riding, so that she fell off and miscarried. Her husband then joined with the other complainants in demanding satisfaction. As the company approached a bridge, Landrea jumped off in despair, but fell into a boat in which two brothers were sitting and killed one of them. The surviving brother demanded justice, and helped to carry Landrea before the judge. The latter decides exactly as did the Marquis of the ballad in regard to the purse. Furthermore he orders that Landrea is to keep the horse until its tail grows out; the woman is to live with him until she is again pregnant; he is to sit in a boat and let the brother jump down on him. The story ends with the four complainants' compromising as they do in the ballad. For a discussion of Sercambi's novella and its parallels see the *Jahrbuch für romanische und englische Literatur*, XII (1871), 349–350. The part played, in stanza 12 of the ballad, by the poor man's crackling sheepskins is duplicated, among other places, in Hans Christian Andersen's tale of Little Claus and Big Claus."

The tune is named from the ballad of "The King & Northern-man . . . o the Tune of *Slut*" (*Roxburghe Ballads*, I, 521), a Bodleian copy of hich (Wood 402 [45]) is signed by Martin Parker.

THE PACK OF AUTOLYCUS

The poor man, the Merchant, and the King;
OR,
The King's brother, his wise Sentence for the poor Man.

To the Tune of *King and poor northern Man.*

1   IT was my chance as I did walk
       a history for to read,
    Solomon wise, when he reign'd King,
       did many a worthy deed.

2   Many a Statute he caus'd to be made,
       and this was one amongst them all,
    It's treason for a man to find out a mans losse,
       and not to restore it to the right owner again.

3   As it chanced there was a rich Merchant,
       as he was riding to the market town;
    It was his fortune to lose his purse,
       and in it there was an hundred pound.

4   Proclamation he caus'd to be made
       if any man could find it plain,
    Restore to him without any doubt,
       and they should have twenty pound for their pain.

5   As it chanced there were a silly poor man
       with two sheepskins on his back to sell,
    It was his fortune to find this purse
       and he took it up and he lik'd it well.

6   When he had took it up into his hand
       he needs must see what in it he would,
    The sum of money he could not understand,
       because there was nought in the purse but gold.

7   Thou horson villain then said the Marchant
       I think it is thou that hast found my purse.
    Why wilt thou not restore it to me again,
       which if thou do not thou shalt fare the worse.

8 My liegh quoth he I found such a purse,
  and gladly to you I'le make it known,
You may have it again it is never the worse,
  pay me for the finding and that's my own.

9 Let me see what's in it then said the Merchant
  he found an hundred pound and no more,
Thou horson villain thou hast payd thy self
  for in my purse there was full six score.

10 But before the King thou shalt be brought,
  I warrant you when I come before our King,
He will not reward me of with nought
  as you your selfe thought to have done.

11 As they were leading him towards the King,
  and as they were going on the way,
There they did meet with a gallant Knight
  and with him was his Lady gay.

12 With hugging and tugging this silly poor man
  his Leather skins they began to crack,
The gelding was wanton and leaped aside,
  and cast the fair Lady quite on her back.

13 The Lady fell down and got a great thwack,
  no harm at all the poor man did mean,
The Lady did light upon the ground,
  and a stub hath struck out one of her eyne.

14 The Knight would needs upon him have been,
  now stay quoth yᵉ Merchant & that is a wrong,
I have an action already against him
  to go [to]¹ the King and he is sure to hang.

15 As they were leading him towards the King,
  the poor man he lik'd not of being led double
But at a sea clift he had thought to have leap'd,
  and to have sav'd both himself and them trouble.

¹ Text omits.

16   As he was leaping at the Sea clift
      thinking no harm at all God wot,
  He met two fishers bound to Sea
      and the leap broke one of their necks in the boat.

17   The other would needs upon him have been,
      now stay quoth the Merchant that is wrong,[1]
  We have two actions already against him
      and to go to the King he is sure to be hang'd.

18   As they were leading him towards the King,
      and as they went to the gallery gay,
  Here is such a villain then said the Merchant,
      as came not before you this many a day.

19   It was my chance to lose my purse,
      and in it was there pounds full six score,
  The villain wil not give me an hundred again
      unless I woold give [him][2] twenty more.

20   I have worse and that then said the Knight,
      I know not what the villain did mean,
  He caus'd my gelding to fling my Lady
      and a stub hath struck out one of her eyne.

21   I have worse and that then saith the Fisher,
      I may sigh and say alas God wot,
  He met with me & my brother was bound to the sea
      and the leap broke my brothers neck in the boat.

22   *Solomon* wise he turn'd him about
      he was not advised in every thing.
  Never such three actions came before me
      never since I was crowned King.

23   *Marquis* his brother he was there,
      I pray you good brother these three you do fear,
  I pray you good brother turn them over to mee
      and their causes I soon will clear.

---

[1] *Text* wrang.   [2] Text omits.

THE POOR MAN AND THE MERCHANT

The second Part to the same Tune.

24 With all my heart said *Solomon* the wise,
   You may have the judgement of them yet,
He turn'd them over to *Marquis* his brother,
   now fainer of them I would have them be quit.

25 *Marquis* heard their judgements all,
   and every one set up his spell,
Come hither poor man, come hither to me,
   and let me hear what thou canst say for thy self.

26 My Leach quoth the poor man then touching this matter
   As I was bound to the market town,
It was my fortune to find this purse
   and in it there was an hundred pound.

27 A proclamation he caus'd to be made
   if any man could find it again,
Restore it to him without any doubt
   & they should have twenty pounds for their pains.[1]

28 Where is thy witness said the *Marquis?*
   I pray you let us hear him soon?
Here is the Merchant's own man,
   and carries the message from town to town.

29 The Merchant's man then he was call'd,
   he swore there was an hundred pound & no more;
And how his Master profered twenty pound,
   to any that would to him his purse restore.[1]

30 Saith *Marquis* this shall be my judgement straight
   yea, and perhaps you will think it strange,
Thou shalt follow him in the heels every day,
   untill thou do find such a bill of Exchange.

[1] The Percy folio inserts a new stanza here. (*In stanza 27 read* pain.)

31 And then keep it to thy self & never give 't him again
  now God forbid then quoth the Merchant,
How should I find a hundred pound [1] of this
  that never had a hundred groats to lose.

32 I had rather give him twenty more,
  if so betyde you wou'd let me stay,
Pay down the money then quoth the *Marquis*,
  so mayst thou quietly go thy way.

33 Now poor man how hindrest thou this Knight?
  thou must needs make him amends I win,
This is against all Laws and Rights,[2]
  the Lady lackt the one of her eyen.[3]

34 Hast thou not a wife at home with two eyes plain,
  yea my Liege an honest poor woman,
And for her living doth take great pains,[4]
  as any one doth in all the town,

35 This shall be my judgement straight,
  yea and perhaps you will think it strange;
The wife with two eyes and the Lady with one
  and as thou hast drest her thou shalt exchange.

36 Now God forbid then quoth the Knight
  that ever so bad should be my choyce,
I had rather give him an hundred pound,
  then to be troubled with his damn'd wife.

37 Pay down thy money then quoth the *Marquis*,
  so mayst thou be going within a while,
The Fisher for fear he should be call'd,
  he was run away halfe a quarter of a mile;

38 Was not there a third man then said the *Marquis?*
  I pray let us hear what he can say?
My Leige quoth they he was here even now,
  but as fast as he can he is run away.

[1] *Text* paund.   [2] *Read* Right.
[3] The Percy Folio inserts two new stanzas here. [4] *Read* pain.

39   I pray let him be called back again,
      if so betyde he be in the sight;
It's never be said you came before me,
      but every man shall have his right.

40   Now Fisher what made thee to run away?
      my Liege quoth he I had a great way home;
And I thought it was time to pack away,
      having spent the most of my coyne.[1]

41   Saith this shall be thy judgement straight,
      yea and perhaps you will think it strange;
Thou shalt set thy boat in the same stead,
      and thou shalt leap at him by way of Exchange.

42   So mayst thou quit thy brothers death,
      now God forbid then quoth the Fisher;
That ever so bad should be my chance,
      I shal either be drown'd or it wil cause me swound.

43   I had rather give him twenty pounds,
      I am sorry my Liege that I came hither:
Pay down thy money then quoth the *Marquis*,
      so may you be packing all fools together.

44   These three they could not well agree,
      but each fell out with one another,
They said they would never come before our King,
      as long as he was in company of *Marquis's* brother.

45   The poor man he was well content,
      and well pleased in every thing;
He said he car'd not how oft he came
      before the Majesty of our King.

𝔉𝔦𝔫𝔦𝔰.

London, Printed for *Charles Tyus* on London-Bridge.

The Percy Folio inserts two new stanzas here.

9

A noble duel

Wood 401 (99), black letter, four columns, three woodcuts, slightly torn.
The eighth and sixteenth stanzas are irregular, thanks to the difficulties the
old printer met with in fitting the letter-press into the form.

James, second Earl of Southesk, killed the Master of Gray in a duel
fought in August, 1660. The latter, the son of an Edinburgh merchant, had
married Hume, Mistress of Gray, a daughter of the seventh Lord Gray, and
had been in command of a regiment of Charles II's army during the years
1650–1651. There are brief notices of the duel in *The Chronicle of Fife* (1810,
p. 158, afterwards printed as Lamont's *Diary*, 1830, p. 126) and in Nicoll's
Diary (1836, p. 300). A detailed account precedes Professor Sir Charles
Firth's reprint of the ballad in the *Scottish Historical Review*, III (1905),
1–5.

The tune comes from the ballad of a duel (in 1609) between Sir George
Wharton and Sir James Steward (*Roxburghe Ballads*, VII, 595) that was
sung to the tune of *Down Plumpton park*. The latter tune is named from
the refrain of "The Lamentation of John Musgrave," of about the same
date (*ibid.*, p. 604), and is apparently unrecorded. It is, however, sung by
Buzzard in Richard Brome's *English-Moor* (III, ii); while in John Fletch-
er's *Captain* (III, iii) Jacomo says, "I can sing nothing But *Plumpton-
park*."

𝔄 𝔑𝔒𝔅𝔏𝔈 𝔇𝔈𝔘𝔈𝔏,

OR,

𝔄n unmatchable 𝔠ombate betwixt 𝔖ir *VVilliam* [*Gray*]
and the 𝔈arl of *Southast*.[1] 𝔅eing a true relation how
this b[loody] 𝔈. of *Southast* 𝔐urthered 𝔖ir *William
Gray*, 𝔖on to the ℜight 𝔥o[norable] the 𝔏ord *Gray*,
which news is sad to the 𝔑acion of *Scotland*, and how
the [𝔈arl] waites for triall for the same.

Tune of, *Sir George VVharton*.

[1] Wood changed to *Southesk*.

1   MY heart doth bleed to tell the wo
      or chance of grief that late befel
At *Biglesworth* in *Bedfordshire*
   as I to you for truth will tell,
There was two valliant Noble men,
   that very rashly fell at words,
And nothing could appease their wraths
   till they betook them to their Swords.

2   The one was called Sir *William Gray*,
   the good Lord *Gray* his Son and Heir,
The other Sir *Iames* as they him call,
   or *Earl* of *Southeist* as I hear,
It seems their quarel they began,
   within the house of Parliament,
And til this Earl had kild Sir *Gray*,
   he could not rest nor be content.[1]

---

[1] *Text* contend, (*sic*).

3   About Religion they out fell,
     the Earl he was a Presbyteir,
Sir *William* did his ways deny,
     he being a Loyall Cavelier,
For our late King as I am told,
     in *Scotland* often kept his court,
At the house of Sir *William Gray*,
     he and his Nobles did their resort.

4   And for his true obedience then,
     as I do wrightly understand
He made was the chiefest Governor,
     in the *Northern* part of fair *Scotland*.
It seems the Earl of *Southeist* calld,
     did kill Sir *William* for this thing,
Because he Governor was made,
     and much advanced by the King.

5   This Earl was governor before,
     out of Commission late was thrown,
Even by this present Government,
     so that he could not call't his own,
And good Sir *Gray* put in his place,
     but truth it brought him into thrall,
For through [1] that cruel bloody Earl,
     his rise [2] was causer of his fall.

6   You see the bloody minds of those,
     which lately had the Sword in hand,
And if they had it so again,
     they quickly would confound the Land.
For to find opportunity
     this wicked Earl he did invent,
How he might Murther Noble *Gray*,
     for truth it was his full intent.

[1] *Text* though.   [2] *Text* rist.

A NOBLE DUEL

𝔗𝔥𝔢 𝔰𝔢𝔠𝔬𝔫𝔡 𝔭𝔞𝔯𝔱, 𝔱𝔬 𝔱𝔥𝔢 𝔰𝔞𝔪𝔢 𝔗𝔲𝔫𝔢.

7 Within the house of Parliament,
     the Earl fell out with Noble *Gray*
But yet before they did depart,
     they loving friends then went away,
It was not known the Earl did ow,
     the least ill will at that same time
To noble *Gray* or unto his,
     or any of his Royall line.

8 They rod together thirty Miles,
     to *Beglisworth* from *London* Town,
And in the way was no distast,
     until they set there at the Crown.

9 They supped together too that night,
     as peacefully as men could do,
But yet a sudden accidence,
     betime ith morning did insue,
The Earl he rose ith morn betime,
     with mischief harbored in his brest,
He come unto the Chamber where,
     sir *William Gray*, he lay at rest,

10 And call'd Sir *Gray* to go with him,
    unto the Fields to take the Ayr,
And he God wot not thinking ill,[1]
    did with him to the Fields repair,
Like to a Lamb that went to dy,
    not thinking death to be so near,
Even so befel the same ye see,
    to Noble *Gray* as doth appear.

11 He left his man abed that morn,
    because he came in late at night,
Desiring them to let him lye,
    till he returned back with the Knight,
His bedfellow and Kindsman too,
    went as a second in the place,
If that the Earl should offer him,
    any abuse or eke disgrace.

12 He did no sooner come in field,
    but both the seconds and the Earl,
Did plot contrive against Sir *Gray*,
    his courage purposely [2] to queal,
The Earl began the quarrel then,
    and Noble *Gray* did so outdare,
And said he was a better man,
    then all the *Grays* in *Scotland* were,

13 And said to him come fight with me,
    thou cowardise which art no man,
Which forced Valiant *Gray* to take,
    his glitering Sword within his hand,
And so the battle fierce began,
    and Noble *Gray* he plaid his part,
But yet at length unhappily,
    the Earl he thrust him to the heart.

[1] *Text* thinkin gill.   [2] *Text* purposel (?)

A NOBLE DUEL

14 This being done they dragd him too
   a stinking ditch which there was by,
And robbed him of his Iewels rich,
   and then they presently did fly,
Unto the Crown whereas there coach,
   stood ready for their safe convay,
But by a man it was found out,
   which did them presently betray.

15 When they was took they did them search
   whereas they found them full of Gold,
A golden watch and ring which cost,
   five hundred pounds his man thus told,
They had them to the Iustice straight,
   and he did send them to the Goal,
Whereas they wait for tryall now,
   I think theres no man will them bail.

16 And thus I will conclude my song,
   I wish all Traytors to be ware,
And not to murder as they do,
   lest they fall in the hang-mans snare.

London, Printed for John Andrews at the White-Lyon
   neer Py-corner.

10

The Jew's high commendation of St. Paul's

Wood 401 (125), black letter, four columns, two woodcuts. There is another copy in Wood 401 (110ᵛ). The date is about 1660.

This ballad was not known to W. S. Simpson, in whose *Documents Illustrating the History of S. Paul's Cathedral* (Camden Society, 1880) it deserves a place. It is particularly interesting because of the strange rumor, credited by many people not only of the Commonwealth period but of later times, that London Jews attempted to buy St. Paul's from Cromwell for use as their synagogue. Sir Edward Nicholas, for example, wrote to the Marquis of Ormonde in the spring of 1649 (Thomas Carte's *Collection of Original Letters*, I [1739], 276): "They [the Commons] are about demolishing and selling Cathedral Churches. I hear *Norwich* is designed already; and that the *Jews* proffer 600,000 *l.* for *Paul's* and *Oxford* Library, and may have them for 200,000 *l.* more." A similar statement was made by Robert Monteth, or Monteith, of Salmonet (*Histoire des troubles de la Grand Bretagne*, 1661, trans. James Ogilvie, 2d ed., 1738, p. 473; cf. D'Blossiers Tovey, *Anglia Judaica*, 1738, pp. 259f.):

> What is very remarkable in this, is, that the *Jews*, who crucify'd the Son of God, by whom Kings Reign, took then Occasion of the Conjuncture [*i. e.*, of the trial of Charles I], which seem'd favourable to them: They presented a Petition to the Council of War, who crucify'd him again, in the Person of the King, his Vicegerent in the Kingdoms, over which God had set him. By their Petition, they requested, that the Act of their Banishment might be repeal'd, and that they might have St. *Paul's* Church for their Synagogue; for which, and the Library of *Oxford*, wherewith they desir'd to begin their Traffick again, they offer'd five hundred thousand Pounds; but the Council of War would have eight. The Brokers employ'd by the *Jews* in the Affair, were [*Hugh*] *Peters* and [*Henry*] *Martin*.

For a discussion of the matter see the work of Simpson already cited (pp. lxiii f.). Paul's steeple, which so impressed the Jew, was proverbial for its height (cf. Chappell, *Popular Music*, I, 117).

The "delicate new tune" and *The repairing of Paul's* are perhaps identical, but apparently the music is not known.

The Jewes high Commendation[1] of the Metrapolitant Cathedrall Church of St. Paul, having view'd the greatest Effiges in the world: With Pauls complaint to his Sacred Majesty of all his sad Losses and abuses in the time of his absence, and his Majesties gracious promise for the Repairing of it to its former state & condition.

To a delicate new tune, Or, *The Repairing of Pauls.*

1 NOw I am constrained[2] to write of a thing
    was builded a thousand yeares agoe,
For all the Effugies that ever was seen
    old *Pauls* still carries the bravest shew.
Indeed I have travel'd Kingdomes farre,
    and seen their famous Fabricks all,
Yet never a one could be compar'd
    unto the Cathedrall Church of *Pauls.*[3]

2 The City of *Roome* I have bin in,
    and many weary step have I trod,
The Tower of *Babel* I have seen,
    in travelling over the world abroad.
Yet never a Monument I found
    of such aspiring height[4] of all,
As is that noble ever renown'd
    the brave Cathedrall Church of *Paul.*

3 The Pilgrims askt me severally
    what manner of thing this Church it was,
Whose height was raised up to the skye,
    and the very walls were beaten brasse.
I answered them these words to the same
    that story I often times had bin told,
And great report I heard of the name,
    which was not the like in all the world.

[1] *Text* Commondation.   [2] *Text* canstrained.
[3] Read *Paul.*   [4] *Text* heigh.

THE PACK OF AUTOLYCUS

4   Then presently I ty'd up my reed,
      it ravished me with so much delight,
And over the Seas I sayled with speed,
      so willing was I for to see this sight.
But when I came to *Pauls Church* yard,
      Lord quoth I what a Church is here.
I thought the *English* people had made
      their way to heaven thorow the spire.

5   I was amaz'd amongst the crouds,
      and staring upwards still did I.
The top of the church did seem in ye clouds
      & I thought ye steeple did reach to the sky.
now hear ye complaint which *Paul* did mak
      unto the King when he came home,
I have bin abus'd my Liege for your sake
      which maks me stand in my rags so torn.

6   FOr in fifty seaven and fifty nine,
      with grief my sids began to crack,
My aged corps did much decline,
      for my cloths were pulled off from my back.
My leaden covering they did take,
      their guns were then so hungry grown,
A purpose Bullets for to make,
      they never would let old *Pauls* alone.

7   They did not care who they abus'd,
      for ruine was their chief intent:
Where Prayers formerly was us'd,
      here they did make a stable in 't.
Yet for all this I still held up,[1]
      though weather-beaten many a yeare,
But severall people were in a doubt,
      this last year I was in great dispair.

[1] *Read* out.

8 But now bespeak our gracious King,
    for all the abuse you received then,
With speed I doe intend to begin
    to give old Paul a new trimming agen.
Then presently I took heart of grace,
    because our Soveraign Lord the King,
Did say he'd make a sacred place,
    and give old *Paul* a new trimming agen.

9 The Service Book shall then be read,
    the Queristers shall sing like men,
The Bishop he shall be the head,
    and all things shal come in old fashion agen.
The Organs merrily they shall play,
    and *Davids* Musick wee shall heare,
The Harps and Timballs all the day,
    which much delighteth then the eare.

10 All these were godly songs [1] that were
    delightfull much in *Davids* dayes,
Which made his Subjects God to feare,
    whilst he was playing with thanks & prais.
The Clergy flourish shall again,
    and Hereticks they must all go down,
True Christian faith wee shall maintain
    and *Pauls* shall be called Sacred ground.

11 As famous as I ever have bin,
    I now shall receive my high renown,
And all my honours return'd me agen,
    I am old Paul of *London* Town.
Now God preserve our Gracious King,
    Lord Mayor and the Aldermen,
which have bin pleas'd in this noble thing
    to give old Paul a new Trimming agen.

printed for F. Coles, T. Vere and W. Gilbertson.

[1] *Text* sons.

II

A most wonderful and sad judgment

Wood 401 (177), black letter, four columns, two woodcuts.

Wood adds, "In the beg. of March 1661." In April George Thomason bought the pamphlet printed by William Gilbertson (E. 1874 [4]) from which the ballad was summarized. It is entitled, *Two most strange Wonders. The one, a relation of an Angel appearing to James Wise, Minister in York-shire; the other being a judgment which befell Dorothy Matley of Ashover, who having couzened a poor lad of two pence, the ground opened and swallowed her.*

Mirabilis Annus (1661, pp. 82 ff.) tells the story of Dorothy Matley at great length. Nathaniel Crouch's *Wonderful Prodigies* (1762 ed., p. 32) and William Turner's *Compleat History of the Most Remarkable Providences* (1697, pt. I, ch. 104, p. 15) each gives a short paragraph to her. Turner notes that there is an abbreviated version in the second volume of Samuel Clarke's *Mirrour, or Looking-Glass for Saints and Sinners* (1671 ed., p. 510). Dr. John Worthington (*Diary*, ed. James Crossley, I, 346) in August, 1661, wrote to Samuel Hartlib: "There is a strange story of a woman that denied she had such money, and wish'd, if she had it, that she might sink into the ground. She sunk some yards into the ground, and was digged out dead. It was not long since, in Derbyshire." John Bunyan inserted a full account of the prodigy in his *Life and Death of Mr. Badman*. There Mr. Wiseman says:

This Dorothy Mately . . . was noted by the people of the town to be a great swearer, and curser, and liar, and thief, (just like Mr. Badman:) and the labour that she did usually follow was, to wash the rubbish that came forth of the lead-mines, and there to get sparks of lead ore; and her usual way of asserting of things was with these kind of imprecations, "I would I might sink into the earth if it be not so; or, I would God would make the earth open and swallow me up." Now upon the 23d of March, 1660, this Dorothy was washing of ore upon the top of a steep hill about a quarter of a mile from Ashover, and was there taxed by a lad for taking of two single pence out of his pocket, (for he had laid his breeches by, and was at work in his drawers,) but she violently denied it, wishing that the ground might swallow her up if she had them. She also used the same wicked words on several other occasions that day.

Now one George Hodgkinson, of Ashover, a man of good report there, came ac-cidentally by where this Dorothy was, and stood still a while to talk with her, as she was washing her ore; there stood also a little child by her tub side, and another a dis-tance from her, calling aloud to her to come away; wherefore the said George took the girl by the hand to lead her away to her that called her. But, behold, they had not gone above ten yards from Dorothy, but they heard her crying out for help; so looking back, he saw the woman, and her tub and sieve, twisting round, and sinking into the ground. Then said the man, Pray to God to pardon thy sin, for thou art never like to be seen alive any longer. So she and her tub twirled round and round, till they sunk about three yards into the earth, and then for a while staid. Then she called for help again, thinking, as she said, she should stay there. Now the man, though greatly amazed, did begin to think which way to help her; but immediately a great stone, which appeared in the earth, fell upon her head, and broke her skull, and then the earth fell in upon her, and covered her. She was afterwards digged up, and found about four yards within ground, with the boy's two single pence in her pocket; but her tub and sieve could not be found.

It may surprise most readers to hear that Dorothy Matley was a real person. They can hardly believe Bunyan's story of her death (can she have been murdered and then slandered by the murderer to conceal his crime?), but her contemporaries believed it; and a reference to her perjury and her punishment went into the burial register of Ashover. The entry (J. C. Cox, *The Parish Registers of England*, 1910, p. 133) follows:

1660. Dorothy Matly, supposed wife of John Flint, of this parish, foreswore herself; whereupon the ground open [*sic*], and she sanke over hed March 1st; and being found dead she was buried March 2d.

After an imprecation similar to Dorothy's, the wife of King Edward I was swallowed by the earth, according to the popular (but, of course, inaccurate) tradition expressed in George Peele's play of *Edward I* (1593) and in "The lamentable fall of Queen El[li]nor" (*Roxburghe Ballads*, II, 69); while in Nathanael Richards's play of *Messallina* (1640), V, i, a striking stage-direction runs, "Earth gapes and swallowes the three murder[er]s by degrees."

For the tune see Chappell's *Popular Music*, I, 162.

𝔄 most wonderful and sad judgement of God upon one *Dorothy Mattley* late of *Ashover* in the County of *Darby*, within fourteen miles of the said Town of Darby; who for so small a thing as two single pennies which she was charged with the taking of from a boy, did most presumptuously with sad imprecations wish and desire, that if she had taken or stole the same, that the ground might open and she sink therein, which by her neighbours relation was an expression very common with her, but so it pleased God to deal, that upon the same words the ground did open, and she with a Tub which she was washing Lead-Oare in sunk into the ground, to the amazement of the beholders, and the ground closed again upon her, as here underneath it is

more fully declared; and this was done upon the 23 of
March 1660. All which may well serve for an example
to all wretches of this age whatsoever, who to advance
themselves by falshood, or for the trifles of this world,
take to themselves assumptions, and imprecations,
nay will not at all stand to forswear themselves to
compass their own ends, as if there was no God or
judgment to be expected; but they may hereby take
notice that some time God will punish such creatures
even in this life for example sake; yet if not here, their
reward will be according to their works hereafter, and
none shall be able to let it.

The tune is, *Fortune my Foe:*

1   Listen a while dear frinds I do you pray,
     And mark the words that I to you shall say
     A wonder strange I mean for to declare,
     In this our time, I think without compare.

2   I'th moneth of *March*, the three & twentieth day
     As we in *England* do compute and say:
     I'th year above exprest, this thing was done,
     To many peoples admiration.

A WONDERFUL JUDGMENT

3 *Ashover* parish in fair *Darby-shire*,
   There God did manifest his dreadful Ire,
   Upon one *Dorothy Matley* called by name,
   As many neighbors can attest the same.

4 This wicked wretch it seems did think to get
   Two single pennies from a boy by cheat
   And when they asked her for them, still yᵉ more
   They were demanded, she the faster swore:

5 She had them not, but would ful sadly scold,
   And with sad imprecations be so bold:
   As to desire from God, if ever She
   The same ere had, she might example be

6 Unto the world, if she such things had done,
   Although there was more then suspition
   To prove the same, yet she did it deny,
   And to her neighbours still would say and cry:

7 IF I this money stole, or it be found
   With me, then let me sink into the ground,
   Ith place whereas I stand and let me be
   Example to you all that do me see.

8   Her neighbours present wishes that she would
Cease imprecations, and not be so bold
As to provoke her Maker, but still she
Did use the same, and never would it flee.

9   But here my pen methinks is at a stand,
To think how God by his revenging hand,
Most justly did this wicked wretch confound,
And she alive forthwith into the ground

10   Begins to sink, a thing it is full sad,
She scrieched & cryed for help, but none she had
One foot she something moved, but suddenly
Straight down she went with a most hidious cry.

11   When she was sunk the ground forthwith did close
And did return unto the first repose.
Which made all for to muse that did it see
And much admire that such a thing should be.

12   Her neighbours some of them would dig to find,
This woful wretch, to satisfie their mind
They found her buried in the ground so deep,
Which would have made the hardest heart to weep.

13   As for the Tub not yet spoke of before
Wherein the wretched woman washed her Oare
It clear was gone, not yet found out by man,
As many of her neighbours witness can.

14   This then may serve to persons of this age,
To warn them from provoking God to rage
By Oaths, Assumptions, and false imprecations,
Least they pull down his vengeance on these Nations.

15   For he it is that can discern aright,
The meanest Subject and the greatest Might.
Each one according to his works shall have
From the just one, he needs it not to crave.

16 Thus have I done what here I did intend
    Nothing but love unto my Country friend,
    Gods won'ders to declare, I think 'tis just
    That they may not lye buried in the dust.

FINIS.

Printed for VV. Gilbertson.

12

Misery to be lamented

Wood 401 (185), black letter, four columns, two woodcuts. Wood adds the date "1661."

Wood has preserved two other accounts of this gruesome calamity. The first is a pamphlet (Wood 365 [17]) printed by J. Jones with the title of *An Exact Relation of the Barbarous Murder Committed on Lawrence Corddel A Butcher, who was Buryed alive At Christ-Church, on Fryday last being the 21 of June, With lamentable Screeks, groans and horrid cryes, made by him in his Grave on Sunday night, and the sad, wounded and mortyfy'd condition he was taken up in on Munday, June 24. Also the Examination and Confession of His Land-Lord and Land-Lady (William Cook and his Wife, at Pill-cock-Lane in Newgate-Market) before the Right Honorable the Lord Mayor of London, by whom they were both Committed to New-Gate* (1661).[1] The second, a broadside printed by Austin Rice (1661), is called *A Sad and Sorrowfull Relation of Laurence Cauthorn, Butcher; who was Buried whilest he was Alive, In Christ-Church-Yard, Upon Friday, June 21. And was taken up, and the Coroners Jury sate on him June 24.* Both accounts declare that William Cook, the landlord, was not at all to blame, but throw vehement suspicion on his wife Sarah, who had "the better of him by wearing the Briches." Like the ballad, with which they agree in every important detail, they were printed immediately after the Cooks had been committed to prison and before their trial.

Somewhat different, and obviously inexact, is the history of Cawthorn given in *The Ladies Dictionary; Being a General Entertainment For the Fair-Sex*, 1694, p. 727 (mispaged 492):

To the knowledge of many hundreds about *London*, in the Year, 1661. One *Lawrence Cawthorn* a Butcher in St. *Nicholas Shambles* who having provided all things for his Marriage, it is doubtful whether too much strong Waters, or Opium given him by his Landlady, who aimed at what monys he had got, and knew she should not be the better for it, if he Married; cast him into a profound Sleep, so sleeping all that night, and all the next day, she got some of her confederates to give out he was dead, so buried him, but the next day being Sunday, as the People passed to Church they heard a strange groaning in the ground, but for a time could not tell what to make of it, growing louder, though a kind of a hollow sound, they informed the Churchwardens of it, who only floutted at it as a delusion of the Senses, but the next day being better informed, and all circumstances considered; this new Grave was opened, and the Body found warm, though dead with the stifling vapours and violent beatings

[1] Another copy of this pamphlet was advertised for sale in Messrs. Dobell's catalogue No. 45, lot 41 (June, 1925).

MISERY TO BE LAMENTED

against the sides of the Coffin, upon news of which the Barbarous Old Woman fled, and we do not hear she ever was found again.

From *The Ladies Dictionary* William Turner quoted the story in his *Compleat History of the Most Remarkable Providences*, 1697, pt. II, ch. 34, p. 33. Cawthorn is referred to as "the Butcher buried alive" in *Gusman's Ephemeris*, 1662, sig. A2ᵛ.

Premature burial, as Edgar Allan Poe's story of that title testifies, has always had a morbid fascination for people of every class. With the present ballad one could profitably compare a book (Wood B 35 [17], Bodleian; E. 356 [13], British Museum) called *A strange and wonderfull Relation of The burying alive of Joan Bridges of Rochester in the County of Kent. Also, The manner of her tearing open of her own belly, the getting of the Cloath off her face, and loosing of her feet in the Grave* (1646). See further *The Untimely Burial: or, Lamentable News from Watford*, May 4, 1676.

For the tune (which is used also for Nos. 26 and 36) see Chappell's *Popular Music*, I, 370, and cf. my note in the *Publications of the Modern Language Association of America*, XXXVIII (1923), 134.

MISERY to bee Lamented: Or,

A Doleful Relation of the sad Accident which befell Lawrence Cawthorn, a Journey-man-Butcher, belonging to the Shambles in Newgate-Market, who being supposed to be dead, was caused to be presently buried by his Lanlady Mris. Cook, in Pincock-Lane, only, as is supposed out of her greedy desire to gain his cloaths. And how hee came to himself again, when hee was in the grave, as appeared when hee was taken up, by the sad consequences of his struling and striving to get out of the Coffin, his arms being beaten black and blew, his head bruised and swel'd as big as two heads, and his eyes starting almost out of his head; It being also certainly reported, that he was heard to utter many grievous shrieks and groans the time he lay under ground, which was from Friday night, June 21. to Monday morning, June 24. 1661.

To the Tune of, *Troy Town.*

THE PACK OF AUTOLYCUS

1 ALL you that spend your precious times
  in sensual pleasures and delights,
In drinking, swearing, and such crimes,
  whom death it self no whit afrights,
Give ear to what I shall declare,
  and well consider what you are.

2 Your daies in length are like a span,
  your life's a vapour, which appears
But for a little while, and than
  death puts a period to your years;
O! therefore now, even whilst you may
  prepare you for your dying day.

3 Let not presumptuous thoughts take place
  within your hearts, but surely know
Your life's but for a little space
  (death is a debt which all men owe)
O! therefore now, even whilest you may
  prepare you for your dying day.

4 Repentance must not be deferr'd
  until old age or sickness come;
Death often meets men unprepar'd,
  and sends them to their longest home;
Therefore so live, that still you may
  be ready for your dying day.

5 It is appointed that all men
  must dye; this truth we know full well,
But in what manner, where, or when
  none but the Lord alone can tell;
Therefore so live, that still you may
  be ready for your dying day.

6 Wee daily by experience see
  that from deaths heavy mortal blow
Nought in the world can set us free,
  but to the stroak wee all must bow,
O! therefore now, even whilst you may
  prepare you for your dying day.

7   A sad Example hath of late
      been evident before our eyes.
    A young man whose unhappy fate
      may teach us all to be more wise
    And live so, that wee alwaies may
      bee ready for our dying day.

8   A Butcher was this young mans Trade
      and *Lawrence Cawthorn* was his name,
    The place where he his lodging had,
      was at a house in *Pincock-Lane*,
    Wherein one Master *Cook* doth dwell,
      in *Newgate-Market*, known full well.

9   When hee his Freedome did obtain,
      a Iourney-mans place hee undertook
    A lively-hood thereby to gain,
      well to his businesse hee did look,
    And very careful hee was still
      to satisfie his Masters will.

10 But now what unto him befell,
      I plainly to you will declare,
    That this is true which I shall tell,
      most certainly it doth appear;
    'Tis strange! yet thus it came to passe,
      alive this young man buried was.

The second Part to the same Tune.

11 ON *Thursday June* the twentieth day,
      as soon as evening-tide was come,
    His work being done, hee went some say
      unto an Ale-house neer his home,
    And tarried certain hours space
      with his companions in that place.

12 Then coming home, to peoples view
  hee seem'd in perfect health to bee
 Much work hee said hee had to do
  next morn as soon as hee could see,
 And told his Landlord to that end
  to rise betimes hee did intend.

13 But when next morning light appear'd,
  and hee not rising as he said,
 To do his work; his Landlord feard
  that sleep his sences had betray'd,
 Therefore hee to his Chamber hies,
  and loudly calls to make him rise.

14 But all in vain, for why alasse,
  the young man heard not when he spake,
 Which to him a great wonder was
  that *Laurence* would no answer make.
 Then down the stairs he did run,
  and told some Neighbors what was done.

15 A Smith was sent for then with speed
  who soon broke ope the Chamber doore:
 Which being done, they then indeed
  began to wonder more and more:
 For why, they surely thought that death
  had quite bereft him of his breath.

16 They found him lying on the bed
  his cloaths were on, his eyes were shut:
 No motion from the foot to head,
  which them into amazement put.
 And all concluded certainly
  his life was past recovery.

17 The Searchers then came up, and view'd
  his body o're in every place:
 And to the people then they shew'd,
  what was their judgement in that case.
 Their Verdict was, that cruel Death
  had by a Quinsey stopt his breath.

18 His Landlady through covetousnesse
    to gain his cloaths I understand:
Did make it her great businesse
    to bury him quickly out of hand.
A shallow Grave was dig'd with speed
    and he therein was laid indeed.

19 But ah! what groans he uttered
    as some report for verity:
For as it seemes he was not dead,
    but only in a trance did lye.
And coming to himself again
    he did endure most grievous pain.

20 With head and feet, and arms he wrought,
    so long as any strength remain'd:
Most earnestly for life he sought,
    which could by no means be obtain'd.
For being underneathe the ground
    to save his life no way was found.

21 From *Friday night* till *Monday morn*
    he lay in earth imprisoned:
Disconsolate and quite forlorn,
    untill his breath was smothered.
And then when as the time was past,
    they dig'd him out o'th grave at last.

22 His Coffin opened was, wherein
    a dolefull sight they then beheld:
With struling he had bruis'd his skin,
    his head and eyes were sadly sweld.
His body over black and blew,
    as many do report for true.

23 His Landlord and his Landlady
    being suspected for this deed:
Examined were most certainly
    and unto *Newgate* sent with speed
And till themselves they well can clear,
    it is suppos'd they must lye there.

24 Now let us all with one consent
      turn to the Lord with heart and mind:
And of our grievous sins repent,
      that so we may Gods mercy find,
And to conclude to God let's call,
      from such a death Lord keep us all.

FINIS.

London, printed for F. G. on Snow-hill.

Entred according to Order.

13

Terrible news from Brentford

Wood 401 (181), black letter, four columns, three woodcuts.

Brentford, or Brainford, has always figured prominently in ballads. Certainly the dreadful punishment that befell Mr. Thompson there should edify or amuse all those who "love a ballad in print o' life."

Drinking healths to the Devil has been always a ticklish business; but, unfortunately, experience is a poor teacher, and not even the doleful and oft-repeated warnings of the ballad-writers succeeded in ending that evil custom. In October, 1642, Andrew Stonesby, a Cavalier, drank a health to the Devil in an ale-house at Listelleth in Cornwall. Immediately Satan appeared and claimed as his own the fellow, who died with horrid ravings and blasphemy on his lips (Thomason Tracts, E. 126 [36]). Nathaniel Crouch ("R. Burton"), in his *Admirable Curiosities* (1702, p. 169) tells of a soldier who drank a health to the Devil in a Salisbury tavern. The horrified bystanders rushed from the room, and presently some one, running up to the chamber, "found the Window broken, the Iron bar bowed in and bloody, but the Man was never heard of after." Crouch quoted from Samuel Clarke's *Mirrour* (1657, p. 148), which relates many similar judgments on cursers and drunkards, as does also Thomas Beard's *Theatre of God's Judgements* (pt. I [4th ed., 1648], 91, 135 ff., 423); but such stories are too numerous to need repeating.

In many of them there is no doubt a modicum of truth. Few men even in this present modernist age would wish to tempt Providence by blasphemy; and perhaps nine persons out of ten would to-day attribute a death like that of Thompson or Stonesby to divine intervention. Compare, for example, this news-story which appeared on the front page of the New York *Times*, November 24, 1923:

May God Punish Me With Death If Guilty, Says Man, Then Dies.

Bregenz, Austria, Nov. 23.—"May Almighty God punish me with instant death if I am guilty," was the final declaration of a man on trial here for the murder of his wife. Immediately after uttering these words he swooned in the courtroom and died before doctors could come to his aid.

His statement was made during a heated cross-examination under which the accused showed great excitement. Doctors certified that heart failure caused his death.

Probably nearly every person who read this dispatch was convinced, at least momentarily, of the unhappy man's guilt.

Health-drinking, whether to devil or man, was bitterly opposed by the Puritans. John Geree, for example, in April, 1648, printed a treatise "wherein the evill of Health-drinking is convinced" (Thomason Tracts, E. 434 [15]). William Prynne was courageous enough to express his feelings on this subject to Charles II shortly after the Restoration (*ibid.*, E. 1040 [4]).

The balladist evidently believed (cf. stanza 12) that the Devil took Mr. Thompson's body as well as his soul. The superstition was generally held: see the examples in Clarke and Beard referred to above. So, too, in Philip Stubbes's *Anatomy of Abuses*, 1583 (New Shakspere Society ed., I, 71 f.), there is a tale of an Antwerp lady who was killed for her pride by the Devil and put into a coffin. "Foure men immediatly assaied to lifte vp the corps, but could not moue it, then sixe attempted the like, but could not once stirre it from the place, where it stoode." Opening the coffin, "thei founde the bodie to be taken awaie, and a blacke Catte verie leane and deformed sittyng in the Coffin."

For the tune see Chappell's *Popular Music*, I, 198. Stanza 11 has only four (instead of eight) lines in the original, and faulty rhymes appear in stanzas 3 and 12.

Terrible News from BRAINFORD:
OR,
A perfect and true Relation of one *Thompson* a Waterman, and two more of that Function, being drinking in excess at *Brainford*, at the House of one Mrs. *Phillpots*, Thursday night, *September 12.* began a Health to the Devil, and another to his Dam; at which falling dead against the Table: With the Devils appearing in the Room visible, the Burial of the sinful Wretch; his Corps seeming heavy at first, but the Coffin afterward as light, as if there had been nothing in it.

To the Tune of, *Chievy Chase.*

1 ALl you which sober minded are,
     come listen and Ile tell,
The saddest story Ile declare,
    which in our dayes befell:
Therefore 'tis for example sake,
    the business written is,
That others may a warning take
    by such lewd lives as these.

2 My matter now I have in hand,
    doth very doleful run;
In *Brainford* you shall understand
    this horrid act was done:
Three Watermen a drinking were,
    some say in *Phillpots* house,
Who very desperately did swear,
    they would have one Carouse.

3 To every friend as they could think,
    abroad the world so wide,
A Glass unto his Health would drink,
    whatever did betide?

So many Healths about did pass,
    which is a shame to tell;
They knew not who to drink unto,
    except the Devil of Hell.

4 Quoth one and swore the Pot shall pass,
    be it to good or evil;
And if thou wilt but pledge a Glass,
    Ile drink unto the Devil:
The other said I willing am,
    call in for Sack about us;
Ile drink another to his Dam,
    it shall not go without us.

5 With that he bowed down his head,
    and suddenly did fall;
He sunk against the Table dead,
    in presence of them all:
His vitals then with death was stung,
    throughout eternally,
His Nose upon the Table hung,
    a ghostly sight to see.

The second Part, to the same Tune.

6 THe others then with fearfulness,
  their legs were smitten so
With horrour and with feebleness,
 they knew not what to do:
But staring in the dead mans face,
 they dolefully did cry,
Good people help us in this place,
 help, help, or else we dye.

7 Which horrid doleful voices then
  put all the house in fear,
Who nimbly up the stairs ran,
 to see what news was there:
And being come, good Lord how then
 they trembled in the place;
And questiond then the living men,
 like wretches void of Grace.

8 How came this horrid dismal fate,
  declare it good or evil;
For we did hear you once relate
 A Health unto the Devil:
Tis very true, quoth they, by stealth
 that act we once began;
And I my self did pledge the Health,
 and drank unto his Dam.

9 At which they all were trembling than,
  though faint and yet unable;
They did endeavour with the man,
 to lay him on the Table:
Which time one knocked at the door,
 but going for to see,
An ill-shap't Devil in did bore
 amongst their company.

10 And being come unto the light,
  their hearts were very cold;
The Devil did appear in sight,
 more wonderous to behold:

But when they on their knees did fall,
    and to the Lord did pray;
The Devil vanisht from them all,
    and quickly went his way.

11   But when the morrow did begin,
        a Coffin then was brought;
    And placed then the Corps therein,
        which all this mischief wrought.

12   The four Bearers did complain,
        and to the people say,
    It seem'd the heaviest Corps that e're
        they carried on the way:
    But yet the case did alter quite,
        e're to the Church they came,
    The Coffin it did seem so light,
        as if nothing had been in.

13   Now let all men a warning take,
        by *Thomsons* dreadful fall,
    And drunken company forsake,
        so God preserve us all,
    And keep us still from great excess
        of drinking which is evil;
    And never in such drunkenness
        drink healths unto the Devil.

FINIS.

Printed for F. Coles, M. Wright,[1] T. Vere, and W. Gilbertson,
1661.

[1] *I. e.*, Master (John) Wright.

14

News from Hereford

Wood 401 (179), black letter, four columns, two woodcuts.

In spite of the impressive list of witnesses whose names W. K. adds to the end of his marvelous story, one has great difficulty in believing it. For one reason, the story had been told as early as 1580 in several pamphlets, whence it was summarized in Anthony Munday's *View of sundry Examples. Reporting many straunge murthers*, 1580 (ed. J. P. Collier, along with Munday's *John a Kent*, Shakespeare Society, p. 90), as follows:

Wee hear also of the fearfull tempest that was at Praga, in Bohemia, wheras on the twenty five of January, 1579, at two of the clock in the after noone, that the people durst not shew themselves in the streets. Three steeples of churches were blowen down, brusing about nineteen houses, and six persons slain therby. At evening again there was a marvelous thunder, wherin fel hail stones that weighed the quantity of 3 quarters of a pound, and therafter fel such an earthquake, during for the space of half an hower, that the houses did shake very wunderfully.

At twelve a clock at night was perfectly viewed a black cloude, wherin were plainely escried a mans two armes and hands naturally, the right hand holding a swoord, the other a bowle which poured foorth blood: therby was perceived a peece of ground with corne standing theron, and therby lay a sickle, and a great voice was heard, but nothing seen, which said, *Wo, wo, to the earth and to the inhabitants therof! for hee commeth that is to come, and all the people shall see him*. This voice caused great terror through al the town, that the infants shriked sucking at their mothers brests, and women were then delivered of children.

Aboove the rest, a woman of lix yeeres olde, named Margaret, her husband called John Bobroth, the Clark of the town. This woman for the space of xxv weeks was diseased, and no help could be had; but through this present accident she was delivered of three Children, their mouthes replenished with teeth, as children of three yeeres olde. The first borne spake, saying —
The day appointed which no man can shun.
The second said, *Where shall we finde living to bury the dead?*
The third said, *Where shall we finde corne to satisfie the hungrie?*

W. K. did nothing but give a local habitation and a name to the Bohemian marvel. Perhaps his immediate inspiration was a book called *A strange and true Relation of a wonderful . . . Earthquake that hapned at Hereford*, a copy of which is preserved in the British Museum. Perhaps he knew also the book of *Strange fearful & true newes, which hapned at Carlstadt, in the kingdome of Croatia. Declaring How The Sunne did shine like Bloude nine dayes together, and how two Armies were seene in the Ayre, the one encountring the other. And how also a Woman was deliuered of three prodigious sonnes, which Prophisied many strange & fearefull thinges, which should shortly come to passe, All which happened the twelfth of Iune, last, 1605.* Cf. also my *Analytical Index*, No. 517.

Tales of children who were born with teeth, and of those who spoke either in the womb or immediately after birth, are collected from many sources in Thomas Bromhall's *Treatise of Specters*, 1658, p. 196, and Nathaniel Wanley's *Wonders of the Little World*, 1678, p. 4. A well-known example of a child born with teeth is — as we are reminded by Shakespeare's tragedy and *A certaine Relation of the Hog-faced Gentlewoman* (1640, sig. A3ᵛ) — King Richard III of England. Similarly distinguished at birth was Robert the Devil, Duke of Normandy, the hero of a celebrated mediaeval romance. To cite a modern instance, the New York *Times* of October 2, 1922, reported the birth of a child in Brooklyn who had "two upper and two lower teeth, perfectly formed, and also two uppers and lowers described as rudimentary." The same paper, for January 11, 1923, printed the following news-item: "The first infant ever born with a full set of teeth, upper and lower, so far as local physicians and medical historians know, was a boy, who came to life Tuesday night [January 9] at Lincoln Hospital, the Bronx. . . . The infant also had more hair than is usual at birth, but with the exception of the teeth appeared normal in every other respect. It died two hours after birth. . . . [The doctors agreed] that so far as known the present case was unique. The only explanation was that the infant was a 'congenital anomaly.'"

For the tune see Chappell's *Popular Music*, I, 162–167. The second line of stanza 24 has a bad reading that violates the rhyme-scheme.

𝕹𝖊𝖜𝖊𝖘 𝖋𝖗𝖔𝖒 𝕳𝖊𝖗𝖊𝖋𝖔𝖗𝖉.

𝕺𝕽, 𝕬 𝖜𝖔𝖓𝖉𝖊𝖗𝖋𝖚𝖑 𝖆𝖓𝖉 𝖙𝖊𝖗𝖗𝖎𝖇𝖑𝖊 𝕰𝖆𝖗𝖙𝖍𝖖𝖚𝖆𝖐𝖊: 𝖁𝖁𝖎𝖙𝖍 𝖆 𝖜𝖔𝖓𝖉𝖊𝖗𝖋𝖚𝖑 𝕿𝖍𝖚𝖓𝖉𝖊𝖗=𝖈𝖑𝖆𝖕, 𝖙𝖍𝖆𝖙 𝖍𝖆𝖕𝖕𝖊𝖓𝖉 𝖔𝖓 *Tuesday* 𝖇𝖊𝖎𝖓𝖌 𝖙𝖍𝖊 𝖋𝖎𝖗𝖘𝖙 𝖔𝖋 *October*, 1661. 𝕾𝖍𝖊𝖜𝖎𝖓𝖌 𝖍𝖔𝖜 𝖆 𝕮𝖍𝖚𝖗𝖈𝖍=𝖘𝖙𝖊𝖊𝖕𝖑𝖊, 𝖆𝖓𝖉 𝖒𝖆𝖓𝖞 𝖌𝖆𝖑𝖑𝖆𝖓𝖙 𝖍𝖔𝖚𝖘𝖊𝖘 𝖜𝖊𝖗𝖊 𝖙𝖍𝖗𝖔𝖜𝖓 𝖉𝖔𝖜𝖓 𝖙𝖔 𝖙𝖍𝖊 𝖌𝖗𝖔𝖚𝖓𝖉, 𝖆𝖓𝖉 𝖕𝖊𝖔𝖕𝖑𝖊 𝖘𝖑𝖆𝖎𝖓: 𝖂𝖎𝖙𝖍 𝖆 𝕿𝖊𝖗𝖗𝖎𝖇𝖑𝖊 𝕿𝖍𝖚𝖓𝖉𝖊𝖗=𝖈𝖑𝖆𝖕, 𝖆𝖓𝖉 𝖇𝖎𝖔𝖑𝖊𝖓𝖙 𝕾𝖙𝖔𝖗𝖒𝖘 𝖔𝖋 𝖌𝖗𝖊𝖆𝖙 𝕳𝖆𝖎𝖑𝖘𝖙𝖔𝖓𝖊, 𝖜𝖍𝖎𝖈𝖍 𝖜𝖊𝖗𝖊 𝖆𝖇𝖔𝖚𝖙 𝖙𝖍𝖊 𝖇𝖎𝖌𝖓𝖊𝖘𝖘 𝖔𝖋 𝖆𝖓 𝕰𝖌𝖌, 𝖒𝖆𝖓𝖞 𝕮𝖆𝖙𝖙𝖊𝖑 𝖇𝖊𝖎𝖓𝖌 𝖚𝖙𝖙𝖊𝖗𝖑𝖞 𝖉𝖊𝖘𝖙𝖗𝖔𝖞'𝖉 𝖆𝖘 𝖙𝖍𝖊𝖞 𝖜𝖊𝖗𝖊 𝖋𝖊𝖊𝖉𝖎𝖓𝖌 𝖎𝖓 𝖙𝖍𝖊 𝖋𝖎𝖊𝖑𝖉. 𝕬𝖑𝖘𝖔 𝖙𝖍𝖊 𝖜𝖔𝖓𝖉𝖊𝖗𝖋𝖚𝖑 𝕬𝖕𝖕𝖆𝖗𝖎𝖙𝖎𝖔𝖓𝖘 𝖜𝖍𝖎𝖈𝖍 𝖜𝖊𝖗𝖊 𝖘𝖊𝖊𝖓 𝖎𝖓 𝖙𝖍𝖊 𝕬𝖎𝖗, 𝖙𝖔 𝖙𝖍𝖊 𝖌𝖗𝖊𝖆𝖙 𝖆𝖒𝖆𝖟𝖊𝖒𝖊𝖓𝖙 𝖔𝖋 𝖙𝖍𝖊 𝕭𝖊𝖍𝖔𝖑𝖉𝖊𝖗𝖘, 𝖜𝖍𝖔 𝖇𝖊𝖍𝖊𝖑𝖉 𝖙𝖜𝖔 𝖕𝖊𝖗𝖋𝖊𝖈𝖙 𝖆𝖗𝖒𝖘 𝖆𝖓𝖉 𝖍𝖆𝖓𝖉𝖘; 𝖎𝖓 𝖙𝖍𝖊 𝖗𝖎𝖌𝖍𝖙 𝖍𝖆𝖓𝖉 𝖇𝖊𝖎𝖓𝖌 𝖌𝖗𝖆𝖘𝖕𝖉 𝖆 𝖌𝖗𝖊𝖆𝖙 𝖇𝖗𝖔𝖆𝖉 𝖘𝖜𝖔𝖗𝖉, 𝖎𝖓 𝖙𝖍𝖊 𝖑𝖊𝖋𝖙 𝖆 𝖇𝖔𝖚𝖑 𝖋𝖚𝖑𝖑 𝖔𝖋 𝕭𝖑𝖔𝖔𝖉, 𝖋𝖗𝖔𝖒 𝖜𝖍𝖊𝖓𝖈𝖊 𝖙𝖍𝖊𝖞 𝖍𝖊𝖆𝖗𝖉 𝖆 𝖒𝖔𝖘𝖙

NEWS FROM HEREFORD

𝔰𝔱𝔯𝔞𝔫𝔤𝔢 𝔫𝔬𝔦𝔰𝔢, 𝔱𝔬 𝔱𝔥𝔢 𝔴𝔬𝔫𝔡𝔢𝔯𝔣𝔲𝔩 𝔞𝔰𝔱𝔬𝔫𝔦𝔰𝔥𝔪𝔢𝔫𝔱 𝔬𝔣 𝔞𝔩 𝔭𝔯𝔢𝔰=
𝔢𝔫𝔱, 𝔱𝔥𝔢 𝔣𝔯𝔦𝔤𝔥𝔱 𝔠𝔞𝔲𝔰𝔢𝔡 𝔡𝔦𝔳𝔢𝔯𝔰 𝔴𝔬𝔪𝔢𝔫 𝔱𝔬 𝔣𝔞𝔩𝔩 𝔦𝔫 𝔗𝔯𝔞𝔟𝔞𝔦𝔩;
𝔞𝔪𝔬𝔫𝔤𝔰𝔱 𝔴𝔥𝔬𝔪 𝔱𝔥𝔢 ℭ𝔩𝔢𝔯𝔨𝔰 𝔴𝔦𝔣𝔢, 𝔬𝔫𝔢 *Margaret Pell-*
more, 𝔣𝔢𝔩𝔩 𝔦𝔫 𝔩𝔞𝔟𝔬𝔲𝔯, 𝔞𝔫𝔡 𝔟𝔯𝔬𝔲𝔤𝔥𝔱 𝔣𝔬𝔯𝔱𝔥 3 𝔠𝔥𝔦𝔩𝔡𝔯𝔢𝔫, 𝔴𝔥𝔬
𝔥𝔞𝔡 𝔗𝔢𝔢𝔱𝔥; 𝔞𝔫𝔡 𝔰𝔭𝔞𝔨𝔢 𝔞𝔰 𝔰𝔬𝔬𝔫 𝔞𝔰 𝔢𝔳𝔢𝔯 𝔱𝔥𝔢𝔶 𝔴𝔢𝔯𝔢 𝔟𝔬𝔯𝔫,
𝔞𝔰 𝔶𝔬𝔲 𝔰𝔥𝔞𝔩𝔩 𝔥𝔢𝔞𝔯 𝔦𝔫 𝔱𝔥𝔢 𝔣𝔬𝔩𝔩𝔬𝔴𝔦𝔫𝔤 𝔯𝔢𝔩𝔞𝔱𝔦𝔬𝔫, 𝔱𝔥𝔢 𝔩𝔦𝔨𝔢 𝔫𝔬𝔱
𝔨𝔫𝔬𝔴𝔫 𝔦𝔫 𝔞𝔫𝔶 𝔞𝔤𝔢.

The Tune is, *Aim not too high.*

1 OLd *England* of thy sins in time repent
   Before the wrath of God to thee is sent,
   For such great wonders in late time have been,
   The like before I think was never seen.

2 But this which here to you I shall unfold,
   It is the strangest thing that ere was told,
   Yet not so strange but that it is as true,
   Yea every word I dedicate to you.

3 On *Tuesday* last *October* the first day,
   In *Herefordshire* there happened such a fray,
   By a most terrible Earthquake that did hap,
   And violent storms too by a Thunder-clap.

4 About two of the clock i'th Afternoon,
   There did arise a violent storm right soon,
   The Air did darken, and did look unkind,
   Then rose the storm and a high mighty wind.

5 Which for two hours space most vehemently
   It made the tyles from off o'th housen fly,
   And vehemently it did blow and roar,
   That people durst not to go out of door.

6 And by this storm Church-steeples were blown down,
   That stood i'th midst of famous *Hereford* Town
   Besides most famous houses great and small,
   Did by this Tempest and the Earthquake fall.

[83]

7   And by the houses fall much blood was spill'd,
For many men and women too were kill'd,
By this most sudden Accident I say
And fearful chance and lamentable fray.

8   After this mighty Tempest it was past
The Air did seem to clear then at the last;
And people did look out upon the Air,
And all the Element began to clear.

9   But presently it overcast again
At six or seven a clock with might and main,
Towards the Evening it began to hail,
Which made yᵉ peoples hearts more sore to quail.

10   The hailstones full as big as Eggs were seen,
The like in *England* nere before hath been,
No tyles nor stones could make yᵉ hardness yield
It did destroy the cattel in the field.

11   Then followed a terrible Earthquake,
Which made the ground and houses for to shake
And did continue half an hours space,
It many famous buildings did deface.

12   And sorely did amaze both all and some,
The people thought that the last day was come.
Immediately a Brightness did appear,
And as Noon-day it seemed 'twas so clear.

13   THen presently the Air again it clouds,
with a thick darkness overspred with clouds
And out of which appear'd two arms and hands,
At which amazement thousands people stand.[1]

14   And gluts their eyes with fulness of this sight,
When they beheld in those two hands that night
In yᵉ right hand was grasp'd a great broad sword
And in the left a cup of crimson blood.

[1] *Read* thousand peoples stands (*cf. stanza 15*).

15 Another wonder appear'd from these Skies,
 Which was beheld by thousand peoples eyes,
 There seem'd to them a piece of Corn to grow,
 And in this sight seem'd ready for to mow.

16 And ready for to mow't a Sythe lay by,
 And from the place came a most mighty cry,
 Which said wo, wo to man that draweth breath
 And the Inhabitants of all the Earth.

17 At the conclusion of this mighty sight,
 It fearfully did men and women fright,
 Women with child which in that town did dwel
 A many into labour present fell.

18 Amongst the rest and strangest too of all,
 Unto one *Margret Pellmore* did befall,
 The Clerks wife of the Town as I am told,
 Who bore 3 children the like was nere unfold.

19 These children they had teeth, and spake as soon
 As ever they into the world did come,
 These words as follows did from them proceed
 The same is verify'd for truth indeed.

20 The first did say this day no man can shun,
 Which is appointed and not yet begun:
 Where will be found the second child it said
 Sufficient men alive to bury the dead?

21 These words did then from the 3d. child proceed
 Where will be corn enough to satisfy your need?
 These were the words they said at that same tyd
 And presently all these three children dy'd.

22 What man is able in our English Land
 The meaning of these things to understand?
 It doth betoken anger great from God,
 How he will smite us with his heavy Rod.

23   Except by prayer we speedily repent,
And of our wicked sins for to relent;
The cup of blood appeared in the Sky,
And sharp edg'd sword great wars doth signifie.

24   The childrens words do mean great sicknesses,
And to this land the Lord will send great cries,
For to fulfill all what the children said,
The living scarce be able to bury the dead.

25   The Famine so shall poverish to the Land,
Thus shall we feel Gods wrathful heavy hand.
These are but warning-pieces to you all,
Therefore repent good people great and small.

26   Your selves be sure fail not to prepare,
To meet the Lord a comming in the Air.
Give praise & thanks so long as you have breath
Vnto your mighty God of Heaven and Earth.

By W. K.

---

*A List of the names of the persons that witnesseth the
truth of this, are as followeth.*

Fran. Smalman.	*James Tully.*
Hen. Cross,	*Geo. Cox Gent.*
Churchwardens.	*John Groom.*
Peter Philpot.	*Robert Mauricee.*
Nich. Finch, Constables.	*Thomas Welford.*

And divers others, too many to be here inserted.

Printed for F. Coles, T. Vere, and W. Gilbertson.

15

A true and perfect relation from the Falcon

Wood 401 (183), black letter, four columns, three woodcuts. Wood adds the date "1661."

There are probably other versions of the remarkable ghost-story of Mr. Powel, but I have not found them. At any rate, it is easy to understand Wood's enjoyment of ballads like this. Real ghost-tales so seldom appear in ballad-form as to make this "True and Perfect Relation" a notable production, but it is equalled by Nos. 29 and 30. The "learned men" mentioned in the title and in stanza 11 were no doubt later members of the Royal Society! Glanvill (who became an F.R.S. in 1665), in particular, would have accepted the story without the slightest hesitation.

Mercurius Democritus, a Commonwealth news-book, in its issue for February 8–15, 1654, told a corking good, if wholly imaginary, story of a ghost, faintly resembling Mr. Powel, that walked "every night among the Butchers at *Smithfield Barrs* the *Shambles*, *White-chappell* and *Eastcheap*, in the habit of *Mallet* [*i. e.*, Sir William Mallet] the Lawyer," and that ate a maid alive!

For the tune see Chappell's *Popular Music*, I, 198.

Here is a true and perfect Relation from the Faulcon at the Banke=side; of the strange and wonderful aperition of one Mr. *Powel* a Baker lately deceased, and of his appearing in several shapes, both at Noon=day and at night, with the several speeches which past between the spirit of Mr. *Powel* and his Maid *Jone* and divers Learned men, who went to alay him and the manner of his appearing to them in the Garden upon their making a circle, and burning of wax Candels and Jenniper wood, lastly how it banished.

The tune of, *Chevy Chase.*

[87]

1 STrange news, strange news, I here have write[1]
    come lissen and Ile tell,
  The strangest news that ever yet
    within our age befell.
  And Ile repeat it word by word
    to let the Nation know,
  The mighty wonders of the Lord,
    which he to them doth shew.

2 For near upon five moneths ago,
    there was a Baker dyed,
  Close by the *Faulcon* many know,
    which is on *Southwarke* side.
  His body after buryed was,
    in earth for to remain,
  But not long sence it came to pass,
    that his Spirit rose again.

3 And walked up and down the place,
    where he before did dwell,
  And lookt most Ghasful in his face,
    that hundreds there can tell.

[1] *I. e.*, writ.

And ratling throw the house would he,
    afrighting people that,
He sometimes like a Goat would be,
    and sometimes like a Catt.

4 He into several shaps would turn,
    with dolful voyces then
He'd like a flame of fire burn,
    streight to a man agen.
This house he constant haunted that,
    at midnight and noone-day
And sometimes seemed like a Catt,
    which scar'd his Son away.

5 Then none within this house did dwell,[1]
    but one poor servant Maid
Which very often did perceive,
    this ghasful Ghost she said.
Whose pale and dreadful glemering sight,
    reduc't her to a fear
For making of the bed one night,
    it to her did appear.

6 She then beholding of his face,
    poor Soul it made her quake
And she lay trembling in the place,
    that every joynt did shake.
He up and down the Chamber ran,
    his hands abroad were spread
His Nose was waxed pale and wan,
    his eyes sunk in his head.

7 At which the Maid cry'd out O Lord,
    I heartily do pray
That by the power of thy word,
    chase this same fiend away.

[1] *Live* would make a passable rhyme.

THE PACK OF AUTOLYCUS

Repeating these same words agen,
 with lifting hands upright
At which the Aperition then,
 quite vanisht out of sight.

8 But on the morrow morning next
  the same appear'd again,
 He on the house so much reflect,
  few durst within remain.
 The Maid a fire making was,
  about the house did stur
 Which time she heard a dolefull voyce,
  one knocking at the door.

9 The Maid reply'd then who is there,
  and to the door did run
 Quoth he thy good old Master's here;
  come tell me where's my Son.
 At which the Maid run backward in,
  and not one word did say
 And for that time the spirit then,
  did vanish quite away.

10 But afterwards it came to pass,
       late in the Evening tyde
    He underneath a Peartree was,
       where he again was spyed.
    For he within the Garden walkt
       where *Jone* came by chance,
    And this same spirit with her talkt,
       that she fell in a trance.

11 Beside her sences they were lost,
       at such a sight to see
    For pure Nature with a Ghost,
       can never well agree.
    Then Learned men of Art came there,
       this Spirit to alay
    Which did immediatele appear,
       and they to it did say:

12 Gods holy Saints did much convert,
       there actions now are blest
    We Conjure thee for to depart,
       unto thy place of rest.
    The aperition in a pause,
       did vanish none knew whether
    Saying woe to them which are the cause,
       of this my coming hether.

13 By skill these Learned men doth see
       and by their art discry
    Some hiden treasure there must be,
       and in the Garden lye.
    And yet these Conjurers doth say,
       their task hath proved so
    The spirit they cannot alay,
       whatever they can do.

14   O what strange wonders now are these;
      the Lord amongst us send
    God grant hereafter they might cease,
    and we our lives amend.

Printed for F. Coles, T. Vere, and *William Gilbertson.*

16

Truth brought to light

Wood 401 (191), black letter, four columns, five woodcuts.

In manuscript Wood added the date "A:D: 1662." The ballad has very great value as an early narrative of the strange series of events that is given at length by Sir Thomas Overbury the Younger in *A true and perfect Account of the Examination, Confession, Trial, Condemnation, and Execution of Joan Perry, and her two Sons, John and Richard Perry; for the supposed Murder of William Harrison, Gent. being one of the most remarkable Occurrences which hath happened in the Memory of Man; sent in a Letter (by Sir T. O. of Burton . . .) to T. S. [Thomas Shirley] Doctor of Physick in London. Likewise Mr. Harrison's own Account, how he was conveyed into Turkey, and there made a Slave for above two Years; and then, his Master which brought him there, dying, how he made his Escape, and what Hardship he endured; who, at last, through the Providence of God, returned to England, while he was supposed to be murdered; here having been his Man-servant arraigned, who falsely impeached his own Mother and Brother, as guilty of the Murder of his Master: they were all three arraigned, convicted, and executed, on Broadway-hills in Gloucestershire*, 1676 (*Harleian Miscellany*, III [1809], 547 ff. A second edition of 1676 and many later editions and accounts are listed in *The Bibliographer's Manual of Gloucestershire Literature*, by F. A. Hyett and W. Bazeley, 1896, II, 135–137, and the supplement to it, II [1916], 347 f. Of these, the editions of 1743, 1750 [?], and 1820 [?] are recorded in the British Museum's catalogue, and a misleading reference is also given there — *s. v.* "Harrison, William, Steward" — to a proclamation by Queen Anne for the discovery of the "murderers of W. H.").

Harrison, steward to the Viscountess Campden,[1] was supposed to have been murdered at Campden, Gloucestershire, on Thursday, August 16, 1660. His servant, John Perry, accused of the crime, not only confessed it but admitted also that he had broken into Harrison's house in 1659 and robbed it of £140. Furthermore, he accused his mother and brother of complicity in the murder. All three Perrys were, after due trial, condemned to death in the spring of 1661, and were executed as the ballad describes.

---

[1] On her husband († 1683) see *The Court and Times of Charles I*, II, 219. In Hazlitt's *Hand-book*, 1867, p. 230, there is listed a book called *The most strangest and unparalleled Account that ever was Printed, or heard of, being to be justified by several Persons Living in Campden in Gloucestershire*, "Cirencester, printed by Thomas Hinton," 1676, that sounds as if it were connected with the Campden Wonder. I have not been able to see it.

THE PACK OF AUTOLYCUS

Joan and Richard died protesting their innocence, while John's own words at the gallows ought to have convinced the auditors of his insanity or, at least, his mendacity. On August 6, 1662 (according to Andrew Clark's *Life and Times of Anthony Wood*, I, 452), Harrison returned to Campden with a wild story of kidnapping and slavery, which the ballad-writer promptly seized on, fully believed, and even added to. Overbury, on the other hand, says explicitly that Harrison made no charges whatever against the Perrys, — indeed he declared that "he saw not his servant Perry, nor his mother, nor his brother the evening he was carried away," — and admits that while Harrison's story may have been true it was doubted by many people. Others, he adds, thought that Harrison's son had his father spirited away in order to succeed him in the stewardship. Few miscarriages of justice more tragical than the execution of the Perrys have ever been recorded.

Anthony Wood (*Life and Times*, I, 452 f.) adds the following interesting facts to the story of the Perrys and Harrison:

> John Perry hung in chaines on the same gallowes. Richard and Joane Perry were after execution taken downe and buried under the gallowes. Three dayes after a gentlewoman, pretending to understand witches, hired a man to dig up the grave that shee might search Joan's body [*i. e.*, for the witch's mark]. Shee being on horseback drew up to the grave when 'twas opened, but the horse starting at the sight of the body ran away under the gallowes and her head hitting against John's feet struck her off from the horse into the grave.
>
> After Harrison's returne, John was taken downe and buried and Harrison's wife soon after (being a snotty covetuous presbyterian) hung herself in her owne house. Why, the reader is to judge.
>
> Upon Harrison's returne to London Sir R. Hyde [the judge who had condemned the Perrys] was at Glocester in his circuit and one that had seen Harrison there brought the news to Gloucester. Which comming to the hearing of Hyde, he became somewhat passionate and commanding his servant to call the messenger chid him for bringing false news and commanded the jailer to commit him to prison.

Another item of interest is furnished by Hyett and Bazeley's *Bibliographer's Manual of Gloucestershire Literature*, II (1896), 136:

> In a Ms. note, on the back of page 43 of the Bodleian copy of this tract [*i. e.*, one of the 1676 editions], it is stated that "Mr. Harrison's wife fell into a deep melancholy and at last hanged herself after the return of her husband; after her dth there was found a letter in her secrtore, which she had recd from her husband, dated before the execution of Joan and her two sons.[1]

For modern studies of the Harrison-Perry story see "The Campden Wonder" in John Paget's *Paradoxes and Puzzles*, 1874, pp. 337-358, and "The Campden Mystery" in Andrew Lang's *Historical Mysteries*, 1904,

---

[1] This information supports Masefield's theory that Mrs. Harrison never believed her husband dead, and would account for the solicitude about Richard Perry's children that Masefield makes her show. In *The Tragedy of Nan*, act II, by the way, "Campden Wonder" is the name of a rose.

TRUTH BROUGHT TO LIGHT

pp. 55–74. Mr. Lang speaks regretfully of the absence of "a ballad or broadside on 'The Campden Wonder.'" The present production would have interested him deeply — as no doubt it would have delighted John Perry himself. Mr. John Masefield — whose one-act play called *The Campden Wonder* was produced at the Court Theatre, London, on January 8, 1907, and, with its sequel, *Mrs. Harrison*, was printed in his *Tragedy of Nan and Other Plays*, 1909 — makes Perry boast in scene iii of the first play, "Us'll have ballads sung — and I shouldn't wonder. Us'll all be in a ballad. 'The bloody Perrys, they was hanged — O, grief!'"

Mr. Masefield's plays, which, according to a reviewer in the *Dial*, "for straight, sullen horror have rarely been equalled in English," seem to have puzzled the critics, who knew nothing of their source.[1] The first play centres about John, Richard, and Joan Perry, who are executed for the murder of William Harrison only a few moments before he actually returns. Especially noteworthy is the motivation of John, a drunken, worthless wretch, who accuses his mother and Richard of being his accomplices in the murder merely to gratify his spite against Richard, a younger brother who has always surpassed him, even in the matter of weekly wages. Mr. Masefield has not taken undue liberties with the traditional story, though he was accused of doing so by a writer in the *Athenaeum* (January 12, 1907, p. 56), who remarked:

> It would seem from the attendant circumstances as if some basis of fact underlay this grim story. If this is the case, tradition must be gravely at fault, or strange liberties must have been taken by the author. At any rate, as exhibited, the circumstances seem inconceivable.

The second play is exceedingly interesting for its characterization of Mrs. Harrison. Anthony Wood damned her in a phrase; but with fine insight Mr. Masefield represents her as helping her callous, brutal husband concoct his tale of kidnapping and Turkish slavery in order to protect him against discovery, and then as committing suicide to escape living with a murderer whom she now despises. The playwright has invented his explanation of Harrison's actions. He makes Harrison tell his wife: "I weren't never more 'n twenty mile away . . . I knowed all about the Perrys . . . What's the Perrys to me? I know my duty, I hope. Hark you to me, missus. It was my Lord [the Viscount Campden] give me that £300. It was to my Lord's advantage I should be away awhile." The *Athenaeum* (November 13, 1909, p. 601) complains, "Why the peer wanted him to conceal himself, or what his lordship could gain by the execution of the Perry family, is never explained." But this complaint is beside the point. As a plausible adaptation of a strange old story, and as a moving human document, Mr. Masefield's plays deserve high praise. Those who know them should enjoy reading the bigoted, prejudiced account of the Perrys given in the ballad.

[1] "It is based on an actual eighteenth-century [*sic*] record of crime," said the *Athenaeum* (November 13, 1909, p. 601) of *Mrs. Harrison*.

Some readers may like to be reminded that the Campden Wonder was paralleled in a few respects by the Colvin mystery of Vermont. Briefly, Russell Colvin, of Manchester, disappeared on May 10, 1812. In August, 1819, Stephen and Jesse Boorn confessed to have murdered him and were condemned to death, but some time later Colvin reappeared, and they were released. The latest account of this affair is that in E. L. Pearson's *Studies in Murder*, 1924, pp. 265–285, 295. One of the numerous pamphlets dealing with it, *The Trial, Confessions, and Conviction of Jesse and Stephen Boorn, for the Murder of Russell Colvin, and the Return of the Man supposed to have been murdered. By Hon. Leonard Sargeant, Ex-Lieutenant-governor of Vermont* (1873), was (as Mr. Pearson fails to mention) the source of Wilkie Collins's novelette, *The Dead Alive*.

For the tune see Chappell's *Popular Music*, I, 162–167.

Truth brought to Light. OR,

Wonderful strange and true news from *Gloucester* shire, concerning one Mr. *William Harrison*, formerly Stewart to the Lady *Nowel* [1] of *Cambden*, who was supposed to be Murthered by the Widow *Pery* and two of her Sons, one of which was Servant to the said Gentleman. Therefore they were all three apprehended and sent to *Gloucester* Goal, and about two years since arraigned, found guilty, condemned, and Executed upon *Broadway* hill in sight of *Cambden*, the mother and one Son being then buried under the Gibbet, but he that was Mr. *Harrisons* Servant, hanged in Chains in the same place, where that which is remaining of him may be seen to this day, but at the time of their Execution, they said Mr. *Harrison* was not dead, but ere seven years were over should be heard of again, yet would not confess where he was, but now it appears the Widow *Pery* was a witch, and after her Sons had rob'd him, and cast him into a Stone Pit, she by her witch-craft conveyed him upon a Rock in the Sea near *Turkey*, where he remaind four days and nights, till a

[1] *I. e.*, Noel.

TRUTH BROUGHT TO LIGHT

Turkish 𝕾𝖍𝖎𝖕 **coming by, took him and sold him into** *Turky*, **where he remained for a season, but is now through the good providence of God returnd again safe to** *England*, **to the great wonder and admiration of all that know the same. This is undenyably true, as is sufficiently testified by the Inhabitants of** *Cambden*, **and many others thereabouts.**

To the Tune of, *Aim not too high.*

1　A Mongst those wonders which on earth are shown,
　　In any age there seldom hath been known,
　　A thing more strange then that which this Relation,
　　Doth here present unto your observation.

2　In *Glocestershire* as many know full well,
　　At *Cambden* [1] Town a Gentleman did dwell,
　　One Mr. *William Harrison* by name,
　　A Stewart to a Lady of great fame.

3　A Widdow likewise in the Town there was,
　　A wicked [2] wretch who brought strange things to pass,
　　So wonderful that some will scarce receive,
　　These lines for truth nor yet my words beleive.

4　But such as unto *Cambden* do resort,
　　Have surely found this is no false report,
　　Though many lies are dayly now invented,
　　This is as true a Song as ere was Printed.

5　Therefore unto the story now give ear,
　　This Widow *Pery* as it doth appear,
　　And her two sons all fully were agreed,
　　Against their friend to work a wicked deed.

6　One of her Sons even from a youth did dwell,
　　With Mr. *Harrison* who loved him well,
　　And bred him up his Mother being poor,
　　But see how he requited him therefore.

---

[1] *Text* Camben.　　　　　[2] *Text* wick.

7   For taking notice that his Master went,
    Abroad to gather in his Ladies rent,
    And by that means it was an usual thing,
    For him great store of money home to bring.

8   He thereupon with his mischevous mother,
    And likewise with his vile ungodly Brother,
    Contriv'd to rob his Master, for these base
    And cruel wretches were past shame and grace.

9   One night they met him comming into Town,
    And in a barbarous manner knockt him down,
    Then taking all his money quite away,
    His body out of sight they did convey.

10   But being all suspected for this deed,
    They apprehended were and sent with speed,
    To *Glocester* Goal and there upon their Tryal,
    Were guilty found for all their stiff denyal.

The second part to the same Tune.

11   IT was supposed the Gentleman was dead,
    And by these wretches robd and Murthered,
    Therefore they were all three condem'd to death,
    And eke on *Broadway-hill* they lost their breath.

12   One of the Sons was buried with his Mother,
    Under the Gibbet, but the other Brother,
    That serv'd the Gentleman was hang'd in Chains,
    And there some part of him as yet remains.

13   But yet before they died they did proclaim
    Even in the ears of those that thither came,
    That Mr. *Harison* yet living was
    And would be found in less then seven years space.

14   Which words of theirs for truth do now appear
    For tis but two year since they hanged were,
    And now the Gentleman alive is found
    Which news is publisht through the Countrys round.

15 But lest that any of this truth shall doubt,
Ile tell you how the business came about
This Widow *Pery* as tis plainly shown
Was then a Witch although it was not known.

16 So when these Villains by their mothers aid
Had knockt him down (even as before was said)
They took away his money every whit,
And then his body cast into a pit.

17 He scarce was come unto himself before
Another wonder did amaze him more,
For whilst he lookt about, he found that he
Was suddainly conveyd unto the Sea.

18 First on the shore he stood a little space
And thence unto a rock transported was,
Where he four days and nights did then remain
And never thought to see his friends again.

19 But as a Turkish ship was passing by
Some of the men the Gentleman did spy,
And took him in and as I understand,
They carried him into the Turkish Land.

20 And there (not knowing of his sad disaster)
They quickly did provide for him a Master,
A Surgeon or of some such like profession,
Whose service he performed with much discretion.

21 It seems in gathering Hearbs he had good skill,
And could the same exceeding well distil,
Which to his Master great content did give,
And pleas'd him well so long as he did live.

22 But he soon dyd, and at his death he gave him,
A piece of plate that so none should enslave him,
But that his liberty he might obtain,
To come into his native land again.

23   And thus this Gentleman his freedom wrought;
     And by a *Turky* Ship from thence was brought;
     To *Portugal*, and now both safe and sound,
     He is at length arrived on English ground.

24   Let not this seem incredible to any,
     Because it is a thing afirmed by many,
     This is no feigned story, though tis new,
     But as tis very strange tis very true.

25   You see how far a Witches power extends,
     When as to wickedness her mind she bends,
     Great is her Malice, yet can God restrain her,
     And at his pleasure let her loose or chain her.

26   If God had let her work her utmost spight,
     No doubt she would have kild the man outright,
     But he is saved and she for all her malice,
     Was very justly hang'd upon the Gallows.

27   Then let all praise to God alone be given,
     By men on earth as by the Saints in heaven,
     He by his mercy dayly doth befriend us,
     And by his power he will still defend us.

London, Printed for *Charles Tyus* at the three Bibles
on *London-Bridge*.

17

A sad and true relation of a great fire

Wood 401 (189), black letter, four columns, three woodcuts. Wood added the date "1662."

In addition to Nos. 17 and 19 Abraham Miles wrote "The Dubbed Knight of the Forked Order" and "Mirth for Citizens," both of which are included in the *Roxburghe Ballads*, IV, 368; VIII, 699. For the tune of the present ballad (itself in the crudest, roughest verse imaginable) see Chappell's *Popular Music*, I, 162.

The terrible fire described in the ballad occurred on the night of December 27, 1662. In the *Obituary of Richard Smyth* (ed. Sir Henry Ellis, Camden Society, p. 57) this entry is given:

Decem. 27. Mr. De Lawn, a merch^t in Lothbury, wth his wife, whole family, and some lodgers, burnt wth his house; not one person saved.

Henry Townshend, of Worcester, had heard of the fire and made a note of it in his *Diary* (ed. Bund, 1920, I, 95):

Dec. 27. M^r ——, a merchant in Lothbury in London, had his house casually in fire about 2 of the clock in the morning, and it being a brick building burnt so all inward that he and his wife, great with child, and all his family, being 3 in number, were all burnt to death, and all his goods except some copper. Another merchant, who lay in his house and to be married that week and parted that night from his mistress at 12 of the clock, was also burnt.

From the Tower, where he was imprisoned, George Wither wrote in 1662, "in *Lyrick Verse*, fitted to the tune of the *Lamentation*, at the end of the singing *Psalms*," a poem called "A Warning-Piece to *London*, Discharged out of a Loophole in the Tower during the *Authors Close Imprisonment* there. It was meditated upon the deplorable consuming of an eminent *Citizen* with his whole Family in the night, by a sad and sudden Fire, at the beginning of our most *Joyful Festival*, in *Decemb*. 1662." This warning was printed in 1662, as well as at the end (pp. 30–41) of his *Memorandum to London*, 1665. A few stanzas may be quoted as an example of Wither's treatment:

> 2. The *Rich man*, heedlesly discerns
> The near approching day of wrath;
> To fill his *Warehouse* and his *Barnes*,
> Is all the present care he hath.

THE PACK OF AUTOLYCUS

At large, he preparation makes
For offrings to his *Belly God*,
Till *Justice* an occasion takes
To mix those *offrings* with his blood;
    When fools in folly most delight,
    They, often, loose their Souls that night.

3. Our *Love* is cold, nigh ripe our sin,
And, in their march, GOD's Judgments be;
At his *own house* they do begin;
Then from them, who shall now be free?
    To make us thereof take more heed,
One house they singled out of late,
And in a bright *flame-colour'd weed*,
Upon the top thereof they sate;
    And when to sleep they laid their heads,
    Consum'd her dwellers in their beds.

5. Oh with what terrors, were they stroke,
How sadly were they discompos'd,
To finde themselves when they awoke
With stifling *fumes*, and *flames* inclos'd?
    It made their terror much the more,
If to remembrance they did call
What they had done, a while before,
And what so quickly did befal.
    More dreadful it appears to me,
    Then Dungeons, Racks, and Halters be.

In the preface to his *Ecchoes From the Sixth Trumpet*, 1666, Wither positively asserts that in "his *Warning-piece to London*, published 1662, occasioned by a *sudden Fire* in the Night at *Lothbury*, near the middle of that *City*, which then consumed the House of an eminent Citizen, with all the Inhabitants therein," he predicted the Great Fire of 1666.

Samuel Pepys heard of the fire two days after it had happened. In his diary, under the date of December 29, he wrote:

> To Westminster Hall, where I staid reading at Mrs. Mitchell's shop. She told me what I heard not of before, the strange burning of Mr. de Laun, a merchant's house in Loathbury, and his lady, Sir Thomas Allen's daughter, and her whole family; not one thing, dog nor cat, escaping; nor any of the neighbours almost hearing of it till the house was quite down and burnt. How this should come to pass, God knows, but a most strange thing it is!

Almost as strange a thing it is that Pepys did not secure a copy of Miles's ballad to add to his collection.

Sir Thomas Allen, Mrs. De Laun's father, was an alderman who had been Lord Mayor of London in 1660. For the family history of Thomas De Laun see *Notes and Queries*, 5th S., XII, 29–30.

A GREAT FIRE

𝕬 𝕾𝖆𝖉 𝖆𝖓𝖉 𝕿𝖗𝖚𝖊 𝕽𝖊𝖑𝖆𝖙𝖎𝖔𝖓 of a great fire or two. 𝕿𝖍𝖊 most terrible and dangerous fire began in the house of 𝕸𝖗. *George Delaun,* an *Hamborough* 𝕸𝖊𝖗= 𝖈𝖍𝖆𝖓𝖙 in *Lothberry,* neer the *Royal Exchange* in *Corn= hil,* 𝖀𝖀𝖍𝖊𝖗𝖊 𝕸𝖆𝖘𝖙𝖊𝖗 *Delaun* and his 𝖀𝖀𝖎𝖋𝖊 being big with 𝕮𝖍𝖎𝖑𝖉, 𝕯𝖆𝖚𝖌𝖍𝖙𝖊𝖗 to 𝕾𝖎𝖗 *Thomas Allen* of *Finchly,* 𝕸𝖗. *Gilbert,* a 𝕸𝖊𝖗𝖈𝖍𝖆𝖓𝖙, two 𝕸𝖆𝖎𝖉 𝖘𝖊𝖗𝖛𝖆𝖓𝖙𝖘, and a 𝕹𝖚𝖗𝖘𝖊 and her 𝕳𝖚𝖘𝖇𝖆𝖓𝖉, were all burned to ashes in the merciless flames of fire.

To the Tune of, *Fortune my Foe,* or *Aim not too High.*

1   GIve thanks, rejoyce all, you that are secure,
     No man doth know how long life may indure
    Regard dear hearts, at the truth the authour aims,
    Concerning those that suffer in fiery flames.

2   On *Friday* night in the month of last *December,*
    Might peirce a stony heart for to remember,
    The sad mishap concerning *George Delaun,*
    And of his friends that he did entertain.

3 This *George Delaun* of whom I do relate,
  A *Hamborough* Merchant a man of great estate,
  He and his Wife for recreation sake,
  Till eleven at night their pleasures they did take.

4 Then did they all prepare for rest,
  Master and Mistris and all the welcome guest,
  And then being in bed so well and warm,
  Sleep closed their eyes & they thought no one harm.

5 But well a day it fils my heart with wo,
  For Timber and Fagots lay in the Seller below,
  Some sparks of fire did light into the same,
  Then Wood and Oyl's soon of a burning flame.

6 Then did these fiery flames presently,
  Brake into the low rooms most vehemently
  Then to the sieling this vehement flame
  Made passage wide and broad still as it came.

7 Most vehemently it burned then upright,
  And fired all along where it did light,
  Less then three hours taking the building round,
  These buildings brave they all fell to the ground.

8 The people too, likewise they perished,
  Were burnd to death as they did lye in Bed,
  Their Spirits to him that gave them is returnd,
  And their Bodies are to Dust and ashes burnd.

9 A Gentle Woman that was there that Day,
  Desired all night she was to stay,
  But she refused, well it went on her side,
  Or else in fiery flames she had sure died.

How the fire was first espyed.

10 It was a womans chance the truth to tell,
  Did sit up late with a Child that was not well,
  Hearing a cracking, to seek she did begin,
  For fear some Villains had been breaking in.

A GREAT FIRE

11 THen she lookt out at window presently,
  And then a mighty light she did espy,
In discontent it made her to admire,
As if an hundred Candles were on fire.

12 In the Merchants lower Rooms she espied,
The Violent flames and then aloud she cryed
Fire, Fire, and being in dread and fear,
And then the Coffee man he did her hear.

13 And then the Coffee man immediately,
Looking out at window heard a doleful cry,
Lord have mercy on us, we are all undun,
We know not how these miseries to shun.

14 These were the words as some do well remember,
About two in the Morn, the 27. of *December*,
But before four the fire did decay,
And burnd these stately buildings clean away.

[105]

15　O this fire it was so fearful hot,
　　Like a Furnace or Refining Pot,
　　But God he raised instruments in the way,
　　To make this vehement fire then obey.

16　They did so lustily water bring in,
　　Into the fire then they did it fling,
　　And with long hooks the fierceness to allay,
　　Or thousands more it would have brought to decay.

17　Mr. *Terils* House and others neer danger lay,
　　Even by these fiery flames to melt away,
　　With wet to quench they many ways contrive,
　　To save their goods, their houses and their lives.

18　That in *Shore-ditch* likewise we may deplore,
　　Three houses burnt with their substance and store,
　　Two or three people that fire did destroy,
　　Some of their limbs in the Rubbish after lay.

19　But now let us Remember *Lothbury*,
　　And of the sad mischance and misery,
　　Where *George Delaun*, was burned to the ground,
　　And four lumps of flesh was after found.

20　About the bigness of a mans hand were they,
　　As black as a Coal, and a skul or two their lay;
　　O little did they think over night being merry,
　　That before morn in fiery flames to fry.

21　All you that are Masters of a family,
　　Govern well your house and fear the God on high,
　　For when to sleep that we do close our eyes,
　　The Lord doth know whither ever we shall rise.

By Abraham Miles.

London, Printed for *E. Andrews* at the White-lyon
neer *Py-corner*.

18

The giants in the Oxford physic garden

Wood 416 (92), roman and italic type, three columns. There is another copy in Wood 423 (38). Wood adds the date "1662."

Jacob Bobart (or Bobert), formerly of Brunswick, Germany, was keeper of the Physic Garden at Oxford. Reporting his death, February 4, 1680, Anthony Wood (*Life and Times*, ed. Andrew Clark, II, 478) describes him as "a servant to the University: an understanding man: the best gardiner in England: hath a book extant." The book in question is *Plantarum historiae universalis Oxoniensis* (1680–1699), part III; the second part (a first part was never published) was by Robert Morison.

The present ballad is an answer (see stanza 12) called forth by Edmund Gayton's ballad "Upon Mr Bobards Yew-men of the Guards to the Physick Garden. To the Tune of *The Counter-Scuffle*," two copies of which are in Wood's collection (Wood 416 [93], Wood 423 [39]. Cf. W. C. Hazlitt's *Hand-book*, 1867, p. 224). A similar broadside, by John Drope, M.A., called "Upon the most hopefull and everflourishing sprouts of valour, the indefatigable centrys of the Physick Garden," has the shelf-marks Wood 416 (107) and Wood 423 (41). Cf. also Abel Evans's *Vertumnus. An Epistle To Mr. Jacob Bobart, Botany Professor To The University of Oxford, And Keeper of the Physick-Garden. By the Author of The Apparition* (1713). The garden itself is described, among many other places, in John Evelyn's *Diary*, July 12, 1654, and in *Mock Songs and Joking Poems*, 1675, pp. 56 ff. The "Ballad on the Giants" hardly lives up to the marvel suggested by the title, for the giants were not monsters of flesh and blood but merely yew-trees clipped to resemble them.

The tune is named from Robert Speed's *Counter-scuffle, Whereunto is added the Counter-rat*, a poem licensed for publication on July 4, 1626 (Arber's *Transcript*, IV, 162), and reprinted many times until the year 1702.

THE PACK OF AUTOLYCUS

𝕬 𝕭𝖆𝖑𝖑𝖆𝖉 𝖔𝖓 𝖙𝖍𝖊 𝕲𝖞𝖆𝖓𝖙𝖘 𝖎𝖓 𝖙𝖍𝖊 𝕻𝖍𝖞𝖘𝖎𝖈𝖐 𝕲𝖆𝖗𝖉𝖊𝖓 𝖎𝖓 𝕺𝖃𝕱𝕺𝕽𝕯, 𝖜𝖍𝖔 𝖍𝖆𝖛𝖊 𝖇𝖊𝖊𝖓 𝖇𝖗𝖊𝖊𝖉𝖎𝖓𝖌 𝖋𝖊𝖊𝖙 𝖆𝖘 𝖑𝖔𝖓𝖌 𝖆𝖘 𝕲𝖆𝖗𝖆𝖌𝖆𝖓𝖙𝖚𝖆 [1] 𝖜𝖆𝖘 𝕿𝖊𝖊𝖙𝖍.

To the Tune of *the Counter Scuffle*.

1 WHat is our Oxford Africa?
  It teemeth Monsters every day
 About East-bridge which is the way
    To *Whately*.

2 In *Boberts* Garden there are two,
 Which lately had nor foot nor shoo,
 Which now have both in publique view
    most stately.

3 That these are Gyants you may guesse,
 Byth' Foot as well as Hercules,
 And as by Tallons nothing lesse
    Than th' Lyon.

4 They'r Grimme as any dogge of Hell,
 Though heads so many we cant tell,
 For only two (and yet that's well)
    We spy on.

5 Two heads are better farre then one
 In any Consultation,
 But these don't joyn but fix like stone,
    Their Noddles.

6 They speak by Figures or by signes
 Without Communication lines,
 Or any Books of deep Divines
    New Moddles.

---

[1] Of this gigantic hero Rabelais (bk. I, ch. xi) says, "Des dents [il] aiguisoit d'un sabot."

7 Without th' Library or the place
   At the South Port, where *Bacons* Face
   A Fryar of our English Race
                              Did venture.

8 On that men call, blesse us! Black Art,
   By which he made the clowns to start,
   And drove some of them with a F——— [1]
                              To th' Center.

9 This *Roger* [2] (so his Forename shews)
   These heads did make, with Copper Nose
   And taught them language that out goes
                              Our knowledge.

10 But how I wonder came their Feet
   So greene, so great, so thick, so neat
   A hundred come them for to greet
                              From Colledge.

11 Nay one [3] from *Ricot* of late dayes
   Who 'mong the Peers may wear the Bays
   These verdant Gallants to their praise
                              Did visit.

12 Whereby these Gyants credit got
   And he [4] that late the Poem wrot,
   But 'tis a Ballad, is it not?
                              Who'le misse it.

13 Our Gyants are familiar
   With Simpling Tribe, and minister
   The Plant, *Tres-humble Serviteur.*
                              And Physick

14 Of Agrimony, Sage, and Rue
   And garden Rhubarb,[5] Dosed true,
   If grieved are the Learned Crue
                              By Tyssick.

---

[1] *Sic.*   [2] Roger Bacon (1214?-1294).   [3] The Duke of Brunswick.
[4] Edmund Gayton.   [5] *Text* Rhabarb.

15 They guard a Book full of such Plants
   And fright out snailes, locusts, and Ants
   And any vermin foule that haunts
                         These places.

16 Apples they doe preserve as good,
   As in Hesperian Orchard stood,
   Which make Lambs-wooll, a lusty food
                         For Races.

17 All sorts of Cherries doe grow here,
   And strawberries frequent appeare,
   Conceive I pray at time oth' yeare,
                         For Winter

18 As well as Time, will nip sweet Face
   And spoyle those Colours Ladys Grace
   When that Grim sire doth set his Mace
                         Or Print there.

19 Here's medc'nall herbs for Galenists,
   Not powders for our new Chymists
   Who are lame *Vulcans* firy Priests
                         And hammer

20 Spirits out of the simple leaves
   And vig'rous dust, which Jesuit gives
   Far worse the patient oft receives
                         From's Gammer.

21 *Alders-gate* street doth not afford
   Such heaps of hearbs for bed, or board,
   Nor piles of Sallats, sawces stor'd
                         For belly,

22 Nor Westminster, nor yet the Strand
   Nor any Garden of the Land
   Such hearbs as come through *Jacobs* hand
                         Can sell yee.

23   Besides the Marvells of *Peru*,
Of most delicious various hue
No Painter can with pencill doe
                    Such colours.

24   There's stemms of Alo's like Whale-bone,
And teeth like Sword-fish every one,
Yet never yet hurt any one
                    Oth' Scholars:

25   For *Jacob* and his Gyants will
Not suffer any thing that's ill
(Unlesse it be for purge or pill)
                    There growing,

26   For all the plants are of his paines,
He diggs, he seus,[1] but heaven raines
But 'las! he has but little gaines
                    For's Sowing.

27   There is a youth call'd little *Jack*
That shall with working break his back
(Unlesse his breakfast he do lack)
                    Hee'l muck it

28   Like any plowman in the field
Untill the ground her fruit doe yeeld,
So oft [2] with water hath he fill'd
                    His Bucket.

29   What would you more then Gyants high
Forbeare yee to approach too nigh,
You'l fright the Lady *Dulciny*
                    TOBOSO.

30   And yet that Lady hath a Knight
That wil drink wine when he should fight
And *Sancho* loves with all his might
                    To doe so.

I. e., sews (sows).   [2] *Text* of't.

31   To all adventures dangerous,
As the Mill nigh can tell to us,
This Knight will some times fiercely rush
               And's Man sterne.

32   Theres no avoiding of that Knight,
Errant yclept, for day and night
He comes these Gyants to affright
               With Lanthorne.

33   Not *Faux*-like on a black designe
To mirth he only doth incline
And hath a Page, if no Moon shine,
               Attending.

34   For hee'l nor carry coales nor light
Nor yet his Squire, who goes upright
But yet they are for any wight
               Defending

35   Or injur'd Lady, or Fleec'd sheepe
Good lack what Racket they doe keep
And never Eat, nor Drink, nor Sleepe
               Till Gyant,

36   And one-eyd Monsters humbled are
Unto their feet, which smell most rare,
With making constant Fewd, and warre
             o Fie on't!

37   What though these Gyants harnest be
Compleatly too, That's Cap a Pe,
And can with Feet deale lustily
               In boxes.

38   Yet Don *Quixot* is arm'd allso
With brasie helmet of *Mambrino*
Hee'l suffer them no harme to do
             To's doxes:

39 So that 'tis prudence to induce
     The Knight and Giants to a Truce,
     That we the Garden still may use
             In quiet,

40 And drink what springs from Scurvy gras
     (Without making a scurvy face,)
     So shall we keep this pleasant place
             From Riot

41 And filthy Routs which spoile soft joyes,
     The sports of the mad Girles, and Boyes,
     When they are in their merry Toyes
             And Ranting.

42 But *Bobert* is a sober soule
     And watches like an *Athens* Oule
     To see of mirth no lawfull jowle
             Be wanting.

43 But if the Poet, as is meet,
     For these his paines you do not greet
     He thus takes pennance in a sheet
             To please you.

44 In Print when he doth next appeare
     He hopes to make it plaine and cleare
     That of your Melancholy feare
             Hee'l ease you,

45 If not hee'l lay another gin
     And try to catch you once therein
     To put you on a merry pin
             And jolly:

46 If then he failes his *Badger* rimes
     Shall to the tune of *Carfax* Chimes,
     Sing *Nought will please the present times*
             But Folly.

FINIS.

19

A wonder of wonders

Wood 401 (193), black letter, four columns. The single woodcut is the well-known picture of Richard Tarlton, the famous Elizabethan comedian, with his drum and tabor. It has been reproduced in J. P. Collier's *Book of Roxburghe Ballads*, p. 54, and in Halliwell-Phillipps's edition of *Tarlton's Jests*, Shakespeare Society, 1844, frontispiece (cf. also pp. xliii f.). Wood dated the ballad "mense februar: 1662" (*i. e.*, 1662/3).

Joseph Glanvill, chaplain of Charles II and Fellow of the Royal Society, published several accounts, each more circumstantial than its predecessor, of the "Daemon of Tedworth." See, for example, his *Blow at Modern Sadducism in some Philosophical Considerations about Witchcraft. And the Relation of the Famed Disturbance at the House of M. Mompesson. With Reflections on Drollery, and Atheisme. The Fourth Edition* (1668).[1] Glanvill's accounts support the ballad (which is perhaps the earliest treatment of the story extant) in every detail. The curious disturbances at John Mompesson's, in Tidworth, Wiltshire, lasted from March, 1661/2, to about the middle of 1663, Glanvill testifies in his *Sadducismus Triumphatus*. Included in that work (1681, pt. II, preface) is a letter from Mompesson himself, dated August 8, 1674, which declares: "When the *Drummer* was escaped from his Exile, which he was Sentenced to at *Gloucester* for a Felony, I took him up, and procured his Committment to *Salisbury* Gaol, where I Indicted him as a Felon, for this supposed Witchcraft about my House. . . . The Assizes came on, where I Indicted him on the Statute *Primo Jacobi* cap. 12. where you may find, that to feed, imploy, or reward any evil spirit is Felony. And the Indictment against him was, that he did *quendam malum Spiritum negotiare*, the Grand Jury found the Bill upon the Evidence, but the Petty Jury acquitted him, but not without some difficulty"; the drummer, it was proved, had said that the disturbances arose "because he [*i. e.*, Mompesson] took my Drum from me; if he had not taken away my Drum, that trouble had never befallen him, and he shall never have his quiet again, till I have my Drum, or satisfaction from him."

[1] The first section of this account of the "Tedworth Demon" is reprinted in John Ashton's *The Devil in Britain and America*, 1896, pp. 47–59. See also George Sinclair's *Satan's Invisible World discovered*, 1685 (1780 ed., pp. 37–51); John Beaumont's *Historical, Physiological, and Theological Treatise of Spirits*, 1705, pp. 309 ff.; *The History of Witches, Ghosts, and Highland Seers*, Berwick, n.d., pp. 12–31; and, for a mere allusion to the story, the prefatory epistle to Scott's *Fortunes of Nigel*.

A WONDER OF WONDERS

According to *Mercurius Publicus*, April 16–23, 1663, the drummer was one William (but sometimes he is called John) Drury, of Uscut, Wiltshire.

Samuel Pepys records that at a dinner party on June 15, 1663, Lord Sandwich, discussing spirits, said "the greatest warrants that ever he had to believe any, is the present appearing of the Devil in Wiltshire, much of late talked of, who beats a drum up and down. There are books of it, and, they say, very true; but my Lord observes, that though he do answer to any tune that you will play to him upon another drum, yet one tune he tried to play and could not; which makes him suspect the whole; and," says Pepys, "I think it is a good argument." Later Pepys found the book "worth reading indeed," though he considered *A Blow at Modern Sadducism* "not very convincing." Samuel Butler laughed at the "Tedworth Demon" in *Hudibras* (II, i, 131 f.), while in *The Displaying of Supposed Witchcraft* (1677) John Webster treated Glanvill with slight respect. "I am sure," he wrote (p. 11), "his story of the Drummer, and his other of Witchcraft are as odd and silly, as any can be told or read, and are as futilous, incredible, ludicrous, and ridiculous as any can be." Such, too, were Addison's sentiments, although the story is the chief source of his comedy, *The Drummer* (1716).

Increase Mather accepted the story *in toto*, retelling it in his *Remarkable Providences* (ed. George Offor, pp. 111 f.), and adding a parallel to it that was supposed to have occurred in 1679 at the house of William Morse, of Newbury, Massachusetts (pp. 101 ff.). Many of the illustrations Mather gives seem like actual borrowings from Glanvill. For instance: "On December 8, in the morning, there were five great stones and bricks by an invisible hand thrown in at the west end of the house while the mans wife was making the bed; the bedstead was lifted up from the floor, and the bedstaff flung out of the window, and a cat was hurled at her; a long staff danced up and down in the chimney," and so forth.

To hear invisible drums beating in the air was no unusual thing — if one is to believe all one reads! There is, to illustrate, a pamphlet called *A true Relation of a very strange and wonderful thing that was heard in the air, 12 Oct. [1658], by many hundreds of people; namely three cannons shot off, a peal of musquets followed, and drums beating all the while* (Thomason Tracts, E. 955 [4]); and wonderful drums are heard a few times in *Mirabilis Annus* (1661). But seldom has so strange a story as that of the "Tedworth Demon" been so elaborately "authenticated." On its truth Joseph Glanvill staked his reputation. Later John Wesley[1] came to be regarded as its chief defender, so that Hogarth, in his print of "Credulity, Superstition, and Fanaticism," made his emotional thermometer, capped with a figure of the "Tedworth" drummer, rest upon volumes written by Glanvill and Wesley. Beside Glanvill's tale, the spirits and ghosts that operated at Woodstock in 1649—cf. satirical pamphlets like *The Woodstock Scuffle* and

---

[1] Cf. especially his *Journal* for May, 1768 (ed. Curnock, V, 266 f.).

THE PACK OF AUTOLYCUS

The Just Devil of Woodstock (Thomason Tracts, E. 587 [5], E. 1055 [10]) and Scott's novel—seem tame indeed.

For a recent discussion of the "Tedworth" affair see Wallace Notestein's *History of Witchcraft in England*, 1911, pp. 273–276.

As for the ballad, it is far superior to any other extant work from the pen of Abraham Miles (cf. No. 17). Its subject gives it real importance. On the very popular, but still unrecorded, tune see the notes in my *Pepysian Garland*, p. 283.

A VVONDER of VVONDERS;
BEING

A true Relation of the strange and invisible Beating of a Drum, at the house of *John Mompesson*, Esquire, at *Tidcomb* [1] in the County of *Wilt-shire*, being about eight of the Clock at night, and continuing till four in the morning, several dayes one after another, to the great admiration of many persons of Honour, Gentlemen of quality, and many hundreds who have gone from several parts to hear this miraculous Wonder, since the first time it began to beat Roundheads and Cuckolds, come dig, come dig. Also the burning of a Drum that was taken from a Drummer: Likewise the manner how the Stools and Chairs danced about the Rooms. The Drummer is sent to *Glocester* Gaol: Likewise a great [2] Conflict betwixt the evil Spirit and *Anthony* a lusty Country fellow.

To the tune of, *Bragandary*.

[1] *Tĭdworth* (Wood's note).   [2] *Text* grea.

1   ALl you that fear the God on high
       amend your lives and repent,
These latter dayes shew Dooms-days nigh
    such wonders strange are sent.
Of a strange Wonder shall you hear
    at *Tidcomb* within fair *Wilt-shire*,
O news, notable news,
    ye never the like did hear.

2   Of a Drummer [1] his use was so
       at great Houses for to beat,
He to one certain house did go
    and entered in at Gate:

---

[1] "He had been a Soldier under *Cromwel*, and used to talk much of gallant Books he had of an old Fellow, who was counted a Wizzard" (*Sadducismus Triumphatus*, 1726, p. 281).

THE PACK OF AUTOLYCUS

At the house of Master *Mompesson*
    he began aloud to beat his Drum.
O news, notable news,
    ye never the like did hear.

3 Alarum, March, and Troop likewise
       he thundered at the Gate,
   The Children frighted at the noise
       forwarned he was to beat:
   But he refused, and his Drum did rattle
       as if he had bin in some battle.
   O news, notable news,
       ye never the like did hear.

4 HE said he would not be forbid,
       neither by his beck nor brall,
   And had power for what he did,
       they did him Rascal call:
   No Sir I am no such quoth he
       two Iustices hands in my Passe be,
   O news, notable news,
       ye never the like did hear.

5 'Twas counterfeit he did understand,
       and then without delay,
   He gave his Servants then command
       to set this fellow away,
   And likewise took away his Drum,
       this you'l repent the time will come.
   O news, notable news,
       ye never the like did hear.

6 About eight a clock that present night
       a Drum beat in every Room
   Which put them in amaze or fright,
       not knowing how it did come:

A WONDER OF WONDERS

The first it beat was this old Iig,
  Roundheads & *Cuckolds* come dig, come dig.[1]
O Wonders, notable wonders,
  ye never the like did hear.

7 From eight till four in the morn
  with a rattling thundering noyse
The eccho as loud as a Horn,
  and frights them many wayes,
To appease the noyse I understand
  they burned the Drum out of hand.
O wonders, notable wonders,
  ye never the like did hear.

8 But still about the same time
  this noyse continued,
Yet little hurt they did sustain
  but Children thrown from bed,
And then by the hair of the head
  they were plucked quite out of bed.
O wonders, notable wonders,
  ye never the like did hear.

9 From one Room to another were they
  tost by a hellish Fiend,
As if he would them quite destroy
  or make of them an end,
And then some ease after their pain
  they'd be placed in their beds again.
O wonders, notable wonders,
  ye never the like did hear.

10 The Gentleman did give command
  to have the Children away
Unto a friends house out of hand
  them safely to convey:

[1] "For an Hour together it would Beat, *Round-heads* and *Cuckolds*, the *Tat-too*, and several other *Points of War*, as well as any Drummer" (*Sadducismus Triumphatus*, 1726, p. 272).

[119]

What ever they did it made them wonder
  a ratling Drum was heard like thunder.
  O wonders, notable wonders,
    ye never the like did hear.

11 A Minister being devout at prayer
     unto the God on high,
    A bed-staff was thrown at him there
     with bitter vehemency,[1]
    He said the Son of God appear
     to destroy the works of Satan here.
    O wonders, notable wonders,
      ye never the like did hear.

12 There's one they call him *Anthony*
     that carried a Sword to bed,
    And the Spirit at him will fly,
     hard to be resisted,
    If his hand out of the bed he cast,
     the Spirit will unto it fast.
    O wonders, notable wonders,
      ye never the like did hear.

13 Both Rooms, Stables, and Orchard ground
     a Drum was heard to beat,
    And sometimes in the Chymney sound
     by night make Cattle sweat,
    Both Chears and Stools about would gig
     and often times would dance a Iig.
    O wonders, notable wonders,
      ye never the like did hear.

14 So powerful were these motions all
     by Satan sure appointed,
    The Chamber floor would rise and fall
     and never a board disjoynted:

---

[1] "A Bedstaff was thrown at the Minister, which hit him on the Leg, but so favourably, that a lock of Wool could not fall more softly" (*Sadducismus Triumphatus*, 1726, pp. 272f.).

A WONDER OF WONDERS

Then they heard a show [1] from high
    three times a witch a witch did cry.
O wonders, notable wonders,
    ye never the like did hear.

𝔉𝔦𝔫𝔦𝔰.

By Abraham Miles.

Printed for William Gilbertson.

[1] *Read* shout.

20

The Devil's cruelty to mankind

Wood 401 (195), black letter, four columns, four woodcuts. Very poorly printed with worn-out, badly blurred type. Wood changed the date in the title to 1662 (*i. e.*, 1662/3) and at the end of the sheet wrote "mense mar: 1662. in y⁰ beg: of y⁰ said mounth."

I can find no other account of the suicide of George Gibbs. In the hands of Charles Hammond the subject-matter becomes almost amusing, thanks to the *naïveté* of the ideas and the language in which they are clothed. Hammond did not always write such doggerel, though his verse was never noted for smoothness or melody.

For the tune see Chappell's *Popular Music*, I, 200.

The Divils cruelty to Mankind.
BEING

A true Relation of the Life and Death of *George Gibbs*, a *Sawyer* by his Trade, who being many times tempted by the *Divill* to destroy himselfe, did on *Fryday* being the 7 of *March* 1663. Most cruelly Ripp up his own Belly, and pull'd out his Bowells and Guts, and cut them in pieces: to the Amazement of all the Beholders, the sorrow of his Friends, and the great grief of his Wife, being not long married: and both young People.

To the Tune of *The Two Children in the Wood*.

THE DEVIL'S CRUELTY

1 GOod Christian People lend an Eare,
    to this my dolefull Song,
A sadder tale you nere did heare,
    exprest by any tongue:
The Divill hath very busie been,
    now in these latter dayes,
For to entrap, and to draw in,
    poor souls by severall wayes.

2 He tempts [1] not only them that be,
    given over to all vice,
But such as lives most Civelly,
    he strives most to entice,
As by this Subject now in hand,
    which I shall here unfold,
As much as I could understand,
    the truth by neighbours told.

3 *George Gibbs* a Sawyer, by his Trade,
    and did in *Hounds Ditch* dwell,
A very civell man tis said,
    and liv'd indifferent well,
Not long time Married as I heare,
    noe charge lay on his hand,
Nor yet noe debts as he did fear,
    as I do understand.

4 His Wife and he liv'd lovingly,
    'twixt them noe discontent,
A very good report hath she,
    her case most do lament,
On *Fryday* being the Seaventh day,
    of *March*, some did me tell,
Gibbs oft his Pen-knife whets they say,
    that night this Chance befell.

[1] *Text* tempt's.

5 A T twelve a clock at night he rose,
      his Wife being then a bed,
   And down to ease himself he goes,
      thus to his Wife he said,
   His Wife perswaded him to stay,
      but he was fully bent,
   The Divill prompting him on's way,
      and out he present went.

6 When he came there he shut the door,
      and out his Penknife slip't,
   His Belly with it Cut and tore,
      and out his Bowells rip't,
   His carefull Wife did present rise,
      but when she did come there,
   And did behold it with her eyes,
      she trembled with such fear.

7 Few words she spake to him but went
      and in some Neighbors brought,
   Thinking the worst for to prevent,
      and save his life they thought.
   Whilst she was gone he made the Door
      fast to himself within,
   But they did break and down it tore,
      and suddenly got in.

8 His Belly he had rip't up quite,
      and out his Bowels tore,
   That such a Devillish bloody sight,
      scarce shown by man before,
   The Divill did do it to be sure,
      elce he could nere proceed,
   His strength and heart could nere endure,
      to do that cruell deed.

9 Some of his Gutts were cut in two,
      and mangled in such sort,
   That he himself could never doe,
      but had some helper for't.

THE DEVIL'S CRUELTY

Eight hours or more this man did live,
   in grievous woe and pain,
What Sustinance they did him give,
   came straight way forth again.

10 The Divil he said did tempt [1] him long,
   and many times before,
For all he did resist him strong,
   he nere would give him ore,
Thus have you heard the doleful end,
   of *Gibbs*, which is too true,
And take this councill from a Friend,
   for fear you after rue.

11 Trust not too much to your own strength
   to God continual pray
Resist the Divil elce at length,
   hee'l lead you his Broad way,
Your Swearing *Dam-me* ranting-boyes
   he minds not them at all,
They are so Wedded to his wayes,
   he hath them at his call,

12 While some strives all the power they have,
   his wayes to flee and shun
For some there be that counts it brave:
   to Hel head-long to run,
Now to conclude I wish you Friends,
   to God for ever pray,
To keep you from untimely Ends,
   and guide you his right way.

C. H.

London [2] *Printed* for *William Gilbertson* at the Bible
in *Giltspur-street*.

[1] *Text* temp't.   [2] *Text* Lonpuo.

21

A true relation of a notorious cheater

Wood 401 (197), black letter, four columns, three woodcuts. There is another copy in Wood 402 (91), which is reprinted, in more or less modernized form, in Andrew Clark's *The Life and Times of Anthony Wood*, I, 504–506. On both sheets Wood made elaborate manuscript annotations, which are reprinted in the foot-notes below. The notes on the Wood 402 (91) copy are taken from Clark's reprint, and are marked with a *C*.

The author, Wood informs us, was Francis Shenton, a drunken Oxford apothecary. Evidently he was an amateur ballad-writer, and his satiric ditty on Robert Bullock was probably intended to embarrass the Oxford people whom Bullock had cozened. No printer's name is given, but the broadside was no doubt printed at Oxford. It is an interesting example of what may be called a non-professional ballad.

I do not know the second tune. The first tune is named from the refrain ("And for mine offence must I dye") of "The Downfal of William Grismond" (*Roxburghe Ballads*, VIII, 70, 120, 145), and is printed, among other places, in the appendix to G. R. Kinloch's *Ancient Scottish Ballads* (1827).

A NOTORIOUS CHEATER

𝔄 True Relation of a Notorious Cheater one Robert Bullock, Lately done in Oxford, to prevent the like.

To the tune of, *And for my Offence I shall die*, or, *For the losse of my goods.*

1   COme listen all good people,
     and here what I can tell,
My name is *Robert Bullock*,
    at *Cheatington* I dwell,
For Rougery in *Oxford*,
    all others I'le excell,
And for mine offence I did flie.

2   That famous ancient City,
    I lately entered in,
To cheat them by the Dozens,
    I thought it no great sin:
And to relate particulars,
    i'le willingly begin.
And for, &c.

3   A Wife and a great Portion
    I did pretend to have,[1]
And thereupon I must
    have all things fine and brave:
I did dissemble with them
    much like a cheating knave.
And for, &c.

4   I took of a rich widdow,[2]
    a house and shop so fair,
That workmen of all sorts
    unto me did repair,
And for their best contrivance,
    I left it to their care,
And for, &c.

---

[1] "From Reading in Berks." "from Reding" *C.*
   "M^ris . . . Robinson widdow of Thom. Robinson bookseller, at the west end of S. Maries church." "Mris. Robinson, widdow of Thomas Robinson, bookseller" *C.*

5   Spoons and Plates, all Silver,
     of a Goldsmith I procured,
And a great Silver tankard,
     which *Banters* [1] booke assured,
My yes,[2] and nays,
     were not to be endured.
And for, &c.

6   A Shute and a fair Cloak,
     I am sure I had of one,
Whose name I have forgot;
     no matter let it alone,
To me hereafter,
     let them make their moan,
And for, &c.

7   A good man a rich Sadler,[3]
     for my custome courted me,
Both Pillion-cloth and Bridle,
     were at my service free,
With Combes,[4] for boots & shoos
     I quickly did agree,
And for mine offences I did flie.

8   MY wedding gloves I bought,
     of honest *Thomas Bland*,[5]
My Brass and eke my Pewter [6]
     I had serv'd me out of hand,
And all poor *Prices* Bodiss [7]
     were at my own command.
And for mine offence I did flie.

---

[1] Baniers *C.*   [2] *Read* yeas.
[3] "Joh. Newman." "John Numan" *C.*
[4] Read *Combes*. "Combes a sho-maker living against S. maries church." "Cumbes the sho-maker over aganst S. Marie's church" *C.*
[5] "living agst S. maries church, father to . . . wife of Rich. Witt. LL. Bac."
[6] "From . . . Sherard the Brasier in S. mich. parish." "from Sherrard the brasier" *C.*
[7] Bodises *C.*

9   My empty rooms were furnisht,
    with all Upholdsterers ware,
Both Beds and all things else
    I left to *Thurstons* [1] care,
And when I pay my debts,
    then he shall have his share,
And for, &c.

10   Bedsteds, and Tables,
    and many a days work to,
I had of a Wooden Ioyner,[2]
    who for the same did sue
As most that I have cheated,
    and now they have time to rue.
And for, &c.

11   I had of *Cox* the Matt man,
    of several sorts, five Chairs,
And Raggs [3] of Bridewel keeper,
    mixt with the finest hairs,
And blankets from a *Witny* man
    who had rather lost his ears,
And for, &c.

12   I was a general marchant,
    for Buttons I did trade,
I cheated brother *Jennings*,[4]
    and a pure Virgin Maid,
My carriage was so wary,
    there's none could me upbraid,
And for, &c.

---

[1] "Edmund Thurston upholsterer in Allsaints parish." "Thurston the upholsterer" *C.*

[2] "Woofield living in S. mich. parish." "Woodfeild the joyner" *C.*

[3] ruggs *C.*

[4] "Jennyngs a Button maker lately the crop-ear'd under-Butler of New coll."
"Jennings, a button-maker, latly under-butler of New Coll., and his sister" *C.*

13 All sorts of several workmen,
    that I in this employ'd,
I paid them all alike,
    dissention to avoid:
If they no better Masters [1] have,
    they'l quickly be destroy'd,[2]
And for, &c.

14 There's two that did escape,
    from my intended plot,
That's honest *Roger Frye*,[3]
    and *Gardiner* [4] the Scot,[5]
I am contented with it,
    seeing it was their Lot,
And for, &c.

15 I gave each what the asked,
    for their commodity,
I made what ready [6] monies,
    I could at *Banbury*,
And then with *Edward Bartlet* [7]
    for carriage did agree,
And for, &c.

16 I hired a good horse,
    in [8] *Holly-well* of one,
May add a great repentance
    (unto his penance done)
That such a rogue and villain,
    with his horse away is run,
And for, &c.

---

[1] *Text* master Masters.   [2] *Text* stestroy'd.

[3] "an Ale-brewer in S. Ebbs parish who was to have served him with ale." "the ale-brewer in St. Ebbs parish," etc. *C.*

[4] "Gardiner a sottish and drunken joyner living in Cat street." "Gardiner a [joy]ner in Cat street" *C.*

[5] In both copies Wood scratches out the *c.*

[6] *Text* rrady.

[7] "The carrier of Oxon. The same who was one of the Citie Ballives an. 1669." "the University carrier" *C.*   [8] of *C.*

17   And when I came to *London*,
      that noble and great City,
   I cheated all my carriage;
      it being not much pity
   That all should loose by me,
      so ends my Ditty.
    And for mine offences I did flie.

              By one of Oxford.[1]

[1] "viz Francis Shenton a drunken and broken apothecary living in the parish of S. Pet. in the Baylie. This cheat was committed in Nov. 1663 & in the same month this ballad was published." "viz. Francis Shenton, apothecary, living in St. Peter's in the Baillye. This buisness was acted and the ballad came out, all in the mounth of November A.D. 1663" *C.*

22

A warning by the example of Mary Dudson

Euing, No. 375, black letter, four columns, three woodcuts.

The picturesque story of Mary Dudson and the adder she swallowed and nourished must surely be told elsewhere, but I have not been able to find any mention of her in works that are accessible to me. Certainly this ballad deals with a genuine marvel, though nobody but a Grub-street journalist would have thought of interpreting Mary's calamity as a warning against the sins of men.

Edward Topsell, in his *History of Four-footed Beasts and Serpents* (1658, pp. 625, 742), declares:

> Serpents do sometimes creep into the mouths of them that are fast asleep. . . . For if a man sleep open mouthed, they slily convey themselves in, and winde and roll them round in compass, so taking up their lodging in the stomach, and then is the poor wretched man miserably and pitifully tormented; his life is more bitter then death, neither feeleth he any release or mitigation of his pain, unless it be by feeding this his unwelcome guest in his guest-chamber, with good store of milk, and such other meats as Serpents best like of.

Topsell further remarks that "it is reported by the *Italians*, that many times while men fall asleep in the fields, Serpents come creeping unto them, and finding their mouths open, do slide down into their stomachs: Wherefore, when the [Green] Lizard seeth a Serpent coming toward a man so sleeping, she waketh him, by gently scratching his hands and face, whereby he escapeth death and deadly poyson." Thomas Lupton, in *A Thousand Notable Things* (1650, bk. VI, no. 68) provides a remedy for snake-swallowers: "To bring them [*i. e.*, snakes] out of ones body, before crept into them by sleeping open mouthed," there is nothing better "then the smoake of old leather, or old shooes burned."

Earlier than Mary Dudson was "a Ladie whiche came from the Peru," and who, according to Dr. Nicolas Monardes, 1574 (*Joyfull Newes out of the Newe Founde Worlde*, translated by John Frampton, 1577, edited by Stephen Gaselee, 1925, II, 18), after taking a dose of "a Joyce clarified of Vervaine . . . cast out from her a worme, she saide that it was a hearie Snake, of more then two spannes long, and verie great, and he had his taile parted, and after she had cast hym out from her, she was well, and whole."

Alleged cases of snake-swallowing in the years 1830–1863 are discussed in *Notes and Queries*, 1st S., VI, 221 f., 338, 466; IX, 29 f., 84, 276 f., 523 f.;

A WARNING

3d S., IV, 358 f. These are fully as remarkable as the case of Mary Dudson and are no more credible. The New York *World* in its issue of November 4, 1924, carried the following dispatch from Chur, Switzerland:

When the stomach of a young nurse who had died in agony was opened a living viper was found.

It is believed the girl, while on a hike in the mountains, drank from a brook and swallowed either a serpent egg or a small living reptile.

The New York *Tribune* on September 28 of the same year skeptically noted that

A London factory girl is reported to have swallowed something while taking a swim, and immediately after was seized with terrible pains. A local doctor and a specialist both failed to diagnose the case, but an X-ray examination finally showed that she had swallowed an octopus egg, which had hatched out inside her anatomy.

The story breaks off at the point where the baffled doctors try to remove the thriving young many-armed octopus. Inquiries in all of the London hospitals have failed to trace the girl in question.

The tune of *In summer time*, which is used also for Nos. 3, 6, 24, 27, 30, 32, 33, 40, may be (as I have shown in *A Pepysian Garland*, pp. 161–162) equivalent to *Maying time*, the music for which is given in Chappell's *Popular Music*, I, 377. Cf. also the notes by Ebsworth in the *Roxburghe Ballads*, VII, 294, and the music printed in *Wit and Mirth, or Pills to Purge Melancholy*, V (1719), 36.

THE PACK OF AUTOLYCUS

A WARNING For all such as desire to Sleep
upon the GRASS:

By the Example of *Mary Dudson* Maid=servant to
Mr. *Phillips* a Gardener, dwelling in *Kent street*, in
the Borough of *Southwark:* Being a most strange,
but true Relation how she was found in a Dead=sleep
in the Garden, that no ordinary Noise could awake
her. As also how an Adder entered into her body, the
manner of her long Sickness, with a brief Discovery
of the Cause at length by her strange and most miraculous Vomiting up of about fourteen yong Adders, and
one old Adder, on *August* 14. 1664. about fourteen
Inches in length, the Maid is yet living. The like to
this hath not been known in this Age.

The Tune is, *In Summer Time.*

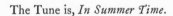

A WARNING

1 GOod Lord, what Age we do live in,
    how many Wonders doth befal?
Yet we repent not of our sin,
    nor unto God for mercy call.
How often to us hath he sent,
    even by the Preachers of his Word,
Intreating us for to repent,
    and turn unto the living Lord?

2 How hard are we for to believe
    Gods Word within the Bible pen'd?
How oft do we our Maker grieve,
    which soul and body doth defend?
Lord teach us to shake off our sins,
    and also to repent with speed:
Good God defend us from those Fiends,
    that would our woe and sorrow breed.

3 The Serpent first did *Eve* beguile,
    causing her *God* to disobay,
So heaps of Sin on us doth pile,
    but Christ hath washt our Sins away.
And ever since old *Adams* fall,
    he still hath sought us to destroy;
And for to bring our Souls in thrall,
    to deprive us of Heavenly Ioy.

4 As in these lines I will relate
    a Story strange, but yet most true,
Of a Maidens sad unhappy fate,
    presented here to publick view.
A Warning fair to those that sleep
    upon the ground, or in the grass,
Lest Serpents into them do creep,
    as to this Maid it came to pass.

5 This *Mary Dudson* wrought by th' week,
    and to the Market loads did bear;
For she was pliant, milde and meek,
    to gain a Living any where.

Her work was in the Garden still,
    for there she spent the pleasant day,
For in such work she had most skill,
    and for the same received pay.

6   But when the pleasant Sun shone hot,
    she would lye down o'th ground to sleep,
Not dreading of any harm, God wot,
    but some Refreshment for to reap.
About the end of *July* last,
    she sleeping in the Garden lay,
In a dead Sleep she lay so fast,
    she eas'ly would not wake, they say.

7   MUch fleam about her mouth did lie,
    in a most sad and dismal sort,
Which did amaze those that stood by,
    as for a truth they do report;

A WARNING

She was so fast asleep they could
    by no meanes wake her suddenly,
After awaked, then behold
    she was sore sick and like to die.

8 Thus she continued many a day,
    in torments strange both day and night,
For she could have ease no way,
    neither in ought could take delight:
The women they did marvel much
    a Maiden should be in such case:
At length the truth appeared such,
    a greater Wonder came in place.

9 Her torments they grew very strong,
    her body was exceeding weak:
It seemed unto her great wrong
    to sit, to lye, to walk, or speak.
Her thirst it was exceeding strange,
    she did drink so abundantly,
Her body all coal black did change,
    which seem'd a wondrous Prodigie.

10 But God that brings all truths to light,
    where means was wanting, did supply,
Before the neighboring peoples sight,
    that all might praise his Majesty.
At times as I do understand,
    fourteen young Adders from her came
By Vomit, and the Lords command,
    no other wight could do the same.

11 These came from her all alive,
    and that in several peoples view:
To get away they all did strive,
    but into the fire they them threw.
The fourteenth day of *August* last,
    the old Adder by Vomit came
Quite through her throat, and out was cast,
    the standers by admir'd the same.

12 This hideous sight put them to flight,
      they judg'd her fourteen Inches long:
Her body thick, and colours bright,
      with seeming legs exceeding strong.
She hist, and back strove to return
      into her mouth with eager speed,
Being withstood, away she run,
      for they had destroyed all her breed.

13 Some Doctors hearing of the same,
      some Potions sent her presently,
To mitigate that poysoned flame,
      which eas'd their Patient by and by.
Still she remains both sick and weak,
      an Object of true Charity:
'Twould make a stony heart to break,
      considering of her misery.

14 Thus have you had this Story true,
      which hundreds [there do] [1] testifie:
God knows what to us may ensue,
      for who knows when that he shall die?
Thus to conclude and make an end,
      of what to you I here do tell,
To Heaven I you all commend,
      and so I bid you all farewel.

Those that desire to be satisfied of the Truth more at large, may repair to this wofull Wight, a Spectacle of Gods mercy, and an Object of true Charity, being a constant Laborer in her health: It is hard to say whether she will live or die. She lyeth over against the sign of the Ship *in* Kent-street *in the Borough of* Southwark. *This Relation the Author had from her own mouth.*

London, Printed for *Charls Tyus* on *London*-bridge. 1664.

[1] Blurred.

23

Nature's wonder

Euing, No. 237, black letter, four columns, two woodcuts.

The question-mark after the title is accidental, for certainly neither the author nor the printer had the slightest doubt that here a genuine wonder of nature was dealt with.

Ballad-writers never tired of describing monstrous children. Although in the second stanza we are assured that news so strange as that of the twins of Fisherton-Anger was never before heard, nevertheless births equally monstrous had often been reported in England. In his continuation of Stow's *Annals* (1615, p. 926) Edmund Howes, for example, writes:

> The 17. of Aprill this yeere 1613. in $\overset{e}{y}$ towneship of *Adlington*, in the parish of *Standish* in Lancashire: there was a mayden childe borne, hauing 4. legs, 4. armes, 2. bellies, proportionable ioyned to one back, one head with 2. faces, the one before, & the other behind, like to $\overset{e}{y}$ picture of *Ianus:* the like of this w^t 2. seuerall faces vnder one scull, I neuer read of before in any Chronicle, except by way of a poeticall report.

The prose pamphlet on this prodigy from which Howes may have got his information is described in the *Harleian Miscellany*, X (1813), 446. Similar to it is the account of the strange twins born to Mr. and Mrs. John Persons as given in *A True and Certaine Relation of a Strange-Birth, which was borne at Stone-house in the Parish of Plimmouth, the 20. of October. 1635* (Hindley's *Old Book Collector's Miscellany*, vol. II). *Gods Judgement from Heaven; Or, A Very Strange Wonder to be declared of a Monster in Flanders, at a place cal'd Sluce*, 1658 (Wood 487), tells of a child with "two heads, two necks, four arms," and so on, that was born to a soldier's wife "at a place called Werted on the elder sconce neer Ardemburg." A "double child" very much like that of Mrs. Waterman was born to Mrs. Grace Batter'd, of Plymouth, on October 22, 1670. A portrait and a discussion of it may be found in the *Philosophical Transactions* of the Royal Society, V, 2096 ff. See further the ballad entitled "The Wonder of this present Age. Or, An Account of a Monster, Born in the Liberty of Westminster, on the 16th. of this Instant September, 1687. Having two Heads, four Arms and Hands; as likewise four Leggs and Feet, yet but one Body from the lower parts to the Breast" (Pepys, IV, 285). Dozens of similar cases could easily be enumerated.

On November 5, 1664 (Eyre's *Transcript*, II, 349), Robert Pauley registered "a picture intituled *The true picture of a monstruous Creature borne neare Salisbury*." This broadside is preserved in the Chetham Library at Manchester (cf. J. O. Halliwell-Phillipps's *Catalogue of Proclamations*,

THE PACK OF AUTOLYCUS

Broadsides, Ballads, and Poems, 1851, No. 978). It is $17\frac{1}{2}$ by $13\frac{1}{2}$ inches in size, with the letter-press in roman and italic type. The "picture" itself has hardly any resemblance to the woodcut that appears on the ballad. The description of the child runs as follows:

THE

TRUE PICTURE

OF A

FEMALE MONSTER

BORN NEAR

SALISBURY.

O N Wednesday the 26. day of *October*, 1664. The Wife of *John Waterman*, a Husbandman, in the Parish of *Fisherton-Anger*, near New *Sarum*, or *Salisbury*, brought forth a wonderful Creature, which cannot be otherwise accounted then a Monster: It having two Heads, four Arms, and two Legs.

The Heads standing contrary each to other, one Head standing where the Feet should be.

There were two perfect Bodies downwards to the Navel, as if there had been two Children, and there they were both joyned together.

The Loyns, Hips and Legs issued out of the sides of the Bodies, just in the middle, where both Bodies were joyned together.

It was dissected, and there were found two Hearts, two Livers, and all the inward parts complete, as the outward to the Navel, except only that it had but two Kidneys.

There was but One Sex to both these Bodies, which was the Female.

This Monster lived two days, and during that time took Sustenance. It would not Suck, but did Eat with both Mouthes; when the one cried, the other did so too, each imitating the other in several actions, and was seen alive by many hundreds of the neighbouring places, which flocked to see so strange a Creature.

NATURE'S WONDER

The Mother had one Child more at the same time, which was born first, and which also is a Female, and a very comely Child in all proportions, and is yet living.

This Monster is intended speedily to be brought to London.
With Allowance, *Roger L'Estrange, Novemb.* 5. 1664.

LONDON,
Printed for *R. P.* at the Sign of the Bible in
Chancery-lane, 1664.

For the tune of the present ballad see Chappell's *Popular Music,* I, 149. The rhyme-scheme of stanzas 1 and 10 is dubious.

Natures Wonder?

OR,

[A True acc]ount [1] how the Wife of one *John Water-man* an Ostler in the Parish of *Fisherton-Anger,* near *Salisbury,* was Delivered of a strange Monster upon the 26th of *October* 1664. which lived untill the 27th of the same Moneth. It had two Heads, foure Armes, and two Legs. The Heads standing contrary each to the other; and the Loines, Hipps, and Leggs Issueing out of the middle, betwixt both. They were both perfect to the Nabell, and there joyned in one, be-ing but one Sex, which was the Female. She had an-other Child born before it (of the Female Sex) which is yet living, and is a very comely Child in all propor-tions. This is Attested for truth, by severall Persons which were eye witnesses.

The Tune is, *London Prentice:* Or, *Jovial Batchelor.*

1   COme take a view good People all,
     observe it well with heed,
  A stranger Wonder Nature did
    ne're frame of Humane Seed;

[1] Text imperfect.

THE PACK OF AUTOLYCUS

A Monster of mishapen Forme
   I here to you present,
By this Example you may learn
   to feare Gods Punishment.

2 Strange Wonders hath been lately shown
   within our *English* Nation;
But none so strainge as this was known,
   you'l find by this Relation;
Then give attention to the same,
   I'le show you how it was,
To tell the truth it is no shame,
   for thus it came to passe.

3 At *Fisherton* near *Salisbury*,
   a Husbandman doth dwell
John Waterman so call'd is he,
   his Neighbours all can tell;
It was his Wife which did bring forth
   this strange Mishapen Thing:
From East to West, from North to South
   the News thereof will ring.

4 It was but in *October* last,
   the Six and twenty day,
No longer since 'twas done and past:
   I can for certaine say
This Woman was Delivered well,
   and with her Life she scap't
Of this same Monster now I'le tell
   how strangely 'twas Mishap't.

The second Part, to the same Tune.

5 TWo Heads it had, grew opposite,
   the Picture plain appeares
With all proportions fair in sight,
   Mouthes, Noses, Eyes and Eares,

NATURE'S WONDER

Two Bodies shaped perfectly,
    down to the Navel seen,
And there they joyned wondrously,
    the Hipps and Leggs between.

6   The bodies being joyn'd in one,
     were of the Female Sex,
The like thereof was never known,
     they strangely did Connex;
Four Armes were on the body plac'd,
     it had of Leggs but two;
Thus Nature had her work defac'd,
     which she doth seldom do.

7   The Women they were all afraid
     to see this fearfull sight,
And eke the Midwife much dismay'd
     when as it came to light,
But most of all the Mother weak
     her grievious Paines was much,
She had not power long time to speak
     her sorrow it was such.

8   Two dayes and nights this Monster liv'd
     in woefull misery,
The Parents they were sadly griev'd,
     the Neighbours came to see;
At length it dy'd, and was convey'd
     for Chyurgeons to Dissect,
And what Report thereof had said,
     they found it in Effect.

9   Another Babe this Mother sad
     brought forth at the same birth,
A comelier Child no [1] woman had
     upon the face o'th Earth;

---

[1] *Text* Ch ld on.

Nature in that did make amends,
   proportioning each Part;
She may bring joy unto her Friends,
   and chear her Mothers heart.

10 Afflictions God doth sometimes send
     to Parents for thier sin,
When they will not their lives amend,
     then doth the Lord begin
With Iudgments for to humble them,
     and make them feel his hand;
O turn unto the Lord in time,
     for none can Him withstand.

11 Our God hath many wayes to make
     vile Sinners come to shame;
If once they do his Laws forsake,
     and wrong his holy Name,
A thousand Iudgments (worse then this)
     he on that People brings,
That will not mend what is amiss,
     but act such hainous Sinnes?

12 Then Parents all Example take,
     at all times seek the Lord;
Fruit of your bodies he can make
     by your own selves abhorr'd:
Your Children which should be a joy
     and comfort in the end,
The Lord in fury will destroy,
     if you do him Offend.

FINIS.

A true Relation of this strange and wonderfull MONSTER.

AT *Fisherton-Anger*, near the City of *Salisbury* (called *New Saram*) near to the sign of the Angel, Liveth one *John Waterman* an Ostler, His Wife (whose name is *Mary*) was Delivered (on *Wednesday* the 26th· of *October* 1664. about two a Clock in the Morning) first of a very comely Daughter (which is yet living) And after of a strange *Monster* which was formed Triangular, two Heads (at either end one) four Eyes, two Mouthes four Armes, two Stomacks, And joyned together at the Navell; and below that two Legges and Thighs, with Natures Passage (as other Female children have) and a Foundament: They were Baptized at 3 a Clock the same Morning, the first was named *Eefelet:* and the Monsters were named *Martha* and *Mary;* they had very comely faces, and both received Sustinance, but not together: This *Monster* lived two dayes and then dyed, and is Imbalmed, and to be brought to *London* to be seen. There hath been both Lords, Ladys, and much Gentry to see it; The Father (being a poore man) had twenty pound given him the first day, by persons of Quality.

I *Josiah Smith*, Practitioner of *Phisick*, saw them all three alive.

With Alowance, Novemb. 12th. 1664. Printed for *E. Andrews*
at White-Lyon in *Pye-corner.*

24

The Devil's conquest

Euing, No. 76, black letter, four columns, four woodcuts.

In this fine ballad the story is told twice: once by the title and again by the verses. The calamity that befell Margery Perry no doubt convinced many seventeenth-century readers that forswearing was a dangerous business. I am sorry that I have been unable to find any further information about her. A story very closely resembling this is told of an Oxfordshire woman in William Turner's *Compleat History of the Most Remarkable Providences* (1697), pt. I, ch. 104, p. 16.

For the tune see No. 22. The rhymes are crude, especially in stanza 16.

The Devils Conquest, or, a Wish obtained: Shewing how one lately of Barnsby-street, in Leg-Ally, in St. Olaves Parish, Southwark, one that Carded Wooll for Stockings, carried home some work to her Mistris, living upon Horsly-Down, who asked her how much shee owed her for; the Maid answered eight pounds; her Mistris said 'twas but six where-upon the Maid began to Swear and Curse, and wisht the Devil fetch her, if there was not eight pounds owing for; the Mistris loving quietness, paid her for eight pound: the Maid, with two of her Companions, walk-ing over Horsly-Down, she having a Childe in her arms, one came and throwed her down, and presently took her up again, which caused her to say, Thou Rogue, dost thou fling me down and take me up again, and suddainly he vanished away, neither she, nor the two women with her, could discern which way he went, which caused them to say, It was the Devil, which for all this, nothing terrified the Maid, who went boldly

THE DEVIL'S CONQUEST

home, and to bed, and the two Women with her; at midnight she heard a voice, which called her by her name
very often; she answered, I come, I come; but the voice
still continuing, she swore she would come, and being
got out of the Bed, fell down upon her face, and was
taken speechless, yet her body moving in most terrible
manner, manifesting her inward pangs; her Mistris
was sent for, who freely forgave her, and wisht God
might forgive her too, and then shee departed, and her
body was found as black as pitch all over; and all this
was for no more than the value of eleven pence, which
was done on the 6th. of this instant May, 1665. and
was written for a warning to all, to avoid the like
course.

The Tune is, *Summer Time.*

1   A Ttend good Christian people all
      to what here I do mean to write,
You Muses nine, to you I call,
   help me these verses to indite.

2   A story true I shall relate,
      I wish it may a warning be,
That all may now avoid that fate,
   and shun that cruel destiny.

3   Full sore & dreadful judgements we
      have often heard and seen abroad,
The righteous God, he doth decree,
   as we have it upon Record.

4   Many a time we do provoke,
      yet still his mercy doth indure,
But at the last hee'l give a stroak,
   which art of man can never cure.

5   Examples many we have had
     in former and in latter years,[1]
  But sure you ne'r heard one more sad
     then this, therefore attend to hear.

6   In *Barnsby-street* of late there dwelt
     one *Margery Perry* called by name,
  With whom it seems the Devil dealt,
     and played his subtil cunning game.

7   In carding wool she imploy'd her self,
     a livelyhood for to obtain,
  But Satan that old subtil Elf,
     tells her 'tis not sufficient gain.

8   TO swear and curse she was inclin'd
     a Vice too common in this Land,
  In this the Devil with her was joyn'd,
     as you shall shortly understand.

9   She carried home some work one day
     unto her Work-Mistrisses home,
  Who asked how much she had to pay
     for all the wool that she did combe.

10   Saith she, you owe me for eight pounds
     nay, saith the Mistris, it is but six,
  But now she goes beyond her bounds,
     to swear and curse she doth not stick.

11   This caused some contest to arise
     between them both, for a short space,
  The Devils flame in her breast fries,
     O woman! what made thee so base?

12   She wisht the Devil fetch her strait,
     if that she had not done eight pounds;[2]
  Ah woman! caught with such a bait,
     that came not all to half a crown.

---

[1] The rhyme requires *year*.   [2] *Read* pound.

13 Her Mistris paid her, away she hies,
  & with her Comrades walk yᵉ streets,
 she little thought how conscience cries
  but now at last the Devil meets.

14 On *Horsly-down* she down was thrown
  and presently caught up again,
 Alas she is so hard hearted grown,
  she can't perceive her inward stain.

15 Those women with her were amazed,
  because he vanished quite away
 That took her up, although they gazed,
  no more of him they saw that day.

16 Then home she hies with her consorts,
  to bed she goes and thinks all well,
 But vengeance will at length arise,
  & death will come with passing bell.

17 Oh little did she think, but she
  should rise again as she was wont,
 Iudgement must come by Gods decree,
  he will not alwaies bear the affront.

18 At midnight then she heard a voice,
  which frequently called her by name,
 Surely she could not then rejoyce,
  knowing her guilt deserved blame.

19 She answered straight, I come, I come,
  and presently begins to swear,
 The Devil hee'l not stay too long,
  but takes her in her chamber there.

20 They took her up from off the boards,
  whereon yᵉ Devil her down did throw
 She speechless was, no breath affords,
  which made yᵉ womens hearts to glow.

21 Then for her Mistris they did send,
      who came immediately to see
    That, which almost her heart did rend,
      a spectacle of misery.

22 Some that were present there did say,
      forgive her though she did forswear,
    I and God forgive her too I pray,
      and so she died whilst she was there.

23 They stript her naked being dead,
      and found her body black as pitch,
    The hellish fiend her prepared,
      according to her cursed wish.

24 Oh that a warning this might be
      to all, that these few lines do read,
    Here plainly we may learn and see,
      and not such wicked paths to tread.

25 Wish for true riches and true grace,
      and labour for it earnestly,
    The Devil he will come apace,
      wish not for him, such courses fly.

26 And now lets study to amend,
      and free our selves from slavery,
    That all our lives may have good end,
      and full assurance when we dye.

27 So to conclude remember still,
      Swearing and Cursing ends in woe,
    If you let the Devil have his will,
      hee'l prove the worst & greatest foe.

Finis.

London Printed for S. Tyus, on London-Bridge. With privilege.

25

The world's wonder

Douce, II, 241ᵛ, black letter, one woodcut, two columns, slightly mutilated and badly wrinkled. I have followed a manuscript copy furnished
through the courtesy of Bodley's librarian.

Certainly no more wonderful fish was ever heard of than this monster
from "Cucanga"! [1] And he, alas, was only a symbol of the triumph of England over Holland and France, not a real fish at all. From stanza 10 it appears that the ballad was written after the cessation of the Great Plague
(May–September, 1665). The Duke of York had defeated the Dutch fleet
under Admiral Obdam on June 13, a victory that no doubt serves to explain
the exultant tone of the balladist towards Holland. Had he waited until
June, 1666, when De Ruyter worsted Monck in a four days' battle, or later
when De Ruyter and De Witt sailed up the Medway and burned the English fleet, he might not have been so sure that "All Down In Holland" was
the meaning of the letters borne by the fish.

In my *Pepysian Garland*, p. 437, one of Wood's ballads on a monstrous
fish is reprinted and a discussion of other prodigious members of 'the finny
tribe that haunts the wat'ry plain' is given. Perhaps mention should also
be made of the whale which in 1645, according to one of George Thomason's tracts (British Museum, E. 308 [24]), "making to Land did strike
upon the Shore, within three miles of Weymouth, where being opened there
was found in the belly of it a Romish Priest, with Pardons for divers
Papists in England and in Ireland"! Narcissus Luttrell, in his diary for
February 25, 1692, tells of a great fish recently seen near Harwich: it was
"as big as a grampas, but painted like a mackrell: the seamen soon mas-
tered him with their grapling irons and other instruments, and pulling him
to shore cutt him open, and to the wonder of many found a man entire with
his clothes on in his belly, and searching his pockets found severall papers
and letters, which they opened, but found nothing materiall in them."

For the tune see Chappell's *Popular Music*, I, 293.

---

[1] Somewhat similar is the fish described in *The Court and Times of Charles I*,
I, 114 f.

THE PACK OF AUTOLYCUS

𝕿𝖍𝖊 𝖂𝖔𝖗𝖑𝖉𝖘 𝖂𝖔𝖓𝖉𝖊𝖗!

OR,

𝕿𝖍𝖊 𝕻𝖗𝖔𝖕𝖍𝖊𝖙𝖎𝖈𝖆𝖑 𝕱𝕴𝕾𝕳.

𝕭𝖊𝖎𝖓𝖌 𝖆 𝖋𝖚𝖑𝖑 𝕯𝖊𝖘𝖈𝖗𝖎𝖕𝖙𝖎𝖔𝖓 𝖔𝖋 𝖙𝖍𝖎𝖘 𝕸𝖔𝖓𝖘𝖙𝖊𝖗, 𝖎𝖙𝖘 𝖑𝖊𝖓𝖌𝖙𝖍 & 𝖇𝖗𝖊𝖆𝖉𝖙𝖍, 𝖜𝖎𝖙𝖍 𝕻𝖗𝖊𝖉𝖎𝖈𝖙𝖎𝖔𝖓𝖘 𝖔𝖓 𝖎𝖙. 𝕬𝖘 𝖎𝖙 𝖜𝖆𝖘 𝖙𝖆𝖐𝖊𝖓 𝖇𝖞 𝕱𝖎𝖘𝖍𝖊𝖗=𝖒𝖊𝖓 𝖎𝖓 𝖙𝖍𝖊 𝕻𝖔𝖗𝖙 𝖔𝖋 *Cucanga*, 𝖓𝖊𝖊𝖗 𝖙𝖍𝖊 𝕻𝖗𝖔𝖛= 𝖎𝖓𝖈𝖊 𝖆𝖓𝖉 𝖐𝖎𝖓𝖌𝖉𝖔𝖒 𝖔𝖋 *China*, 𝖎𝖓 𝖙𝖍𝖊 𝖞𝖊𝖆𝖗 1664. 𝖆𝖓𝖉 𝖘𝖊𝖓𝖙 𝖙𝖔 𝖙𝖍𝖊 𝕰𝖒𝖕𝖊𝖗𝖔𝖚𝖗 𝖔𝖋 *Germany*, 𝖆𝖓𝖉 𝖋𝖗𝖔𝖒 𝖙𝖍𝖊𝖓𝖈𝖊 𝕮𝖔𝖓𝖛𝖊𝖞'𝖉 𝖙𝖔 𝖍𝖎𝖘 𝕽𝖔𝖞𝖆𝖑 𝕸𝖆𝖏𝖊𝖘𝖙𝖞, 𝖙𝖍𝖊 𝕶𝕴𝕹𝕲 𝖔𝖋 *Great Brittain*, &𝖈.

To the tune of, *When Stormy Winds do blow.*

1   I De [1] tell you of a Wonder,
     that lately hath been Shewn,
  [A]s strange as Winters Thunder;
     or Frost and Snow in *June:*
Fish by Fishermen was catch'd
     late in *Cucanga* Bay,
Where Health, and Wealth,
     their Plenty do Display.

2   [I]n Sixteen hundred sixty four,
     this Monstrous Fish was caught,
  [S]ent to the *German* Emperour,
     then from him it was brought
  [T]o *Charles* the King of *England*,
     a Prince of high Renown,
  [W]hich well, doth tell,
     much wellfare to his Crown.

3   This monstrous Fish is twelve Foot long,
     and likewise six foot broad:
Upon his back (so firme and strong)
     he bears a pondrous load,

---

[1] *Text* ... De (*torn*).

THE WORLD'S WONDER

A Piece of Ord'nance mounted,
   upon a warlike Carr,
Whose Charge, at large,
   doth threaten woful War.

4   The Face of it, is like a man,
      upon its [1] head a Crown;
   A Cross for *England*, in the Van,
      Presaging all's our own;
   The Cross doth issue from his mouth,
      which he seems to disgorge;
   And cry, Wee'l die,
      for *England*, and St. *George*.

𝕿𝖍𝖊 𝖘𝖊𝖈𝖔𝖓𝖉 𝖕𝖆𝖗𝖙, 𝖙𝖔 𝖙𝖍𝖊 𝖘𝖆𝖒𝖊 𝖙𝖚𝖓𝖊.

5   THis rarity in Nature,
      Doth all mens wits controule,
   This strange Prodigious Creature,
      Is Flesh, and Fish, and Fowle:
   The Flesh is meant for *England* sure,
      The Fowle is meant for *France*,
   The Fish, a Dish,
      For *Hollands* mainteynance.

6   His Back is full of Fish-like Finns,
      his Legs have Eagles Clawes,
   And Cock-like Spurs, as sharp as Pinns,
      which blood in Battel drawes:
   The Eagle is a Princely Bird,
      and never Fights for *States;*
   But flyes, at th' Eyes,
      of such Confederates.

7   Upon his very Shoulder-bone,
      he bears two Flaggs a crosse;
   A. D. I. H. is writ on One,
      importing some great losse:

[1] *Text* 'its.

Which I shall now Expound to you,
   the next ensuing Lines;
If this, do miss,
   Ile leave it to Divines.

8 *A. D. I. H.* doth seem to teach,
   the *Dutch-man* shall have no-Land;
  A. D. doth stand for *All Down*, and [1]
   I. H. doth mean *In Holland:*
  A. D. I. H. doth plainly shew,
   All Down In Holland falls;
  [I]f they, obey
   not *England's* Brazen Walls.

9 There are Three Muskets and a Sword,
   display'd upon the Rump;
  Which shews the *Hollander* Aboard,
   is beaten to the Stump:
  Death's Head on his Left-side is,
   and like so many Shots;
  [A]ll round, 'tis Crown'd,
   with *Pestilential Spots.*

10 Which doth demonstrate unto men,
   our wofull *Plague* of late;
  And will, we fear, renew agen,
   if we Repent not strait:
  This Fish hath Arrows in the Tayle,
   which he 'gainst *Holland* drawes,
  And slights, the Flights,
   their *Lyon* hath in's Pawes.

11 Thus have I plainly painted out
   the Picture of this Fish;
  Pray God all things may come about,
   as we do desire and wish:

[1] No rhyme here.

[154]

THE WORLD'S WONDER

Three Nations against *England* come,
    it is not Nobly done;
I hope, they'l stoop,
    and find inough of One.

12 Let us but move, in truth and love,
    and prove good Friends at home,
That Sacred Power that is above,
    will give them all their doome.
If we by Factions spoyl our Selves,
    and on each Other Fall,
The Foe, will grow,
    too Powerful for us all.

13 But if wee hold together,
    nor *French*, nor *Dutch*, nor *Dane*,
With *Butter-box*, and *Feather*,
    shall make our Fortunes wain:
VVee'l whip the Frisking *Frenchmans* tail,
    which would possesse our Land;
The *French*, shall Flinch,
    and bow to *CHARLES* Command.

14 God blesse the King, the Queen, the Duke,
    with all the Peeres beside,
And may the Lord of Host rebuke
    the *Dutch* and *French-mans* pride:
Wee need not fear the Powers that come
    from *Paris*, nor from *Delf*,
If we, then be,
    at Peace within our Self.

FINIS.

London, Printed for *R. White* at the *Bible* in *Giltspur-street*.

26

Mount Etna's flames

Wood 401 (199), black letter, four columns, one woodcut.

The ballad and the tabular data appended to it are summarized from a pamphlet that contains an account of the eruption of Mount Etna in March-April, 1669, which the Earl of Winchilsea sent to Charles II (Wood D. 28 [19]). John Evelyn heard "a description of the prodigious eruption of Mount Etna" read at a meeting of the Royal Society on October 21, 1669 — probably Winchilsea's pamphlet. The latter was registered for publication by Thomas Newcomb on June 5, 1669 (Eyre's *Transcript*, II, 401), and is reprinted in Lord Somers's *Tracts*, ed. Sir Walter Scott, VIII (1812), 605 ff. From it also came the summaries given in Samuel Clarke's *Mirrour or Looking-Glass for Saints and Sinners* (1671, II, 583–589) and Nathaniel Crouch's *Surprizing Miracles of Nature and Art* (2d ed., 1685, pp. 161 ff.).

For the tune see No. 12. The rhyme-scheme is faulty in stanzas 2 and 11 and somewhat dubious in stanza 15.

Mount Ætna's Flames.
OR,
The *Sicilian* Wonder,

Really manifesting, and plainly demonstrating, the prodigious effects of that dreadfull Spectacle of those furious Flames of Mount *Ætna* (an Island call'd *Sicily* in the King of *Spain's* dominions,) which in 40 days time destroyed the Habitations of twenty seven thousand persons, made two hills of one a thousand Paces high a peice, and hath allready much indanger'd the famous City of *Catania* which the Inhabitants are forc't to desert for fear of ruine and destruction.

Tune of, *Troy Town.*

1 COme hear a wonder, people all
    Of an vnwonted prodigy,
A mountain that destroys up all
    within the *Isle* of *Sicily*,
The flames are fierce, no stop can be
Put to its fury as we see.

2 Of all the wonders in the world
    of which the learned men do write,
Not one like this is to be found
    and brought to view and publick sight
Though strange, 'tis true I witness can
'Tis known to many a learned man.

3 In *Sicily* an *Island* fair
    under the rule of *Spain's* great King,
A mountain is, without compare
    which doth to many sorrow bring,
Sad is their fate that lives so nigh
These sad conclusions[1] for to try.

---

[1] *Text* conclusion.

THE PACK OF AUTOLYCUS

4   *Mount Ætna* it is call'd by name
     a fearfull sight for to behold,
Old Authers hath describ'd the same
     therefore to speak I may be bold
The flames which do from thence proceed
Makes many a melting heart to bleed.

5   *Catania* that City fair
     full fifteen miles from this same place
Is threatned with the flames so near
     the people in a wofull case,
Least they [1] should fear, as neighbours do
Which makes their heart, be full of woe.

6   The fiery flames from thence proceed
     and cinders, they fly up amain,
Whilst Sulphur mines the same doth feed
     and rolling stones, return again.
A sad and dismall sight to see
Poor souls in that perplexity.

7   From out the rock a river slides
     like burning streames unto the eye,
And in a Channell strange it glides
     with flames that seem to scale the sky,
Nothing is seen but smoak and fire
Which makes the people all admire.

8   Six hundred yards into the Sea
     this burning river drives by force,
Still flaming most impetuously
     it keeps it's dreadfull fiery course.
No fish nor fowl, the same comes nigh
But presently fall down and dye.

[1] *Text* thy.

MOUNT ETNA'S FLAMES

9   TWo Rocks in one this flame hath put
      each one a thousand paces high,
And what dame nature wisely cut
     it doth deface most furiously:
Water and fire, good servants are
But once being Masters, rage and tear.

10   Do but observe and you shall find
      that former ages nere did know,
Nor e're did see, time out of mind
      such flames from *Ætna's* mount to glow
A dreadfull sight it is to see
Huge stones like *Atomes* tost should be.

11   In forty dayes it did destroy
      the habitations and the home,
Of twenty seven thousand men,
      and left them all abroad to rome,
Castles and Towns it Swallows down
A fearfull sight as ere was shown.

12   The hideous noise and roarings loud
      which ecchoes from this dreadfull place
Whilst flames ascend as in a cloud
      poor people are in wofull case,
The ayre, and water do conspire
To show themselves like flames of fire.

13   The towns, this earthquake hath destroy'd
      was worth some Millions of good gold.
People of all sorts it anoy'd
      by lodging in the fields so cold,
Poor souls what pitty they deserve
Which now for want do lye and starve.

14 Then do but take a serious view
        of what do follow in this place,
    And all your greif it will renew
        to see what towns it down did race,
    And then give thanks to God on high
    That we such sorrows are not nigh.

15 And last of all observe the form
        of this prodigious mountains birth,
    Which rocks and hills doth overturn
        and doth deface, our Mother earth.
    And then conclude this story's true
    Which I have set forth to your view.

A List of the most considerable Towns and places ruin'd
    and destroyed by the dreadful Earth-quake and Erup-
    tions.

The Town of *Nicolosi* wholly Ruin'd by the *Earthquakes*.

The Towns of { *Padara* / *Tre Castagne* } the greatest part destroyed by the Earthquake.

The Towns of { *La Guardia,* *Malpasso* *Campo Rotundo,* *La Potielli,* St. *Antonino,* St. *Pietro,* *Mostorbianco,* *Montpileri,* *La Annunciato,* *Falicchi,* *Placchi,* } Wholly Over-flowed, Consu-med and lost in this Fiery Inun-dation, with all the Lands be-longing to them no Footsteps of them remaining.

The Towns of { *Mascalucia* / *St. Giovanni de Galermo.* } Ruin'd in part.

The large *Gardens* and *Vineyards* of *Albanelli Overflown* and *Destroyed*.

MOUNT ETNA'S FLAMES

The Famous Piece of *Antiquity* of *Marcus Marcellus* much
    Ruin'd.
Madonna de Monserrato destroyed, besides many *Castles*,
    Farms, and other Places, which have run the same
    Fortune, whose Names we for brevity pass over.

Printed for *F. Coles*, *T. Vere*, and *J. Wright*.

27

Strange and true news from Westmorland

Euing, No. 341, black letter, four columns, two woodcuts. There are other copies in the Roxburghe collection, II, 432; Bagford, II, 54; Pepys, II, 155. The date of the ballad is about 1670.

The Roxburghe copy has been reprinted twice (in *Roxburghe Ballads*, VIII, 79 f., and John Ashton's *The Devil in Britain and America*, pp. 13–16; cf. also the British Museum *Catalogue of [Satirical] Prints and Drawings*, I [1870], 253). But the ballad is such a fine example of a marvel that I have felt almost obliged to include it in this book, following a different copy from that of the earlier reprints.

In spite of the impressive list of witnesses at the end of the ballad, one may have difficulty in believing the story of Gabriel Harding, a murderer who was killed by the Devil at the express command of an avenging angel. Of that unfortunate man I have found no other trace. Certainly the story told of his death shows an amazing degree of credulity. It also illustrates very clearly the dangers that were popularly supposed to attend forswearing.

For comments on the tune see the introduction to No. 22.

STRANGE NEWS FROM WESTMORLAND

𝕾trange anð true 𝕹ews from *Westmoreland.*
𝕭eing a true 𝕽elation of one *Gabriel Harding,* who
coming home ðrunk, struck his 𝖂ife a blow on the
breast, anð killeð her outright, anð then ðenyeð the
same: 𝕷ikewise how a 𝕾tranger ðið come to the
𝕳ouse clotheð in green, the people that were eye wit=
nesses saið it was an 𝕬ngel; anð how the 𝕾tranger or
𝕬ngel ðið give 𝕾entence on the man for killing of his
𝖂ife: 𝕬lso how 𝕾atan ðið break the mans neck that
ðið forswear himself, anð the 𝕾tranger or 𝕬ngel ðið
command 𝕾atan to hurt none else, anð to banish; 𝕿hen
ðið the 𝕾tranger cloatheð in green take his leave of the
people; whereof the chiefest in the 𝕻arish ðesireð it
might be put into 𝕻rint, anð have hereunto set their
hanðs.

Tune is, *In Summer time.*

1   A Ttend good Christian people all,
      Mark what I say both old and young
    Unto the General Iudgment day
    I think it is not very long.

2   A wonder strange I shall relate,
    I think the like was never shown,
    In *Westmoreland* in *Tredenton*
    Of such a thing was never known.

3   One *Gabriel Harding* liv'd of late,
    As may to all men just appear,
    Whose yearly Rent by just account
    Came to five hundred pound a year.

4   This man he had a Virtuous Wife,
    In Godly ways her mind did give:
    Yet he as rude a wicked wretch
    As in this sinful Land did live.

THE PACK OF AUTOLYCUS

5   Much news of him I will relate,
     The like no mortal man did hear:
     'Tis very new, and also true,
     Therefore good Christians all give ear.

6   One time this man he came home drunk
     As he us'd, which made his wife to weep,
     Who straightway took him by the hand,
     Saying, Dear Husband lye down & sleep.

7   She lovingly took him by the arms,
     Thinking in safety him to guide,
     A blow he struck her on the breast,
     The woman straight sunk down and dy'd.

8   The Children with mournful cries
     They run into the open street,
     They wept, they wail'd, they wrung their hands
     To all good Christians they did meet.

9   The people then they all ran forth,
     Saying, Children why make you such moan?
     O make you haste unto our house
     Our dear mother is dead and gone.

10   Our Father hath our Mother kill'd,
     The Children they cryed then,
     The people then they all made haste,
     And laid their hands upon the man.

11   He presently denied the same,
     Said from guilty Murder I am free,
     If I did that wicked deed he said,
     Some example I wish be seen by me.

12   Thus he forswore the wicked deed,
     Of his dear wifes untimely end,
     Quoth the people let's conclude with speed,
     That for the Coroner we may send.

13   Mark what I say, the doors fast shut,
The people the Children did deplore,
But straight they heard a man to speak,
And one stood knocking at the door.

14   One in the house to the door made haste,
Hearing a man to knock and call,
The door was opened presently,
And in he came amongst them all.

15   By your leave good people then he said,
May a stranger with you have some talk,
A dead woman I am come to see,
Into the Room I pray Sir walk.

16   His eyes like to the Stars did shine,
He was clothed in a bright Grass green,
His cheeks was of a Crimson red,
For such a man was seldome seen.

17   Vnto the people then he spoke,
Mark well these words which I shall say,
For no Coroner you shall send,
I'm Iudge and Iury here this day.

18   Bring hither the man that did the deed
And firmly hath denied the same.
They brovght him into the room with speed
To answer to this deed with shame.

19   Now come O wretched man quoth he,
With shame before thy Neighbours all,
Thy body thou hast brought to misery,
Thy soul into a deeper thrall.

20   Thy chiefest delight was drunkenness
And lewd women, O cursed sin,
Blasphemous Oaths and Curses vile
A long time thou hast wallowed in.

21 Thy Neighbours thou wouldst set at strife
And alwaies griping of the poor:
Besides thou hast murdered thy wife,
A fearful death thou dy'st therefore.

22 Fear nothing good people, then he said
A sight presently will appear,
Let all your trust be in the Lord,
No harm shall be while I am here.

23 Then in the Room the Devil appear'd
Like a brave Gentleman did stand;
Satan (quoth he that was the Iudge)
Do no more than thou hast command.

24 The Devil then he straight laid hold
On him that had murdered his Wife,
His neck in sunder then he broke,
And thus did end his wretched life.

25 The Devil then he vanished
Quite from the people in the Hall,
Which made the people much afraid,
Yet no one had no hurt at all.

26 Then straight a pleasant Melody
Of Musick straight was heard to sound,
It ravisht the hearts of those stood by,
So sweet the Musick did abound.

27 Now (quoth this gallant man in green)
With you I can no longer stay,
My love I leave, my leave I take,
The time is come, I must away.

28 Be sure to love each other well,
Keep in your breast what I do say,
It is the way to go to Heaven
When you shall rise at Iudgment day.

29   The people to their homes did go,
      Which had this mighty wonder seen,
      And said it was an Angel sure
      That thus was cloathed all in green.

30   And thus the News from *Westmoreland*
      I have related to you o're;
      I think it is as strange a thing
      As ever man did hear *before*.

Here are the Names of some of the chiefest men that live in the Parish: Christopher Rawly, Esq; James Fish, Gent. William Lisse, Gent. Simon Pierce, Ambrose White, Oliver Craft, Robert Bord, Thomas Clifford, Yeomen; George Crawly, Peter Vaux, Philip Cook, Francis Martin, George Horton, Husbandmen.

Printed for *P. Brooksby* at the Golden Ball
in Py-corner.

28

Robbery rewarded

Wood E. 25 (108), black letter, three columns, three woodcuts.

Further information about these highwaymen is contained in a booklet called *The Confession of the four highwaymen . . . J. W., alias T. Matchet, F. Jackson, alias Dixie, J. White, alias Fowler, W. Parkhurst*, etc., 1674 (British Museum, 1132.b.63). In the same year appeared also a pamphlet by Richard Head called *Jackson's Recantation, Or, The Life & Death of the Notorious High-Way-Man, Now Hanging in Chains at Hampstead* (Hindley's *Old Book Collector's Miscellany*, vol. III). In J. C. Jeaffreson's *Middlesex County Records* (IV, 52–53) there are fourteen indictments, dated March 16 and March 18, 1674, against Parkhurst, Jackson, White, Williams, and Slader (*sic*) for highway robberies committed at Bedfont, Hendon, and Hampstead. Two further indictments charge James Slader with having murdered Edward Kemp with a pistol on March 18, and charge Francis Jackson with having murdered Henry Miller with a sword on the same day. Slader died in jail before trial. The other four outlaws were found guilty and sentenced to be hanged, according to a gaol-delivery record dated April 10. The details given in the ballad are, on the whole, reliable.

For the tune see Chappell's *Popular Music*, I, 123.

Robbery Rewarded,

OR,

An Account of Five Notorious High-way-men's Exploits: Viz, JAMES SLAUTER, JOHN WHITE, JOHN VVILLIAMS, alias, MATCHET, FRANCIS JACKSON, VVALTER PARKHURST. The manner of their taking on the 17th. of March last past, one of their Company, Viz. James Slauter being since dead in Newgate, the tryal of the other four at the old Baly the 10th. and 11th. of April, they were found Guilty of fifteen several Indictments for Robery and Murther, the persons Kill'd

ROBBERY REWARDED

by them, were one **Edward Kemp** of **Henden**, and **Henry Miller** of **Hamstead**, for which facts three of them were sentenced to be hang'd at the comon place of Execution, & **Jackson** to be Gibited at **Hampsted**.

Tune is, *packington's pound.*

1 ADieu vain delights, and bewitch us no more,
   Our former ill courses we now do deplore;
Our Crimes upon Earth hath bereav'd us of hope,
The thread of our lives is spun out in a Rope:
     We Rob'd Night and Day,
     Upon the High-way,
     And spent it on Wine, and on wenches & play.
But to this sweet meat sowre sauce must be had,
For the Gallows is still the reward of the Padd.

2 Neer *Colebrook* & *Windsor* our scene we did lay,
Each purse that came there Contribution must pay
we scorn'd to compound with the great or the smal,
For the game yᵗ we play'd at, was nam'd have-at-al.
     With Pistol in hand,
     We made them to stand,
     And deliver you Dogs was the word of Command,
But with this sweet meat sowre sauce must be had,
For the Halter attends all the Kts. of the padd.

3 We made our selves valiant with full flowing flagons,
To Examine Portmantues, and ransack the waggons,
VVho travel'd in Coaches, if we came in sight,
They presently bid all their moneys good-night.
     But alas all in vain,
     For now we are ta'ne,
     And must finish our lives in sorrow and pain,
Destruction still treads on the heels of the bad,
And a Halter attends all the Knights of the padd.

4   Each sort, and Sex must submit to our Doom,
The Gallants were Hector'd the Ladys o'recome,
VVhose fine tempting Iewels we soon made a prize,
Though never so guarded with languishing eyes,
      Rich Cloaths and good Lace,
      We made them uncase,
      And left them behind to complain on the place.
but with such sweet meat sowre sauce must be had,
For the Gallows is still the reward of the padd.

5   The renowned *Du Vall* [1] with his Kt. arrant fame,
Henceforward shall yield to our gallanter name;
He jilted the people with tricks and with words,
VVe made them submit to the charms of our swords.
      Yet alass to our shame,
      Our ends prove the same,
      The Hangman and *Tyburn* our merits proclaim.
Destruction still treads on the heels of the bad, &c.

6   Our work we so ply'd, that in very few days,
VVe resolv'd a good round sum of money to raise,
VVhich being obtained a plot we design'd,
To trip o're the Ocean, where none should us find,
      But alas our hard fate,
      Has quite alter'd our state,
      VVe find by sad proof now although 'tis too late,
That to our sweet meat sowre sauce must be had,
For the Halter attends all the Knights of the padd.

7   The Country Alarum'd with what we had done,
They came in each man that could handle a Gun,
VVith swords, & with Flayls, & with Halberts al rusty
VVith dead-doing Rapiers and Cudgels were trusty,
      In Van, Flanck, and Reer,
      They round us appear,
      VVhich yet could not cause our bold Spirits to fear.
Destruction thus, &c.

[1] "This day [January 21, 1670] was publickly executed at *Tyburn, Claude du Val*, to the great grief of the women." — Samuel Clarke's *Historian's Guide*, 1688, p. 77. See also *The Memoirs of Monsieur Du Vall*, 1670 [by Dr. Walter Pope], re-

8 A couragious retreat we resolved for to make,
For well we perceiv'd that our lives lay at stake,
And thence we conclude it a nobler thing,
To fall by the Sword then to peep through a string.
VVe fought all the way,
To *Hampstead* that day.
And often shifted Horses to make the less stay,
but still 'tis in vain, &c.

9 Two poor men we slew whose deplorable sake,
VVith grief fills our souls, & it makes our hearts ake,
VVith sighs & with tears we beg mercy of Heaven,
That Crime and all others may quite be forgiven.
VVhich if we procure,
VVe will gladly endure,
Our punishment here, and esteem them a Cure:
Though vile we have been, & most shameful our story
True repentance may waft from the Gibit to glory.

10 Though long we resisted yet wounded full sore,
At last we grew faint and could hold out no more,
But streightly confined to *Newgate* we came,
VVhere one by his death was released from shame.
The rest on fair Tryal,
Beyond all denyal,
VVere clearly convicted & now they must die all.
Thus to our sweet meat, &c.

11 Thus may our Example to all be a warning,
And serve for each young-mans instruction & learning;
Be honest & Iust, & not wast time and leisure,
In Ryot, Debauchness, and wantoning pleasure:
For see what sad gains,
One of us obtains,
His body it must be consumed in Chains.
Destruction still treads on the heels, &c.

Printed for P. Brooksby in VVest-smith-field.

rinted in the *Harleian Miscellany*, III (1809), 308–316, and the sketch in the *Dictionary of National Biography*.

29

The disturbed ghost

Douce, I, 56ᵛ, black letter, two woodcuts, four columns, slightly torn. I have followed a manuscript copy furnished by the kindness of Bodley's librarian.

I have not seen the original pamphlet called *A Faithful Narrative of the Strange Appearance of E. Aven to T. G., his Son-in-Law*, 1674 (W. C. Hazlitt's *Hand-book*, 1867, p. 677), on which this ballad is perhaps based; but it is reproduced in *Satan's Invisible World discovered*, 1685 (1780 ed., pp. 69–73), by George Sinclair, "Late Professor of Philosophy in Glasgow"; in William Turner's *Compleat History of the Most Remarkable Providences*, 1697 (pt. I, ch. 4, pp. 36–37); in *The History of Witches, Ghosts, and Highland Seers* (Berwick, n. d. [*ca.*1780?], pp. 137–142); and in several other places. Sinclair's reprint runs thus: —

Thomas Goddard of Marleborough, in the county of Wilts, weaver, on the ninth of November 1674, going to Ogburn, at a stile on the high way, about nine in the morning, met the apparition of his father-in-law, one Edward Avon of this town, glover, who died in May last, having on, to appearance, the same clothes, hat, stockings, and shoes, he did usually wear when he was living, standing by, and leaning over that stile; which when he came near, the apparition spake to him, with an audible voice, these words, "Are you afraid?" To which he answered "I am, thinking on one who is dead and buried, whom you are like." To which the apparition replied with the like voice, "I am he you were thinking on; I am Edward Avon your father-in-law: come near to me, I will do you no harm." To which Goddard answered, "I trust in him that bought my soul with his precious blood, you shall do me no harm." Then the apparition said, "How stands cases at home?" Goddard asked, "What cases?" Then it asked him, "How do William and Mary?" Meaning, as he conceived, his son William Avon, a shoemaker here, and Mary his daughter, the said Goddard's wife. Then it said, "What? Taylor is dead;" meaning, as he thought, one Taylor of London, who married his daughter Sarah, which Taylor died at Michaelmas last. Then the apparition held out his hand, and in it, as Goddard conceived, 20 or 30 shillings in silver, and then spake with a loud voice, "Take this money, and send it to Sarah; for I shut up my bowels of compassion toward her in my lifetime, and now there is somewhat for her." And then said, "Mary (meaning the said Goddard's wife, as he conceived) is troubled for me; but tell her, God hath shewed mercy contrary to my deserts" But the said Goddard answered, "In the name of Jesus, I refuse all such money." Then the apparition said, "I perceive you are afraid, I will meet you some other time." And immediately it went up the lane to his appearance. So he went over the same stile, but saw it no more that day.

He saith, The next night, about seven of the clock it came and opened his shop windows, and stood in the like clothes, looking him in the face, but said nothing to him. And the next night after, as Goddard went forth into his back-side, with a

[172]

THE DISTURBED GHOST

candle in his hand, it appeared to him again in the same shape; but he being in fear ran into his house, and saw it no more then.

But he saith, That on Thursday the 12th instant, as he came from Chilton, riding down the hill, between the manor-house and Axford farm-field, he saw somewhat like a hare crossing his way, at which his horse frighted, threw him into the dirt, and as soon as he could recover on his feet, the same apparition met him there again, in the same habit; and there standing about eight feet before him in the way, spake again to him, with a loud voice, "Source (a word he common-[ly] used when living) you have staid long;" and said to him, "Thomas, bid William Avon take the sword that he had of me, which is now in his house, and carry it into the wood, as we go to Alton, to the upper end of the wood, by the wayside; for with that sword I did wrong thirty years ago, and he never prospered since he had that sword; and bid William Avon give his sister Sarah twenty shillings of the money which he had of me. And do you talk with Edward Laurence; for I borrowed twenty shillings of him several years ago, and did say, I had paid him, but I did not pay it him; and I would desire you to pay him twenty shillings, out of the money which you had from James Elliot at two payments." Which money, the said Goddard now saith, was five pounds, which James Elliot, a baker here, owed the said Avon on bond; and which he, the said Goddard, had received from the said Elliot, since Michaelmas, at two payments, viz. thirty-five shillings at one, and three pounds five shillings at another payment. And it further said to him, "Tell Margaret (meaning his own wife, as he conceived) that I would desire her to deliver up the little money which I gave to little Sarah Taylor the child, or any one she will trust for it; but if she will not, speak to Edward Laurence to persuade her; but if she will not, then, tell her, that I will see her very suddenly: and see that this be done within a twelve-month and a day after my decease, and peace be with you." And so it went away over the rails into the wood there, in the like manner as any man would go over a stile, to his apprehension: and so he saw it no more at that time. And he saith, that he paid the twenty shillings to Edward Laurence of this town, who, being present now, doth remember he lent the said Avon twenty shillings about twenty years ago, which none knew but himself and his wife, and Avon and his wife; and was never paid it again, before now by this Goddard.

And this Goddard further says, that this very day, by Mr Major's order, he, with his brother-in-law, William Avon, went with this sword; and about nine o'clock this morning, they laid down the sword in the copse, near the place the apparition had appointed Goddard to carry it: and then coming away thence, Goddard looking back, saw the same apparition again, in the like habit as before; whereupon he called to his brother-in-law, and said, "Here is the apparition of our father," who said, "I see nothing:" then Goddard fell on his knees, and said, "Lord, open his eyes that he may see it, if it be thy blessed will." And the apparition, to Goddard's appearance, beck'ned with his hand to come to it, and then Goddard said, "In the name of the Father, Son, and Holy Ghost, what would you have me to do?" Then the apparition said to him, "Thomas, take up the sword, and follow me." To which he said, should both of us come, or but one of us? To which it answered, Thomas, do you take up the sword; and so he took up the sword, and followed the apparition, about ten poles in length, further into the copse; and then turning back he stood still, about a pole and a half from it, his brother-in-law staying behind, at the place where they first laid down the sword; then Goddard, laying down the sword upon the ground, saw something stand by the apparition, like a mastiff dog of a brown colour. Then the appari-

[173]

tion coming towards Goddard, he stept back about two steps; and the apparition said to him, "I have a permission to you, and a commission not to touch you;" and then it took up the sword, and went back to the place, at which before it stood, with a mastiff dog by it, as before; and pointed the top of the sword into the ground, and said, "In this place, lies buried, the body of him whom I murdered in the year 1635, which is now rotten, and turned to dust." Whereupon Goddard said, "I do adjure you, in the name of the Father, Son, and Holy Ghost, When did you commit this murder?" And it said, "I took money from the man, and he contended with me, and so I murdered him." Then Goddard asked him, Who was confederate with him in the said murder? And he said, "None but myself was accessary thereto." Then Goddard said, "What would you have me to do in this thing?" And the apparition said, "This is, that the world may know that I murdered a man, and buried him in this place, in the year 1635."

Then the apparition laid down the sword, on the bare ground there, whereon grew nothing, but seemed to Goddard, to be as a grave sunk in; and then, the apparition, running further into the copse, vanished, and he saw it no more; whereupon Goddard, and his brother-in-law, Avon, went away together, leaving the sword there. Avon told Goddard he heard his voice, and understood what he said, and heard other words distinct from his, but could not understand a word of it, nor saw any apparition at all; which he now, being present, affirmeth; and all which the said Goddard then attested under his hand, and affirmed, he will depone the same, when he shall be thereto required.

From this pamphlet the ballad itself differs in a number of important details. Perhaps it was written up from hearsay. The average reader will view "the said Goddard" and his incredible tale with grave suspicion.

The tunes are given in Chappell's *Popular Music*, I, 162–164.

The Disturbed Ghost: Or,
The Wonderful Appearance of the Ghost, or Spirit of
Edward Avon, late of *Marlborough* in *Wiltshir[e]*[1]
to his Son-in-law *T. G.*[2] and his own Son *W. A.* the
23, 25, and 26. of *November* last. With the co[n]fes-
sion of money he in his life time borrowed of *E. L.*
Which he denyed, and forswore, when [it][1] was de-
manded. Also how[3] he committed a Robbery and
murder 39. years ago in *Boru[m]*[1] Wood and other
Remarkable passages.

Tune *Aim not two High*, or *Kings Tryal*.

[1] Torn.   [2] Text *F. G.*   [3] *Text* how how.

THE DISTURBED GHOST

1 GOod Christian people all pray lend an ear,
  And hearken to the words I shall declare;
  A stranger wonder late hath not been known,
  As in this Song shall presently be shown.

2 The truth of which is known both far and wide
  And hath by many men been justified,
  Though folks so unbeleeving now are grown
  That what there eys do see theyl hardly own.

3 The subject which Ime going to declare,
  Is of a truth and many men there are;
  Have justified the same as it is known,
  Before the Magistrates of *Malborrough* town.

4 There *Edward Avon* as it came to pass,
  An Officer or under *Bayly* was:
  An honest man who was by Law his son,
  He married *Avons* daughter as tis known.

5 This *Avon* was about some business sent,
  And nine or ten miles out of town he went:
  In May last he to *Collingbourn* did goe,
  Not dreaming what should follow to his woe.

6 He went full well and seem'd his health to hav[e.] [1]
  When he came their *Tobacco* he did crave:
  Because that he was hot with going fast,
  Not thinking that same pipe should be his la[st.] [1]

7 FOr suddainly the pipe in's mouth tis said,
  He being in his chair did fall down dead:
  To the amazement of his dearest friend,
  Who little thought of his so suddain end.

8 Thus he in deasent manner was convayd,
  [A]nd [1] in the earth in Burial he was laid:
  None thinking of disturbance as they say,
  Nor thought to see him eare the judgment day.

[1] Torn.

9   But he who *Avons* daughter had to Wife,
[A] [1] person well approv'd of honest life:
Walking towards *Ogburn* there a town hard by
Met one of his acquaintance by the way.

10   To whom he said have you your Father seen,
[I] [1] met him as I came by yonder green:
My Father said the sun alass hees dead,
And hath these seaven months been buried.

11   To which the man reply'd I durst have sworn,
The cloaths that you have on by him was worn;
And so they parted on there way each one,
But mark what follows after shall be shone.

12   This son had not gon fields ore passing two,
But met his Father whom so well he knew:
That taking courage thus his mind exprest,
What ist saith he desturbs thy quiet rest.

13   Speak in the name of God what ist thoudst have
Or what disturbs thy quiet in the Grave:
Let me but know thy mind and Ile fullfill,
Unto my utmost power all thy will.

14   Speak for I fear no ill thou wandring guest,
What makes thy spirit thus to be opprest:
To which the ghost it presently reply'd,
Some mony I did owe before I died.

15   In *Marlburrough* town I borrowed of one,
Just twenty shillings which I did disown:
And when for that same som he to me came,
I did deny it, and forswore the same.

16   And stretching, forth his hand unto him then,
Said he her's mony goe and pay the man:
To which the sun reply'd Ile see it payd,
But will not take your mony or your aid.

[1] Torn.

THE DISTURBED GHOST

17   Accordingly as to the ghost he said,
      He went next day and there the mony paid:
      That so his Fathers ghost might be appeas'd,
      And his disturbed spirit should be eas'd.

18   A little after rideing on the way
      The likeness of a hare did make him stay:
      Which starting up before his horses head,
      The horse did start and down his burden laid.

19   But geting up found standing by his side,
      The old mans ghost as formerly he spy'd:
      Said he my sun in law be not a frayd,
      I will not hurt thee be not thou dismayd.

20   But to my story lend attentive heed,
      The grief of which would makes ones hart to bleed,
      Said he my own son *William* hath at home,
      A *Sword* which I could wish he nere had known.

21   Which if he keep it will much mischief breed,
      Heel never thrive till from it he be freed:
      To morrow bring it if that you think good,
      And meet me both of you at *Borum* wood.

22   Next day the Brothers both together went,
      And took the *Sword* to give the ghost content:
      When both unto the wood side they repaird,
      Where presently the ghost to them apeard.

23   He bid them lay the *Sword* upon the land,
      VVhich presantly he took into his hand:
      And wished them to follow him full fast,
      And mark the place where he should lay it last.

24   Into the wood they came close by an oak
      And further yet the ghost unto them spoak,
      Theres nine and thirty years by past and gone,
      Since in this place I rob'd and kill'd a man.

25   Close by this oak I did his corps convay
      And from him this same *Sword* was tane away
      And that's the reason I am so oprest,
      Till I declared it, (I could take no rest.)

26   This it declared to do all men right,
      And then it vanished out of there sight:
      The truth of which is known both far and wide
      In *Malburrough* and in all Wiltshire beside.

London, Printed for Phillip Brooksby at the Ball
in West Smith-Field.

30

Strange and wonderful news from Northampton

Wood 401 (203), black letter, four columns, two woodcuts. Wood added the date "1674," which should be changed to 1674/5.

This delightful ghost-story is no more incredible than many of the "fully authenticated" ghost-stories included in, say, the *Sadducismus Triumphatus* of Joseph Glanvill. In details it varies considerably from the account given in an eight-page pamphlet called *The Rest-less Ghost: OR, Wonderful News from Northampton-shire, and Southwark. Being a most true and Perfect Account of a Persons Appearance that was Murdred above two Hundred and Fifty Years ago, First about three weeks since, to one William Clarke at Hennington in Northampton-shire, whom it appointed to meet in Southwark, and did there appear to him again, and several others, on Sunday last the 10th. of this instant January. Where it Discovered a great parcel of Money, and some writings buried in the ground, which were disposed off by his Order, and then seeming satisfied it disappeared. This Relation is taken from the said Will. Clarks own Mouth, who came to London on purpose, and will be Attested and Justified by Will. Stubbins, Iohn Charlton, and John Stevens, to be spoken with any day, at the Castle Inn without Smith-Field-Barrs, and many others. Printed for John Millet.* The pamphlet, which is reproduced in *Tracts (Rare and Curious Reprints, MS., etc.), relating to Northamptonshire,* 2d Series, 1881, may be summarized as follows:

William Clark (or Clarke), "by Profession a Maulster," lived in a farmhouse, "usually called Old *Pells* house," at Hennington, four miles from Northampton. For a year his house had been subjected to violent supernatural disturbances, but the ghost first appeared to him some three weeks ago. In reply to Clark's questions the ghost said: "I am the disturbed Spirit of a person long since Dead, I was Murthered neer this place Two hundred sixty and seven years, nine weeks, and two days ago, to this very time, and come along with me and I will shew you where it was done." The ghost further declared that he had lived in Southwark, "where he had some Money and Writings that had ever since lain buried in the Earth, and that till the same was taken up and disposed of according to his mind, he should never be at rest." The reason why he had not appeared before, he said, was because for 250 years he had been prohibited from appearing on earth "by the Magical Art of a certain Fryer." Clark agreed to meet the ghost in Southwark within a fortnight, and on Sunday afternoon, January 10, 1675, he went to the rendezvous. The ghost "in the common habit of a man" met him at the bridge, took him to the house, and there told Clark and the owners of the house "the whole story aforesaid, & that they were some of his posterity, & then shewed them a place, bidding them dig there next day. . . . Next day *Clark* going over early, they dug accordingly in that place, and about 8 foot deep, found a pot and in it a considerable quantity of gold, & at the bottom of that some Writings, some of paper which did moulder away & crumble to dust if they touched them, but others of parchment were whole, by whose dates it appeared they had lain there as long as he had said before it was since he was Murthered . . . the Spirit . . . gave him particular order how he should dispose of what he found, which he distributed accordingly, and then the spirit appeared to him again in a very joyful contented manner, saying, Thou hast done well, and henceforth I shall be at rest, so as never more to trouble thee." On January 14 Clark returned to Hennington "very well satisfied."

The ballad perhaps appeared before the pamphlet, and it may have been based on oral, rather than written, reports. It is a fine piece of journalism.

For notes on the tune see No. 22.

Strange and wonderful News from
Northampton-shire,
OR,
The discontented Spirit.

Being a true Relation of a Spirit that Appeared to one *Richard Clarke* **of** *Hinnington* **in** *Northampton-shire*, **That had been Murthered, 267 years and odd days, he was seen several times about** *Richard Clarkes* **yard: and at last he comming from turning his Mault, the spirit met him at the door and shob'd him into the Orchard, and there spoke to him, Saying that he must go to** *London*, **and so to** *Southwark* **to be his Messenger, and he would be his guide to go with him, (which the said** *Clarke* **did) and what he saw, is expressed in this following Ditty.**

The Tune is, *Summer time.*

STRANGE NEWS FROM NORTHAMPTON

1 GOod people all pray listen well,
    i'le here lay open to your veiw,
  A Song most wonderful and strange,
    and it is known for to be true.

2 You have heard of spirits for to walk,
    though many be, you ne'r did see,
  And with some men do seem to talk
    about their hidden treasurie.

3 As by this story very strange,
    the which to you I shall declare;
  Of *Richard Clark* of *Hinnington*,
    a town that's in *Northampton-shire.*

4 This man a Farmer is, 'tis known,
    and well beloved of his neighbours by;
  Although he lives not on his own,
    yet he doth live sufficiently.

5 About that house where he did dwell,
    a spirit did appear also,
  Which did amaze him very much,
    for it was murdered long ago.

6 The spirit much amazement bred,
    as it did walk too and again,
  His cattel it much troubled,
    because it could not speak with him.

7 For when he walkt the Yard ith night,
    either was untied his shooe or hose;
  Or else unbutton'd it had no power,
    what it walkt for for to disclose.

8 But it finding an opportunity,
    one night he turned his malt o'th flowre,
  To's house he went most speedily,
    but it did meet him at the Door.

THE PACK OF AUTOLYCUS

𝕿𝖍𝖊 𝖘𝖊𝖈𝖔𝖓𝖉 𝖕𝖆𝖗𝖙, 𝖙𝖔 𝖙𝖍𝖊 𝖘𝖆𝖒𝖊 𝖙𝖚𝖓𝖊.

9 INto the Orchard it him shove,
    in the name of *Jesus* Christ, said he,
Crying out, was much amaz'd
    whither wilt thou shove me.

10 Be not afraid, the spirit said,
    no harm shall come to thee at all,
But to thee I must declare my mind
    and look thou dost fulfil it all.

11 Two hundred sixty and seven years
    since a servant man there did him slay,
But conjur'd down it now appears
    as the spirit unto him did say.

12 I was a man the which was kil'd
    two hundred sixty seven years ago,
By a servant man that dwelled here
    for that I had the truth is so.

13 He also did cut off my head,
    and wounded me very sore,
And in this place me buried
    what could he against me a done more.

14 Then after was I conjured down
    for so many years as I tell thee;
But now my time is expired,
    and thou my messenger must be.

15 Prepare and go thy ways (said he)
    to *Southwark* Ile be thy guide;
To such a house to set things strait,
    which I so long ago did hide.

16 And in a celler thou shalt find
    some money and some Writings too,
To the right owner thou shalt them give,
    Ile be with thee the place to shew.

17   So go thy ways unto thy house,
         and mark these words that are so plain:
      Be sure you perform all what I say,
         but do not you look back again.

18   So he to London went with speed,
         and on his Iourney made no stay,
      Much like a man of forty years,
         the spirit met him by the way.

19   And smiling unto him it said:
         what on thy Iourney thou dost go:
      And upon London-bridge again
         the spirit met him there also.

20   And to the house in Southwark
         the spirit it did him convey:
      And was his guide to go with him,
         and would not let him make no stay.

21   But when he came unto the house
         he declared the thing in solemn wise,
      And when the Women was sent for,
         the tears did trickle from their eyes.

22   Then into th' celler he did go
         and dig'd not above two foot i th ground
      Whereas the spirit did him show,
         and there the money strait he found.

23   In a brass pan this Money was,
         and the writings in the same did lye:
      But the papers did crumble away
         so that they could not them descry.

24   But the Parchment it was safe & sound,
         the which did signifie some Land:
      But the money was so eaten with rust,
         the same they could not understand.

25 So the money and the writings too
    to this poor woman he did give:
Who from that Relation did spring out,
    who at his hand did it receive:

26 The spirit stood by all the while
    and gave him directions what to do,
That he should no ways her beguile
    the which the same belong'd unto.

27 And when its mind he had fulfill'd
    the spirit vanished away
Vnto the place from whence it came,
    and seen no more unto this day.

28 Thus friends and neighbours you do see,
    that wilful murther will come out,
Though it be done ne'r so long ago,
    yet time and years will bring it about.

29 Therefore lets fear the Lord on high,
    that we may be of the flock which Christ hath,
And then we need not fear to dye,
    our souls no doubt will be at rest.

30 So to conclude what here is pend,
    and is laid open to your view,
Although it be a story strange,
    yet hundreds knows it to be true.

Printed for R. Burton, and are to be sold by W. Whitwood,
in Duck-Lane.

Wood E. 25 (104), black letter, four columns, one woodcut.

T. L., the author, was no doubt Thomas Lanfiere, a well-known ballad-writer "of Watchat town in Somersetshire," as he sometimes signs his work. Perhaps he was the person jocularly referred to in the line,

Since my strong friend *T. L.* was kikt, and poasted,

that occurs in "A brief computation of some things very memorable till this year 1654," given in Raphael Desmus's *Merlinus Anonymus*, 1654, sig. A4^v. The monstrous birth that Lanfiere here versifies is described also by Laurence White in the ballad next following (No. 32). It occurred about 1675, if one may judge from the dates at which Lanfiere, White, and their respective printers flourished.

But, although T. L. several times remarks that the like of this "strange example" was never before told, he was entirely mistaken. Such examples, on the contrary, were fairly common. Thus on May 8, 1646, the Reverend Ralph Josselin (*Diary*, Camden Society ed., p. 32) heard of "a monster borne about Colchester, first a child, y^n a serpent, y^n a toad which lapped." (The monster referred to may be that discussed also in Thomas Edwards's *Gangræna*, 1646, pt. II, pp. 4–5.) *A certaine Relation of the Hog-faced Gentle-woman* (1640, sig. A4^v) reminds us that "it hath beene knowne also in our knowne [*sic*] Country, when a Gentlewoman of good discent and quality hath brought an infant into the World with a live Snake wrapt about the necke and body: in memory of which, that Noble Family in the emblazon of their Armes, give the Snake ever unto this day."[1] In book II of his *Natural Magic*, 1558 (English translation, 1658, p. 28), Giovanni Battista della Porta remarked that "neither is it hard to generate Toades of women . . . for women do breed this kind of cattel, together with their children"; and he instanced the women of "Salerium" (Salerno) who often gave birth to lizards, toads, and frogs, and who "were wont to use the juice of Parsley and Leeks, at the beginning of their conception, . . . to destroy this kind of vermin." James Howell (*Familiar Letters*, I, § 2, letter 13, April 10, 1623) had heard that in Holland women always gave birth to "a living Creature besides the Child . . . likest a *Batt* of any other Creature; which the Mid-

[1] Cf. Thomas Churchyard (*The Worthines of Wales*, 1587, H3, Spenser Society ed., p. 65), who in describing the tombs of "the auncient house of *Gams*" mentions

Three fayre boyes heads, and euery one of those
A Serpent hath close lapt about his necke. . . .

wifes throw into the Fire." Edward Topsell, in *The History of Four-footed Beasts and Serpents*, 1658, pp. 595–596, gives many examples of serpent-bearing women. "Women conceiving with childe," he says (p. 728), "have likewise conceived at the same time a Frog, or a Toad, or a Lizard." People call "a Toad the Brother of the *Salernitans*, and the Lizard the Brother of the *Lombards*, for it hath been seen that a woman of *Salernum*, hath at one time brought forth a Boy and a Toad, and therefore he calleth the Toad his Brother; so likewise a woman of *Lombardy*, a Lizard, and therefore he calleth the Lizard the *Lombards* Brother. And for this cause, the women of those Countries, at such time as their childe beginneth to quicken in their womb, do drink the juyce of Parsley and Leeks, to kill such conceptions if any be." All this, says Topsell, merely shows God's judgment on Popery, "for surely, none but Devils incarnate, or men conceived of Serpents brood, would so stiffely stand in *Romish* error as the *Italians* do."

William Turner (*A Compleat History of the Most Remarkable Providences*, 1697, pt. II, ch. 7, p. 9) tells of one Anne Tromperin, who was delivered of "a Boy and two Serpents upon St. *John's* Day, *Anno* 1576." Many other examples are brought together in his chapters on "Monstrous Births and Conceptions of Mankind" and "Monstrous Animals" (*ibid.*, chs. 7, 27, pp. 8–9, 25–26). Thomas Heywood's *The Hierarchie of the blessed Angells*, 1635, pp. 540 ff., and Thomas Lupton's *A Thousand Notable Things*, 1595 (see the 1650 ed., bk. VIII, no. 52), should also be consulted. Perhaps the most remarkable yarn of all (for yarn it was) is that told in *The Several Depositions . . . Relating to the Affair of Mary Toft, Of Godalming in the County of Surrey, being deliver'd of Several Rabbits* (1727).

For comments on the tune see No. 3.

The wonder of wonders, or, the strange Birth in *Hampshire*. Being an exact, true, and perfect relation of one *A. B.* living in a Country parish neer the Town of Rumsey in Hampshire: relating how the said person was strangely brought to bed the 18th. of November last; with a live Toad, a terrible Serpent, and a dead Child, having some part of its head and face, and other parts devoured by the serpent in the Mothers Womb, where at this strange birth the Midwife and other Women sounded at the delivery of the said Monsters; but some of the other Women being more bolder in spirit took the Toad

THE WONDER OF WONDERS

and Serpent and burned them, and buried the child in a
decent manner: the said Midwife and other women have
testified for the truth of this relation.

By T. L.

Tune of, *My bleeding heart.*

1   ATtend good Christians young & old,
    Observe what hear I shall unfold,
 A strange example i'le rehearse,
 The like was never put in verse.

2   'Tis such a wonder strange indeed,
 Would make a stony heart to bleed,
 When as I have the same declared,
 You'l say the like was never heard.

3   Strange wonders God to us doth send,
 For to make us our lives amend,
 But some so unbelieving be,
 They'l not believe unless they see.

THE PACK OF AUTOLYCUS

4   All in the West of *England* fair,
    Near unto *Rumsey* in *Hampshire*,
    At *Shervel* Parish call'd by name,
    From thence this true relation came.

The second Part, To the same Tune.

5   IN this same place which I you tell,
    An honest man and his wife did dwell,
    They lov'd each other very dear,
    As by relation doth appear.

6   This Woman she with child did prove,
    By her husband whom she did love,
    He on her had a special care,
    All things in order to prepare.

7   Her time being come she call'd in hast,
    In travel she then fell at last,
    The neighboring women came with speed,
    For to help her in time of need.

8   The Midwife she came with good will,
    To use her chiefest art and skill,
    Some present help for to procure,
    To her that torment did endure.

9   The child-bed woman with pain and woe,
    Much misery did undergo,
    In bringing forth of such a birth,
    Which almost brought her unto death.

10 The first monster which came to sight,
    Was a live toad, which did them fright,
    It sprauled and creeped all about,
    Which put the women all in doubt.

11 It had four legs as it is told,
    A loathsome creature to behold,
    In ugly shape it did appear,
    The like no woman e're did bare.

12 The next that came unto their view,
  As for certain it is just and true,
  It was a Serpent and a dead child,
  Whose life the Serpent did beguile.

13 For why some of it's face and head,
  By this monster was devoured,
  And it's body injured full sore,
  The like was never seen before.

14 The Serpent had ears like a Pig,
  Which was considerable big,
  It had a long great tail likewise,
  With a pair of wings, and eke two eyes.

15 This Monster joyn'd to the childs side,
  Which they endeavour'd to devide,
  But before they could bring it to pass,
  The Midwife sunk down in the place.

16 But other Women in the room,
  Who having stouter hearts then some,
  Without delay they did contrive,
  To burn these 2 Monsters alive.

17 Into the fire they did them throw,
  whereas they burnt them with much ado,
  And there they were consumed quite,
  To dust and ashes in their sight.

18 The poor weak woman and Midwife too,
  For to recover had much a do,
  The thoughts of this same terrible thing,
  Much grief and sickness did them bring.

19 Thus have you heard me briefly tell,
  This judgement which of late befell,
  Unto this woman in *Hampshire*,
  The like before did near appear.

20 Then let us serve the Lord on high,
 And praise his name continually,
 Let us keep still the right path-way,
 Then we his blessings shall enjoy.

𝔉𝔦𝔫𝔦𝔰.

Printed for J. Hose, and E. Oliver, and are to be sold at
their shops, in Holbourn, and on Snow-hill.

3²

True wonders and strange news

4to Rawlinson 566, fol. 117, black letter, four columns, two woodcuts, one of which is used also in T. L.'s ballad (No. 31).

Laurence White, the author of this doleful ditty, wrote a number of ballads (*e. g.*, "The Dutchman's acknowledgement of his errors. Or a Dutch ballad translated into English," *circa* 1672, Luttrell collection, III, 88), but got most of his popularity from such chapbooks as *The Charitable Farmer of Somersetshire* (1675). A considerable list of his writings will be found under his name or initials in the British Museum catalogue.

In the present ballad White deals with the wonder of wonders of which in the foregoing production (No. 31) Thomas Lanfiere also sings. The two ballads resemble each other closely, but have enough variations to indicate that each, the publication of a rival printer, followed a different prose booklet. To such a source White plainly refers in stanza 6. Judged as news, his ballad is less satisfactory than Lanfiere's. Both are the cheapest of doggerel.

For comments on the tune see No. 22. The rhyme-scheme is most irregular.

True Wonders, and strange news from *Rumsey* in *Hampshire*.

Being a full and true relation of a woman that lately was delivered of a Toad, a Serpent, and a child, to the admiration of all beholders. The Toad and Serpent came from her alive, but the Child dead, having some part of it's head and face devoured by the Serpent in the Womb; the two foul ugly creatures was burned, but the child descently buried; this being the wonder of all the west of England, and has been sent in several Letters by Persons of quality to their friends in London.   *By L. W.*

The Tune is, *In Summer time.*

THE PACK OF AUTOLYCUS

1   GOod people all to me draw neer,
  and to my Song a while attend,
Such wonders here I shall declare,
  may cause some wicked lives to mend

2   Forswearing and to drunkenness,
  too many in it takes delight,
All filthy sins some do commit,
  and glories in them day and night.

3   Strange miracles the Lord has sent,
  that we our sins may lay aside,
but our hearts are so we can't repent
  yet still for us he doth provide.

4   But now I much amazed stand,
  to think what here I shall reherse,
My Pen doth shake, and eke my hand,
  to bring my subject now in verse.

5   'Tis such a wonder that the like,
  in any age was never known,
And did some people sore affright,
  when first unto the world 'twas shown.

6   A Corporation in *Hampshire*,
  and *Rumse* is the places name,
My news is true which I declare,
  as Letters testifie the same.

7   A woman there lives in that Town,
  that lately was but made a Wife,
Her husband with her all along
  lived a sweet peaceable life.

8   This woman being big with child,
  her Husband loved very dear,
He humoured her with speeches mild,
  and on her had a loving care.

9   Her Reckoning-day it drawing nigh,
        all things provided were with speed
The Mid-wife with a many more,
        promist to help in time of need.

10   At last the hour being come,
        poor woman, torments did indure,
The Neighbouring Women flocked in,
        ·to see what help they could procure.

11   With shrieks and crys, poor woman, she
        in labouring travel groaned sore,
Poor wretch indured misery,
        good women judge the cause therefore.

12   For now behold the seed being ripe,
        the Mid-wife eas'd her heavy load,
And first which did appear to sight,
        was a foul loathsome crawling Toad.

13   It crawled in the Midwifes lap,
        which did affright the Women there,
They pittied her hard mis-hap,
        she such a loathsom thing should bare.

14   The woman she lay screetching out,
        whilst they lay gazing on the same,
The Midwife was in such a doubt,
        that she forgot from whence it came.

15   Once more again to work she goes,
        the Womans life for to secure,
With eight or nine most heavy throws,
        more miracles she did procure.

16   For now behold came to their view,
        a dead child, and another thing,
Likened¹ unto a Serpent, which
        tempted a Woman first to sin.

¹ *Text*, Linkened.

17 The Serpent grew unto the child,
     and rapt about it's little arm,
  The Babies life it did beguile,
     likewise the mother suffered harm.

18 Two large staring eyes it had,
     which in the room gave such a light,
  It made the Mid-wifes heart full sad,
     and did the Women sore affright.

19 It had two ears much like a Pig,
     the Nose was shaped like a Dog,
  The Serpents tail was long and big,
     and coloured over like a Frog.

20 It did affright the Women all,
     and made their spirits much decay,
  Some of them on the Lord did call,
     whilst others swounded quite away.

21 Some having better hearts then some,
     so far as I can understand,
  The Serpent and the Toad likewise,
     they took and burned out of hand.

22 The child was buried descently
     within the ground that very day,
  The Mother, and the Midwife both,
     poor wretches, very sick they lay.

23 What is the meaning of those things,
     there's none can tell but the most high.
  'Twas sent to wean us from our sins,
     or else eternally we dye.

24 How are we bound to praise the Lord,
     which perfectly has shap'd us here,
  Then let us all, both great and small,
     the living God for ever fear.

FINIS.

Printed for F. Coles, T. Vere, J. Wright, and J. Clarke.

33

The world's wonder

4to Rawlinson 566, fol. 95, black letter, four columns, three woodcuts. The sheet is slightly mutilated.

Alice Griffithes, of Leominster, Herefordshire, gave birth to four male children, so the ballad informs us, on April 25, 1677. The ballad-writer considered this "the world's wonder," and saw in it a warning from heaven against the sins of men. When four children were born at a birth in London on September 26, 1575, John Stow thought the event worthy of a prominent place in his *Annals* (1615 ed., pp. 679–680); but it is doubtful whether at the present time unusual attention would be attracted by a mere quadruple birth when so many cases of five children at a birth have been reported (see Narcissus Luttrell's diary for May 16, 1704, and the discussion in *Notes and Queries*, 2d S., II, 226, VI, 179; 8th S., III, 308, etc.). For a ballad reporting seven children at a birth, in London, see the *Roxburghe Ballads*, I, 355. The New York *Times* for December 12, 1921, carried a press dispatch from Mexico City reporting that at Tampico "Senora Enriquita Ruibo at that place gave birth yesterday to eight children, all still-born. The mother is well." The same paper, on October 26, 1922, printed a "story" about an Indiana couple who were the parents of "five sets of triplets and two sets of twins" after ten years of marriage. But to return to England: George Hakewill, in his *Apologie*, 1635, p. 253, speaks of "a woman buried in the Church at *Dunstable*, who (as her *epitaph* testifies) bore at three severall times, 3 children at a birth, and five at a birth two other times"; while Henry Townshend (*Diary*, ed. Bund, 1920, I, 62) heard "a report made to his Majesty [Charles II, in 1660] of a man now living and his wife that had at 25 births 50 sonnes, 2 at a birth and all living at this present, and are to present themselves to the King."

These stories are mild! More wonderful is Marcin Kromer's statement, in his history *De Origine et Rebus Gestis Polonorum* (1568, liber IX, p. 162), that on January 20, 1269, Countess Margaret of Cracow bore thirty-six children at a burden. Samuel Clarke, in his *Mirrour or Looking-Glass for Saints and Sinners* (1657, p. 249), asserts that Mrs. Anne Hutchinson, of New England fame, growing "big with childe," for her thirty monstrous heresies "at last brought forth thirty monstrous births, or thereabouts at once"! For a record-breaker — a world's wonder of 365 children born at one birth to Countess Margaret of Henneberg at Loosduinen, Holland — see my *Pepysian Garland*, pp. 121 ff., and my article in *Notes and Queries*, 12th S., XI (1922), 351 ff.

THE PACK OF AUTOLYCUS

In Pliny's *Natural History*, VII, iii, the subject of multiple births is discussed, but Pliny was completely outdone by the credulity of his followers. His treatment, for example, should be compared with that in Boaistuau's *Histoires prodigievses*, 1568 ("Des Femmes Qvi Ont enfanté grand nombre d'enfans," fols. 247ᵛ–252); in William Turner's *Compleat History of the Most Remarkable Providences*, 1697 ("Examples of the Fruitfulness of some Women," pt. II, ch. 4, pp. 5–6); and in *A Description of Holland*, 1743 (pp. 300–301). The comparison is all to Pliny's advantage.

No doubt Mrs. Griffithes figured in contemporary pamphlets, but the collections that ought to contain them are not now accessible to me. The British Museum has a pamphlet of *Strange News from Leominster* (1679), which tells of the "opening of the earth in divers places thereabouts. Also, a true relation of several wonderful sights," but which, I suppose, does not mention the present wonder.

On the tune see No. 22. The rhyme-scheme is somewhat irregularly carried out.

The Worlds Wonder.

Being strange and true News from *Leompster* **in** *Hereford-shire* **of one** *Alice Griffithes*, **that had four men children at a birth, upon the 25***th***. day of April last past, 1677.**

> *Good people all that hear this song,*
> *give good attention to the same;*
> *And do not strive your selves to wrong,*
> *but alway, praise his holy name.*

With Allowance.

To the Tune of, *In Summer time.*

1 I Pray good People all draw near,
   & mark these lines that here are pen'd,
See that the living Lord you fear,
   and strive your lives for to amend.

2 For here to you I will make known,
   and lay it open to your view,
And what is penned in this song,
   I can approve it to be true.

3 Of one *Alice Griffithes* call'd by name,
    the which doth live in *Leompster* town,
That had four men children at one birth,
    as is by many hundreds known.

4 All perfect children they were seen,
    as ever any woman did bear,
I think it is as strange a thing,
    as ever any man did hear.

5 They all received Baptism,
    as the blessed will of God was so;
Let the Parents now give thanks to him,
    and praise his holy name therefore.

6 In *Leompster* Church-yard they now do lye
    as I to you for truth can tell;
I trust to God that sits on high,
    that now in heaven they do dwell.

7 The first his name was *Abraham*,
    as I to you for truth do tell;
I trust to God in heaven above,
    with *Lazarus* his soul doth dwell.

8 The second Son was *Isaac* call'd,
    a dainty lovely Babe was he,
I trust to God in heaven above,
    that now his soul doth rest with thee.

9 The third his name it was *Jacob*,
    which was the [next dis]centing [1] one;
'Tis known [to be a wonder strange] [1]
    as any on [the earth was shown.] [1]

10 THe Fourth was *Jeremiah* call'd,
    indeed it was his Fathers name,
I trust unto my heavenly God,
    that now their souls do rest in fame.

[1] Torn.

[197]

11 These Babes they all alive were born,
     according as they are pen'd here,
And all some Sirrups did receive,
     I can for truth make it appear.

12 The Woman blest be God is safe,
     and past her trouble of the same,
God give her grace to serve the Lord,
     and always praise his Holy Name.

13 This same fell out in *April* last,
     upon the five and twentieth day,
The Lord this wonder strange did send,
     for which to him they have cause to pray.

14 For as he sent them in the World,
     upon the five and twentieth day;
So likewise he upon the sixth,
     did take them to himself away.

15 Therefore we have cause to praise him still,
     and call upon his holy name;
For to preserve us still from ill,
     and keep our souls in health and fame.

16 For he doth send us wonders strange,
     to make our souls for to relent;
But always we along do range,
     and never strive for to repent.

17 But still he is a gracious God,
     for to preserve our souls from thrall,
Else he might strike us with his rod,
     because on him we do not call.

18 Therefore good people all I pray,
     you strive your lives for to amend,
And not Gods words to disobey,
     but strive to make a godly end.

19   For God he is a Righteous Iudge,
       which will preserve us still from ill,
   If that at him we do not grudge,
       but still his mind for to fullfil.

20   So to conclude and make an end,
       God give us grace to serve the Lord,
   That we our wicked lives may mend,
       and serve him still with one accord.

FINIS.

Printed for *F. Coles*, *T. Vere*, *J. Wright*, and *J. Clarke*.   1677.

34

Strange news from Staffordshire

Wood E. 25 (125), black letter, four columns, four woodcuts.

The ballad is summarized from a pamphlet called "*Strange and true News from Staffordshire; or a true Narrative concerning a young Man lying under Almighty God's just Vengeance, for imprecating God's Judgment upon himself, and pleading his Innocency, though he knew himself Guilty. Written by W. Vincent, Minister of God's Word at Bednall, in the County of Stafford, aforesaid; who saw and discoursed the said Person, upon the 26th Day of April, 1677. The saddest Spectacle that ever Eyes beheld.* Licensed, May 11, 1677, Roger L'Estrange. London, printed in the Year 1677" (*Harleian Miscellany*, 1809, II, 327–329). To the tune of *Aim not too high*, one J. C. (Ebsworth mistakenly identifies him with John Cart and dates his work 1633) wrote on this subject: "A Warning for Swearers. By the Example of God's Judgments shewed upon a man Born near the Town of Wolverhampton, in Stafford-shire, who had stolen a Bible; and being examined before a Justice, deny'd the fact, and falsely forswore it; wishing he might Rot, if he were Guilty of the Theft; which (according to his desire) immediately fell upon him; and is at this time a sad Spectacle to Hundreds that have beheld him" (*Roxburghe Ballads*, VIII, 76).

In the New York Public Library I have found another account of this marvel in a pamphlet called "*A Genuine Account of the Man, Whose Hands and Legs rotted off, In the Parish of King's-Swinford in Staffordshire; Where he died, June 21, 1677. Carefully collected by Ja. Illingworth, B. D. To which is added, (Occasion'd by this remarkable Instance of Divine Vengeance) A Discourse concerning God's Judgments; preach'd (in Substance) at Old Swinford in Worcestershire, a neighbouring Parish to King's-Swinford. By Simon Ford, D.D. And Rector of the said Parish. To the Whole is prefix'd, The Rev. Mr. William Whiston's remarkable Mention of this extraordinary Affair; with his Reasons for the Republication thereof, taken from his Memoirs. London, Reprinted, from the first Edition in 1678.*"[1] According to this book, the man in question was named John Duncalf. "About January the 6th, 1676–7, coming to the House of *Humphrey Babb*, living at the *Grange-Mill*, about three miles from *Wolverhampton*, he begged of *Margaret*, the said *Humphrey's* Wife, Victuals and small Drink." Duncalf stole

---

[1] The first edition (1678), a copy of which I have seen in the Harvard Library, is far less elaborate. In it, *A Just Narrative, Or, Account Of the Man whose Hands and Legs rotted off*, is merely an appendix to Simon Ford's *A Discourse Concerning Gods Judgements*.

1er Bible, and sold it for 3s. to "a Maid of *John Downings*, who lives near
the *Heath-Forge*." Accused of the theft, Duncalf "did not only deny it with
some Fierceness, but execrated and cursed himself, *wishing his Hands
might rot off*, if that were true." He died on June 22 after having gradually
"rotted" since the end of April. The whole story is told graphically in some
ninety pages; many letters from eye-witnesses are included, so that this
book is far better than Mr. Vincent's modest tale. John Duncalf's story
is told at length also in William Turner's *Compleat History*, 1697 (pt. I,
ch. 104, p. 16), and in Nathaniel Crouch's *Wonderful Prodigies*, 1762
(pp. 36–38).

A similar wonder was written up by one I. H. about 1600 and printed by
John Wright in a ballad, unique and unreprinted, entitled "An Example
for all those that make no conscience of swaring and forswearing: Shewing
Gods heavy Judgement upon a Maid-servant in London, who forswore
herselfe, & now lies rotting in S. Bartholomewes Hospitall in Smithfield,
where many resort daily to see her. To the tune of, *Aime not too high*"
(James Tregaskis, Catalogue No. 838, lot 155). To the same person Samuel
Clarke probably referred in his *Mirrour or Looking-Glass for Saints and
Sinners*, 1657 (p. 428):

A certaine maide in *London* that had stolen many things from her Mistris, being
examined, forswore them, wishing that she might rot if ever she touched them, or
knew of them: notwithstanding which she was carried to prison, where she began so
to rot, and stink, that they were forced to thrust her out of prison into a common
hospital.

Beard's *Theatre of God's Judgements* (pt. I, 4th ed., 1648, p. 140), supplies
another example:

Iohn Peter sonne in law to *Alexander* that cruel Keeper of Newgate being a
most horrible swearer and blasphemer, used commonly to say, If it be not true, I
pray God I may rot ere I die: and not in vaine, for he rotted away indeed, and so
dyed in misery.

The tune of *My bleeding heart* is named from the first line of a ballad
by Martin Parker (*Roxburghe Ballads*, III, 23), and is equivalent to *In
summer time* (cf. No. 3).

𝔖trange 𝔑ews from *Stafford-shire;*
OR,
A Dreadful Example of Divine Justice.
𝔖hown upon a young-man in that County, who having
stolen a 𝔅ible, and being taxed therewith, fell to im=
precating 𝔊ods Judgements upon himself, wishing
that his hands might rot off, and that he might rot alive

𝔦𝔣 𝔥𝔢 𝔱𝔬𝔲𝔠𝔥𝔢𝔡 𝔦𝔱; 𝔴𝔥𝔦𝔠𝔥 𝔥𝔢𝔞𝔳𝔶 𝔧𝔲𝔡𝔤𝔢𝔪𝔢𝔫𝔱 𝔦𝔫 𝔞 𝔰𝔥𝔬𝔯𝔱 𝔱𝔦𝔪𝔢 𝔣𝔢𝔩𝔩 𝔲𝔭𝔬𝔫 𝔥𝔦𝔪, 𝔥𝔦𝔰 𝔥𝔞𝔫𝔡𝔰 𝔞𝔫𝔡 𝔥𝔦𝔰 𝔞𝔯𝔪𝔰 𝔯𝔬𝔱𝔱𝔦𝔫𝔤 𝔞𝔴𝔞𝔶, 𝔞𝔫𝔡 𝔥𝔦𝔰 𝔩𝔢𝔤𝔤𝔰 𝔣𝔯𝔬𝔪 𝔥𝔦𝔰 𝔟𝔬𝔡𝔶, 𝔥𝔢 𝔟𝔢𝔦𝔫𝔤 𝔫𝔬𝔱 𝔰𝔦𝔠𝔨, 𝔶𝔢𝔱 𝔞𝔭𝔭𝔢𝔞𝔯𝔦𝔫𝔤 𝔱𝔬 𝔞𝔩𝔩 𝔱𝔥𝔞𝔱 𝔰𝔢𝔢 𝔥𝔦𝔪 𝔱𝔥𝔢 𝔰𝔞𝔡𝔡𝔢𝔰𝔱 𝔰𝔭𝔢𝔠𝔱𝔞𝔠𝔩𝔢 𝔱𝔥𝔞𝔱 𝔢𝔳𝔢𝔯 𝔢𝔶𝔢𝔰 𝔟𝔢𝔥𝔢𝔩𝔡. 𝔗𝔥𝔦𝔰 𝔪𝔞𝔶 𝔴𝔞𝔯𝔫 𝔬𝔱𝔥𝔢𝔯𝔰 𝔣𝔯𝔬𝔪 𝔴𝔦𝔰𝔥𝔦𝔫𝔤 𝔣𝔬𝔯 𝔧𝔲𝔡𝔤𝔢𝔪𝔢𝔫𝔱𝔰 𝔱𝔬 𝔣𝔞𝔩𝔩 𝔲𝔭𝔬𝔫 𝔱𝔥𝔢𝔪, 𝔴𝔥𝔢𝔫 𝔱𝔥𝔢𝔶 𝔨𝔫𝔬𝔴 𝔱𝔥𝔢𝔪𝔰𝔢𝔩𝔳𝔢𝔰 𝔤𝔲𝔦𝔩𝔱𝔶. 𝔗𝔥𝔦𝔰 𝔕𝔢𝔩𝔞𝔱𝔦𝔬𝔫 𝔴𝔞𝔰 𝔤𝔦𝔳𝔢𝔫 𝔞𝔫𝔡 𝔞𝔱𝔱𝔢𝔰𝔱𝔢𝔡 𝔟𝔶 𝔐𝔯. *Vincent*, 𝔐𝔦𝔫𝔦𝔰𝔱𝔢𝔯 𝔬𝔣 𝔅𝔢𝔡𝔫𝔞𝔩, 𝔴𝔥𝔬 𝔡𝔦𝔰𝔠𝔬𝔲𝔯𝔰𝔢𝔡 𝔴𝔦𝔱𝔥 𝔱𝔥𝔦𝔰 𝔪𝔦𝔰𝔢𝔯𝔞𝔟𝔩𝔢 𝔶𝔬𝔲𝔫𝔤=𝔪𝔞𝔫.

Tune of, *My Bleeding heart, &c.*

1　GOod people all come cast an eye,
　　Upon a doleful Tragedy;
　　For this relation here is pen'd,
　　That sinners may their lives amend.

2　We never strive for to prevent
　　Our iust deserved punishment;
　　Nor to appease an angry God,
　　Until we feel his heavy rod.

3   Those that the Devil doth possess,
      He leads them on to wickedness,
      From Sin to Sin they post it fast,
      Vntil destruction come at last.

4   This sad example makes appear,
      The true event for to be clear;
      Where Iustice here is plainly shown,
      That scarce the like was ever known.

5   A wicked wretch in *Stafford-shire*,
      Who of the Lord had little fear,
      A Bible chanc't to steal away,
      For which he now may rue the day.

6   The Bible being mist and gone,
      They did inquire of each one,
      And this young-man among the rest,
      They taxed, but he ne'r confest.

7   The same he stiffly did deny,
      Although he gave himself the lye;
      And like a villain bold and stout,
      These imprecations did belch out.

8   He wisht if he the Book did take,
      The Lord would him example make;
      And so that he alive might rot,
      Which came to pass too true God wot.

9   FOr in a very little space,
     He found himself in a sad case;
  His hand which did commit the fact,
  Did first rot off, for that same act.

10   Likewise the flesh we may presume,
    Vp to his elbow doth consume;
  So that he is in woful plight,
  Exposed to all peoples sight.

11   His other hand shrunk up and dry'd
    Like a Beasts Hoof, lyes by his side;
  His knees do rot, and legs decay,
  And from his body fall away.

12   It is a dreadfull sight to see
    A person in such misery,
  Vpon a pad of Straw to lye,
  And so consume insensibly.

13   A Minister in *Stafford-shire*,
    Who of this spectacle did hear;
  Vnto the place he did repair,
  The truth thereof for to declare.

14   When as he came unto the place,
    And see him in that wofull case;
  Yet sensible he did remain,
  As if that he had felt no pain.

15   The Minister admonisht him,
    By all means to confess his sin:
  That so he might redeem his Soul;
  Though his offences were so foul.

16   To which he did confess in brief,
    That like a wretch he plaid the Thief,
  And had the Bible stole away,
  Which brought his body to decay.

17 And that he did the same deny,
   For which he's now in misery,
   Repeating of his wishes o're,
   As he had done the same before.

18 Good peoples prayers he did desire,
   To mittigate Gods wrath and ire;
   Acknowledging his punishment,
   For his offence was justly sent.

19 A Keeper constantly doth stay
   For to attend him night and day,
   Vntil the Lord shall see it fit,
   For to release him out of it.

20 Let his example warn us all,
   Least we into such sins may fall,
   Forbear such wishes too which may
   Bring soul and body to decay.

Printed for, F. Coles, T. Vere, J. Wright, and J. Clark.

35

A strange storm of hail

Pepys, II, 137, black letter, three columns, one woodcut.

The ballad is a disappointing story that does not at all live up to its title. Nothing, for example, is told of the "several men" who were hurt; and though one man is "stricken dead" in stanza 5, even he is revived in the seventh stanza. Just why hail should have burned this man's hat and scorched his breast is not explained — but one is to assume that lightning accompanied and added to the terror of the hail-storm. That information, and a great deal more besides, is given in the book called *An Account of a Strange and Prodigious Storm of Thunder, Lightning and Hail, Which Happened in and about London* (1680), to which the reader may be referred. Narcissus Luttrell calmly wrote in his diary: "On the 18th, between ten and 11 of the clock in the morning, was a most violent storm of hail, tho' it lasted not long; the hailstones many of them as big as pidgeons eggs, and did great mischeif to the glasse-windowes in London, and killed several birds." See also the discussion of hail-storms in the introduction to No. 7. The ballad-writer, although he felt certain that so prodigious a tempest had never before swept over London, was more interested in drawing a moral than in adorning his tale.

For the tune see Chappell's *Popular Music*, I, 162–167.

A STRANGE STORM OF HAIL

A Ballad of the Strange and Wonderful Storm of Hail, Which fell in *LONDON* on the 18*th*. of *May* 1680, which hurt several men, killed many Birds, and spoiled many Trees; with other strange Accidents, the like never before known in *ENGLAND*.

To the Tune of, *Aim not too High.*

1 GOod Christians all attend unto my Ditty,
　　And you shall hear strange News from *London* City;
　　The like before I think you ne'r did hear,
　　Which well may fill our hearts with Dread and Fear.

2 Vpon the Eighteenth of this present *May*,
　　A Tempest strange, pray mind me what I say:
　　So strange, I think the like was never known,
　　As I can hear of yet by any one.

3 Hail-stones as bigg as Eggs a pace down fell,
　　And some much bigger, as I hear some tell:
　　Who took them up as they lay on the ground,
　　And Measur'd, they were found Eight Inches round.

4 And Fourteen Ounces two of them did Weigh,
　　As one who weigh'd them unto me did say:
　　It is so strange, and yet so very true,
　　The like before no mortal ever knew.

5 Much mischief by these Hail-stones there was done,
　　For in St. *Leonard Shorditch* there was one
　　Who as he was a dressing Hemp, 'tis said,
　　All on a sudden he was stricken dead.

6 His Child being by at this was terrifi'd,
　　My Father he is dead, the Child he cry'd:
　　At this Out-cry Neighbours came in amain,
　　And found the man as they supposed slain.

7   Great care was taken by his friends and Wife,
All Art they us'd to bring him unto Life:
So that at last they found that he had breath,
And God preserv'd him from that sudden death.

8   He in his Bed in trembling manner lies,
A stranger sight ne'r seen with mortal eyes:
His Hat was burnt, the Hair scorcht off his breast,
With Limbs struck lame, full sad to be exprest.

9   The very Fowls that flew up in the Air
Were stricken dead, it plainly doth appear:
Wings from their bodies parted by this Hail,
A Story true, although a dreadful Tale.

10   Trees of their Branches then was stripped quite,
Some people from their Houses put to flight:
Such Terrours then possest the hearts of men,
The like I hope they'l never see agen.

11   Let all good people keep this in their minds,
He'l nothing lose who for his Sins repines:
For this I fear fore-runs some stranger things,
And's sent for warning by the King of Kings.

12   Who only knows what there is yet to follow,
And when the Grave each sinful man shall swallow
Repent in time and fit your selves for Death,
Then do not fear how soon you lose your breath.

13   Fitted for Death, you fitter are to Live,
Dispise not then this counsel which I give:
You do not know when Death shall give the stroke,
But that once done, your hearts is quickly broke.

14   He that's prepar'd, grim Death cannot affright,
What man doth fear what doth his heart delight:
A Christian true desires Dissolv'd to be,
That he may Live with God Eternally.

A STRANGE STORM OF HAIL

15 These things as judgements surely they are sent,
That all poor Sinners timely may Repent:
E're vengeance fall, for then 'twill be too late,
For to Deplore your Sinful wretched state.

16 But them who boldly say, There is no GOD,
Shall surely taste of his sharp scourging Rod:
Vengeance shall overtake them e're they know,
Into the Pit of Darkness they must go.

FINIS.

Printed for *F. Coles*, *T. Vere*, *J. Wright*, *J. Clarke*, *W. Thackeray*, and *T. Passinger*.

36

A new wonder

Wood E. 25 (97), black letter, four columns, four woodcuts.

According to this ditty, on May 4, 1681, a terrific rain of corn (or wheat) poured from the skies upon Shrewsbury, presaging some dire calamity. Whatever may have been true of the author, it seems probable that the six printers had published entirely too many reports of sad and terrible news to be in this instance unduly impressed or frightened. The curious delusion that led to the ballad was widespread. Showers of wheat, indeed, had been so often seen (or, what amounts to the same thing, said to have been seen) that the Shrewsbury shower should have created little commotion. In February, 1583, one William Averell, student in divinity, wrote *A Wonderful and Strange News which Happened in the County of Suffolk and Essex the first of February . . . where it rained wheat the space of six or seven miles compass*, concluding his narrative with the signatures of four eye-witnesses (cf. also Philip Stubbes's *Anatomy of Abuses*, 1583, New Shakspere Society ed., I, 188). Before 1612 Sir John Harington asserted, in lines called "Of the corne that rained" (*Epigrams*, bk. II, no. 18):

> I handled, tasted, saw it with mine eyes,
> The graine that lately fell downe from the skies.

Showers of wheat were reported at Ashley, Staffordshire, in 1637 (*Notes and Queries*, 2d S., III, 398); at Brotherton, Yorkshire, in 1648 (cf. No. 7); at Tuchbrooke, near Warwick, and in Shropshire and Staffordshire in 1661 (Thomas Birch, *History of the Royal Society*, 1756, I, 32; Andrew Clark, *Life and Times of Anthony Wood*, I, 400); at Spalding, in Lincolnshire, in 1661 (Nathaniel Crouch's *Admirable Curiosities*, 1702, p. 118); and in Yorkshire in June, 1681. Sir Thomas Browne, in his *Pseudodoxia Epidemica* (2d ed., 1650, II, vii, 5), remarks: "In the history of prodigies we meet with many showers of wheat; how true or probable, we have not room to debate: only thus much we shall not omit to inform, That what was this year [1650?] found in many places, and almost preached for wheat rained from the clouds; was but the seed of Ivy berries, which somewhat represent it, and though it were found in Steeples and high places, might be conveied thither, or muted out by birds." Ralph Thoresby, F. R. S. (*Diary*, I, 85 f.), was in like manner uncertain whether natural or preternatural causes explained the Yorkshire shower of 1681. On the subject of wheat-showers in general, see John Gadbury's *Natura Prodigiorum*, 1660, and *Notes and Queries*, 8th S., IV, 508, V, 114.

For the tune see No. 12.

A New Wonder:

OR,

A strange and True Account from *Shrewsbury* of a Dreadful Storm, which happened on the 4ᵗʰ of *May* last, 1681. at or about Mid-night, which the people that heard it supposed to be Hail, but finding their mistake by the Day-light, were all possessed with Astonishment. The Truth thereof is attested by several of the place, as being Eye-witnesses of the Premises.

To the Tune of, *Troy Town*.

THE PACK OF AUTOLYCUS

1   IT is well known for some years past,
    strange wonders we have often seen;
A Wonder very lately past,
    more Strange in *England* hath not been:
Such Miracles let's keep in mind,
Least we an Angry God do find.

2   Mind well my Words, and you shall hear
    a Wonder that is Strange and True,
Which did in *Shrewsbury* appear,
    to the amaz'd Spectaters view:
And in the dead time of the Night,
Which many hundreds then did fright.

3   A mighty Storm of Hail, as they
    did by the noise it made suppose;
For long time it went not away,
    while Wonders in the hearers grows:
It clattered so against the Glass,
That all that heard it troubled was.

4   But when the dawning of the day,
    brought proof to their deceived ears;
That knew not what to think or say,
    they more and more were fill'd with fears:
For that which Hail they thought to be,
Resembled Corn, they all did see.

5   Some looked White, and some lookt Red,
    and some was of a sadder hue,
Some almost black, as it is said,
    by those that did this Wonder view:
A Husk upon't there was likewise,
No humane Art could this devise.

6   And some that little patience had,
    to try experience soon made haste;
Although their hearts were dull and sad,
    they of this new come Corn would taste:
And trying if 'twas good to eat,
They said it was exceeding sweet.

A NEW WONDER

7 And what this mighty wonder means,
 there's none can tell but God alone;
'Tis he that sends things in extreams,
 'tis he [1] that makes such wonders known:
Then let our hearts to him incline,
He's good and just, and all Divine.

8 But doubtless all the Wonders which
 we have in *England* lately seen,
Strange things portends to poor and rich,
 although we know not what they mean:
O let us then for Death prepare,
Lest it doth seize us unaware.

9 How gracious is he that Creates
 the World and all that is therein;
All kind of Cruelty he hates,
 and still fore-warns us from our Sin:
But we like sinful Wretches bold,
Walk on in Sin as uncontroul'd.

10 No dreadful Signs of Blazing-Stars
 can rouze up *England* to awake,
The Fire, the Pestilence, nor Wars,
 can make your Stubborn hearts to ake:
O *England* then in time Repent,
For fear you may too late Lament.

11 And though this Corn to some may seem
 no dreadful Sign, mind what I say;
As none can tell what it doth mean,
 to *England* it prove Fatal may:
Let no Strange things forgotten be,
Lest they'r the last that e're you see.

[1] *Text* he he.

12 And when a Dreadful Sign is sent,
    without all doubt 'tis sure to give
All timely notice to Repent,
    that they in peace may longer Live:
If of these Signs you take no care,
England I say, beware, beware.

Printed for *F. Coles*, *T. Vere*, *J. Wright*, *J. Clarke*, *W. Thackeray*,
and *T. Passenger*, 1681.

37

Sad and dreadful news from Horsleydown

Pepys, II, 152, black letter, three columns, three woodcuts.

Horsleydown, once a large open space in the parish of St. Mary Magdalen's Bermondsey used for grazing horses, was, it will be recalled, the place where Margery Perry (No. 24) met and was killed by the Devil. Even more terrible was the encounter that Dirty Doll, the heroine of the present ballad, had with Satan and two of his devils. She was so severely bruised in the fight that gangrene set in and soon caused her death, the manner of which aroused so much public curiosity that hundreds of people attended the funeral. But, no doubt to their disappointment, no unusual happening disturbed the burial-service.

Doll Winterbottom was a tally-woman. Her male counterpart is thus described in *Four for a Penny: Or, poor Robin's Character . . . of an oppressing Tally-man*, 1678 (*Harleian Miscellany*, 1809, IV, 148):

The unconscionable Tally-man . . . is one that eateth up the poor (to use a sacred phrase) even as bread; and yet under a charitable pretence of serving and accommodating them: for he lets them have ten-shillings-worth of sorry commodities, or scarce so much, on security given to pay him twenty shillings by twelve-pence a week. Then his wandering Mephistophilus, with the bundle of rattles, whom we may call the devil's rent-gatherer, haunts them more diligently, than a revengeful ghost does a murderer . . . and if they happen to fail the first or second week, snaps them or their security, and makes them, forthwith, pay the utmost farthing; alleging, now their former agreement was void.

The ballad, then, is a warning to harsh creditors, usurers, and other "caterpillars."

The tune of *Packington's pound* is in Chappell's *Popular Music*, I, 123; the tune of *Now, now the fight's done*, which is named from the first line of "Love's Conquest" (Pepys, III, 105), is given in John Playford's *Choice Ayres*, III (1681), 41.

On Josiah Blare see Plomer's *Dictionary of Printers* (1668–1725), p. 38.

THE PACK OF AUTOLYCUS

Sad and Dreadful News from *Horsly-Down*, **in the Parish of St.** *Mary Magdalen Bermondsey;* **or, A Warning to Brokers, Tally-Men, and such like unconscionable Catter-pillars; by the sad Example of** *Dorothy Winter-bottom*, **Alias** *Dirty-Doll*, **late of** *Horsly-Down*, **who according to her own Report, as 'tis Credibly attested, by contending with the Devil, received such mortal Bruises, as occasioned her death, she dying on the 27**th. **of** *August*, **and was buried at St.** *Olaves*[1] *Southwark*, **on the 28**th. **of the same month, 1684.**

Reader, behold what Mortals are, when sin
Opens the Gate and lets the Tempter in,
As by this Story may too plain be seen.

To the Tune of, *Now now the Fights done;* Or, *Packingtons Pound*.

1 A Story most strange I shall to you declare,
   The like in past ages will hardly appear,
So sad and so dreadful that but to relate,
May fear in the hearers and wonder create:
'Tis of a wretched woman that lately did dwell,
In *Horsly-Down* as thousands know full well;
Who upon the Tally's put Money to use,
Which oft the poor ruines when turn'd to abuse.

2 And *Dorothy Winterbottom* was her name,
   Though by Dirty *Doll* she was known most to Fame,
Her vices were many as people express,
Being given to curse and to drink to excess:
Which gave the foul Tempter a way to get in,
And still urge her on for to multiply sin:
To covetousness she was likewise inclin'd,
For though she had store, yet she griev'd in her mind,

---

[1] Text apparently *Olives*.

SAD NEWS FROM HORSLEYDOWN

3 That she had no more, and so sparing was seen,
That victuals she'd begg, where abroad she had been,
Or Candles, or Shooes, or what else she could get,
For her heart on her money was wholy now set:
Which in her extravagant talk she would say,
The Devil had lent her, and she must repay,
But one day with her Tally's abroad having been,
And not to her mind her extortion got in,

4 She wish'd as 'tis said, if she then did fail,
To arrest them and lay them to rot in a Iale:
The Devil might mortifie her at his will,
Not minding that God does rash wishes take ill:
And oft in his anger lets Satan prevail,
O're those that before he'd no power to assail,
When almost at midnight sometime after that,
She staggering home at last to her house got.

5 But scarce was she entred when with doleful cries,
She call'd out for help, when strait at the sad noise,
And murthers repeating her daughter came there,
But being surpriz'd and amazed with fear
Her self durst not enter, till other did hast,
To know what the matter was, but found all fast,
So that the sad cry still increasing the more,
With instruments fit they broke ope the back-door.

6 When entring with lights they might plainly percieve
Beneath the old Lumber poor *Dorothy* heave,
For o'rewhelm'd with its weight she was struling for life,
Yet threatning as if she had then been at strife,
With some dreadful foe, and no sooner reliev'd,
But as one distracted she flounc'd and she reav'd;
And in an extravagent manner 'tis said,
She confess'd an encounter with Satan she had

7 And that she two Devils had worsted, but then
A third coming in, had o'recome her again,
And that the sad Quarrel for money was made,
Which she had borrow'd and lent in her trade:

That they came in humane shapes she did confess,
Two in mens cloathing, the third in womans dress;
Nor would she be perswaded that it was a dream,
But angry with those that so told her did seem.

8 When neglecting the bruises, and using no art,
The gangreen increasing, soon reach'd to her heart,
In spight of Chirurgeons who came all to late
But could not reprive her from death and sad fate;
Though raveing she lay and oft ideley she talk'd,
As if Hells black spirits about her had walk'd:
Not minding advice though many it gave,
In hopes her poor soul from the Tempter to save.

9 Her talk of her money was mostly her care,
Still asking those absent the time they wou'd pay her,
When falling asleep she soon fainted away,
And groaning her last she no more had to say:
When dead her own daughter to her husband did send,
Who long had absented him, but in the end,
He refusing to Bury her, her Daughter seiz'd
On what there was left, to dispose as she pleas'd.

10 And for her Funeral straight did provide,
As Duty enioyn'd her, when hundreds beside,
Attended the Corps to the Church-yard, and there,
The Sexton did decently Old *Doll* Interr:
To rest in her Grave now in spight of the Fiends,
Vntil the great day comes, in which the world ends:
Then by her take warning you that Tally's keep,
Least Satan chastise you, and make you to weep.

𝔉𝔌𝔑𝔌𝔖.

Printed for J. Blare, at the Looking-glass in the New-Buildings
on London-Bridge.

38

Man's amazement

Pepys, II, 175, black letter, three columns, three woodcuts.

John Deacon first published at the sign of the Rainbow, Holborn, about 1682, and shortly afterwards at the Angel in Giltspur Street. This ballad, which was printed in 1684, was, therefore, one of his earliest publications. It helped to start him on a career of "marvelous ballading" that he abandoned only at his death.

The story of Thomas Cox and his devil-fare is certainly a genuine marvel. In a country where prohibition obtains, it could perhaps be satisfactorily explained on rational grounds; but, considering the time and the place, to attempt no explanation of it might be best. Probably Thomas Cox did make to "hundreds" of people the explanation that is given in the ballad, and possibly some of them believed it. Nevertheless, the story is sheer fiction from beginning to end, written and printed to take advantage of popular credulity. Even as fiction it lacks plausibility, though it is none the less fun for that! The flaming eyes and the bear-like form of the Devil are conventional, but it is odd to find him unsubstantial. He should have had a fleshy hand with real money in it; and if Cox had taken the money from the Devil's hand his sickness would have been entirely plausible. Nobody could touch the Devil with impunity!

The ballad is merely a summary of a pamphlet (British Museum, 8630. bb. 24) which has the following title-page (with its verso blank):

A Strange, True, and Dreadful/Relation,/of the Devils appearing to/Thomas Cox/a Hackney-Coach-man;/Who lives in Cradle-Alley/in Baldwins-Gardens./ First, in the habit of a Gentleman/with a Roll of Parchment in his hand, and/then in the shape of a Bear, which after-/wards vanish'd away in a flash of Fire, at/Eight of the Clock on Friday Night,/October the 31th. 1684./London: Printed by E. Mal-let, 1684./

The body of the pamphlet (typographical errors being corrected in my reprint but indicated in the foot-notes) runs thus:

[A₂] THE TRUE RELATION OF THE DEVILS APPEARING
TO THOMAS COX A HACKNEY–COACH–MAN

Amongst the variety of those strange Discourses, which have appeared in pub-lick; I presume nothing ever yet issued from the Press more remarkable than this present Relation, which is so strange and surprizing in it self, that I do not question, but some curious and scrupulous Wits of this Age will discredit the Truth of it, and think it altogether fabulous in it self, considering the dreadful Circumstances

[219]

which attend it: but I would advise those whom *Atheism* and *Infidelity* has so far prevailed upon to amend their own vicious Lives, for fear a greater mischief does correct their insolence, to whom this [A2ᵛ] may be a fair warning. As to the reality of this Relation, I would so far engage the Readers good Opinion of the Truth of it, that I do assure him, the Person himself has related this from his own mouth; confirm'd it in the presence of all those Numerous Visitants who daily croude to see him, with all the solemn and sober protestations an honest man, and a good Christian can averr the truth. And as I do not question, but several persons will give themselves the satisfaction of inquiring out the truth; so *I* am well assured it will give an advantage and repute to this present *Paper*; when from all hands the whole world shall be satisfied in the candour Truth and Integrity [1] of this Discourse.

Had not *Thomas* [2] *Cox* himself lived so near, that any person may satisfie himself of this Truth, several persons who were present, both Divines & other Gentlemen of good Quality and Estate, would attest the Truth under their own hands.

Thomas Cox now lives in *Cradle Alley* in *Baldwins-Gardens*, and was formerly a *Labourer*, and served *Masons* and *Bricklayers*, but leaving that imployment has since drove a *Hackney Coach*; a man of a fair Life and Conversation in the esteem and reputation of his neighbours.

On *Friday* the last of *October* he took up a *Faer* at *White-Hall Gate*, which he [3] drove into *Water-Lane* in *Fleet-street*, which having set down, he was forced to drive to the bottom of the *Lane* to the *Thames side* to turn his Coach, and at his coming up called in at a *Victualling* [4] *house*, where he drank a *Pot or two of drink* [A3] going into his *Coach-Box* he gently drove up the *Lane*, and within three or four doors of the upper end he saw a person standing by one of the Posts, near the Wall, in the habit of a Gentleman with a *Roll of Paper or Parchment in his hand*; it was then dark and about *Eight of the Clock* at *Night:* The Gentleman called Coachman, and he immediately stop'd and opened the door of his Coach; the Gentleman went in, and bid him drive to the *lower Church Yard* by *Fleet-Ditch*, which [5] belongs to *St.* [6] *Brides Church*; he went up into the Box [7] again and giving his Horses a Lash, they started and his *Hat* fell off which forced him to light, & after he had some time in vain felt for it in the dark, the Gentleman asked him what he wanted; he told him he had drop'd his *Hat* and could not find it, and had rather have lost *eight Shillings out of his pocket*; the Gentleman bid him look under one of his Horses feet, which he directed him to and there he should find it, he did so, and found it accordingly; though it was so dark he could not see it before: At this the Coachman was a little surpriz'd, [8] wondering how the Gentleman could tell where his *Hat* was, who sat in the Coach, and the Night so dark he cou'd not see it, but drove on and observed all the way he went, his Horses were very unruly and started upon every lash he gave them, and were very Resty and unwilling to go forward; when he came by the *Ditch side* he drove very slow. Being now within some few paces of the *Church-Yard*, they started again, and were so unruly, that in a passion the Coach-man descended from the Box, and in a great fright said he would drive him [A3ᵛ] no farther, and opened the door of the Coach, holding the Reins of his Horses in his Whip, which he had made in a Bow [9] to lengthen them that he might reach the door, the Gentleman told him he had money enough, and should have what he would, reaching out his hand, which the Coach

[1] *Integrity.*	[2] *Thomos.*	[3] be.
[4] *Victuallng.*	[5] whieh.	[6] *St.*
[7] *Box.*	[8] supriz'd.	[9] *Bow.*

man saw, but no money in it; but when he went to take it could feel no hand, though he saw the same shape of the Gentlemans person in the Coach as before, who presently stept out, at which the Horses started and flying out drew the Coach-man back, who having stopped his Horses and looking back to his fare, he saw a great black thing in the form of a Bear with great flaming Eyes which lay by the Wall side and made up to him, at which the Horses press'd forward, and the Coachman with much ado stop'd them, and taking the Reins from his Whip into his Hand, as it approached him whip'd at it, and as he thought lash'd it; when on a sudden it vanished away in a terrible flash of Fire with great sparks, as if a Flambeaux had been dashed against the Wall and all flashed in his face,[1] that he was so stoun'd that he did not know where he was, and lost all Sense in the Horrour and Consternation he was in.

Being come home so amazed that he knew not where he was (the horses as he suppos'd going of their own accord as they usually would do) he was taken out of the *Box* speechless and carried to his Bed, where he so remained till *Thursday Morning* the 6 of this Instant, without speaking a word, though he knew at the same time those several friends who came to visit [A4] him, as he hath since declared. On *Thursday* very early in the Morning, his Wife came into his chamber to see how he did, and as she heard the *Cock* crow his Speech returned to him at that instant: He was visited by several Divines who much pitied his sad & deplorable condition, and with their Pious exhortations much comforted his poor afflicted Wife, who was almost distracted to see the lamentable estate her Husband was in. Since [2] he recovered his speech multitudes of persons have been to see and discourse him, to all which he has given the same relation as to every particular circumstance of this Narration, and is ready to confirm it to any person who is desirous of further satisfaction from his own mouth; and he does further say, that though the person in the Coach when he refused to carry him any farther, did tell him he had money enough, and he should be well satisfied for his pains, yet he could not perceive any in his hand, nor did receive any from him.

Since he has been able to speak his limbs are so benumn'd that he has no sense or feeling in them, but are as if they were dead, or no part of his body, he is not sensible of any heat though fire is applied to them which you may burn his flesh withall, without making him sensible of any pain or anguish; and it is very much fear'd by his friends that he will never recover the use of them again, but remain in that sad condition as long as he lives. For fear any person should apprehend this was only a vain and idle fancy of a swimming Brain occasioned by drunkenness: he does declare he was very sober, and had been very moderate [A4ᵛ] in his drinking all that day, and as free from being fudled as ever he was in his life; and till this strange accident happened to him, without any fear or apprehension of such a danger, which by the strong impression it then made upon his Spirits, and yet remains so firmly fix'd, to any sober and considering person it is apparent somthing more than ordinary, was the cause of so strange and sudden a consternation.

It [3] has so nearly affected him, that he has resolved never to drive Coach again, if he does so far recover his Limbs as to be able to do it, tho' it was an imployment he very much delighted in before, and lived very happy and contentedly by those lawful gains his honest labour and industry had acquired by it.

I hope no person how strange and improbable [4] this Relation may seem, will be so unkind to imagine any man would be so disingenuous for his own private advantage

---

[1] facc.   [2] *S*ince.   [3] *I*t.   [4] improable.

to impose a Romance upon the world, with so much confidence as this is averr'd to be a Truth; and as it has already furnished the Town with Discourse of wonder and amazement, it is no *Wapping* Apparition, but published with mature consideration and scrutiny: whose Truth renders it as remarkable as it's surprising Circumstances does strange and wonderful.

FINIS.

For the tune — which is elaborately discussed in the *Roxburghe Ballads*, IV, 392 f., VI, 36 ff. — see John Playford's *Choice Ayres*, I (1676), 10.

𝕸𝕬𝕹𝕾 Amazement:

It being a true Relation of one Thomas Cox, a Hack-ney-Coach-man, to whom the Devil appeared on friday night, it being the 31st. of *October*, first in the likeness of a Gentleman, seeming to have a role of Paper or Parchment in his hand, afterwards in the likeness of a great Bear with glaring eyes, which so affrighted him, that it deprived him of all his Sences.

To the Tune of *Digbys Farewel.*

1   GOod People attend now, and I will declare,
A wonder as strange as you ever did hear;
It hath been apparent to many ones view,
For though it is strange, yet 'tis certainly true;
The last of *October*, on Friday at night,
A strange apparition a Coachman did fright,
In such a strange manner the like was ne'r known,
As here by these lines shall plainly be shown.

2   That night near *White-Hall* he had took up a fair,
And then unto *Water-Lane* he did repair,
And when he had set his fare down in the Lane,
He drove to the end to return back again:
And as he was driveing then easily on
The Devil appear'd in the shape of a man,
And leaning against a great post he did stand,
With likeness of Parchment rol'd up in his hand.

MAN'S AMAZEMENT

3 He call'd to the Coach-man as it did appear,
The Coach-man Supposing he had been a Fare;
He stopped his horses and came down therefore,
And stept to his Coach and then open'd the door,
He bid him to drive him to *Brides* Low Church yard,
The Coachman observ'd him with reverent regard;
For little he thought of that infernal sin,
And therefore to drive him he then did begin.

4 The Horses possest with a Habit of fear,
They snorted and startled as it did appear,
The Coachman his hat it fell of to the ground,
The night being dark it could not be found:
This gentleman told him though he did not see it
His hat it lay under his horses fore-feet;
There finding his hat and the words to be true,
He then was amazed to think how he knew.

5 But when he got into his Coachbox again,
His horses they startled and could not refrain,
Thus snorting and flouncing being frighted withal,
At length he came near to St. *Brides* church-yard-wall
The coach-man came down from his box in a fright,
And said he would drive him no further that night:
The Devil he held out his hand and did say,
Here's mony enough I will bountiful pay.

6 Then as he did proffer to feel for his hand,
Yet there was no substance he could understand
Nor there was no mony the coach-man could see,
The Devils a lyar and so he will be,
Still he in the shape of a man did remain,
Till he from the coach had desended again;
The Coach-man he turning about to his fare,
He then did appear in the form of a Bear.

7 Which did both his heart and his sences surprize,
It staring upon him with great flaming eyes
And also did seem to make at him amain
But he with his whip lashed at it again,

And then he did seem to give back and retire,
And vanisht away in great flashes of fire,
O this was a sad and deplorable case,
The flashes did seem for to fly in his face.

8 He then stepped into his Coach-box straightway,
The horses run homeward without there delay,
The coach-man was speechless like one almost dead
But they took him down and convey'd him to bed
Where five or six days he did speechless remain,
But then at the length it returned again.
Now from his own mouth he hath made it appear,
And briefly declared the things mention'd here.

9 He has lost both the sence and the use of his Limbs,
Which is a great cut and a grief to his friends,
To see how he lyes in a languishing state,
Alas this affliction and sorrow is great:
To see how he lyeth and still doth remain,
'Tis fear'd that he ne'r will recover again,
He says if the Lord will his Limbs now restore,
He never will follow the calling no more.

10 There's many hath seen him from both far and near;
From whose just Relation the truth did appear,
Now in *Baldwins* Gardens there in Cradle Court,
This man still is living as hundreds report,
And those that will take but the pains for to go
A further Account of the truth you may know,
Yea from his own mouth he will freely unfold,
The sum and the substance of what I have told.

FINIS.

Printed for I. Deacon, at the Angel in Guilt-spur street.

39

The distressed gentlewoman

Pepys, II, 74, black letter, three columns, three woodcuts, slightly torn.

A pious young lady who dwelt near Lincoln's Inn Fields was, by the implacable malice of Satan, suddenly possessed of a devil — "a dæmon of High Germany." No efforts, medicinal, surgical, or spiritual, could dislodge him, and the ballad-writer calls upon all Christian people to pray for the gentlewoman's relief. The devil refused to permit her to take the sacrament, shouting out, to the horror of the congregation, "She shall not take it; no, she shan't." At the Savoy church he rudely interrupted Dr. Anthony Horneck (1641–1697) in the middle of a prayer.

Horneck was appointed at the Savoy in 1671, where (stanza 12) he preached for many years and gained great popularity, becoming the King's Chaplain in 1689. That the ballad appeared about February, 1691, is shown by a reference in one of Richard Lapthorne's letters in *Fifth Report of the Royal Commission on Historical Manuscripts*, app., pt. 1, p. 381. For the tune see Chappell's *Popular Music*, I, 162–167.

THE PACK OF AUTOLYCUS

The Distressed Gentlewoman;

Or, *Satan's* Implacable Malice. Being a True Relation of a young Gentlewoman near *Lincolns-Inn-Fields*, who is possess'd with an Evil Spirit, which Speaks within her most Blasphemous Words, to the grief of her Friends and Relations, and all good Christian People.

The Tune is, *Aim not too High.*

Licensed according to Order.

1 GOod People all, I pray you now draw near,
  Unto these Lines lend an attentive Ear;
  While I a dismal Story do unfold,
  Which is as true as ever Mortal told.

2 A Youthful Damsel now near *London* dwells,
  Whose Birth and Education far excells
  Some thousands, for it is well known, that she
  Has been a pattern of true Piety.

3 This is well known, it was her constant care,
  Still to frequent the Holy Home of Pray'r;
  To Worship God according to his will,
  His Holy Laws and Precepts to fulfill.

4 All kind of Pride she hated and abhor'd,
  Her care and study was to serve the Lord;
  Therefore the Holy Scriptures did she Read,
  And eke an upright Christian Life did lead.

5 Now while she was Religiously inclin'd,
  Satan, the Enemy of all Mankind,
  He study'd how he might her soon Possess,
  And blast that sweet Celestial Happiness.

6 The which he thus endeavour'd by degrees,
  First Melancholly did her Sences seize;
  Which did her former Glory soon expell,
  But yet what was the cause she could not tell.

THE DISTRESSED GENTLEWOMAN

7   At length it did to strange Distraction grow,
While her dear friends beheld with grief and woe.
All means were us'd for a Recovery,
And free her from this sad Calamity.

8   Learned Physitians us'd their chiefest Skill,
Tho' all in vain, for she remained still
Distracted, as she had been long before,
Her Sence and Reason they could not restore.

9   This done, all former means they laid aside,
And did in God alone their hopes reside;
To whom they had recourse by fervent Pray'r,
And many faithful Ministers came there.

10   Which she receiv'd with joy and sweet content,
But as they offer'd her the Sacrament,
Her very Teeth were set, and clenched fast,
And eke a Voice was heard in her at last.

11   In these like words the Hellish Fiend did taunt,
Saying, *She shall not take it, no, she shan't:*
Then Barking like a Dog, it did Revile,
Her Mouth and Eye-lids being clos'd the while.

12   Next day she to the *Savoy*-Church was brought,
Where Dr. *Horneck* many Years has Taught;
And in the time of Pray'r this Fiend did Roar,
More veh'ment than at any time before.

13   Nay, in the hearing of all People there,
He Curst the Minister in time of Pray'r;
And said, *Come down, black Dog, this shall not do:*
This said, his Barking Tone he did renew.

14   Next way ¹ to her a Learned Doctor went,
Who after he some time in Pray'r had spent,
Demanded of the Fiend in Gods great Name,
Now what he was, and eke from whence he came.

¹ *Read* day.

15   At which the Spirit did in short reply,
      I am a *Dæmon* of *High-Germany;*
      And having found a Habitation here,
      It is not any such as you I fear.

16   No Tongue is able to express her Grief,
      While thus she does remain, void of reliefe:
      Let sober Christians pray to God above,
      That he will manifest his tender Love

17   To this poor Creature which is thus possest,
      Who at this time is wofully opprest:
      O that her Glory he once more will raise
      That she may live to speak his lasti[ng praise.] [1]

FINIS.

Printed for P. Brooksby, J. D[eacon, J. Blare, J. Back.] [1]

[1] Torn.

40

The happy damsel

Pepys, II, 81, black letter, four columns, two woodcuts, slightly torn.

Maria Anna Mollier (Marian, or Mary, Maillard, to give her real name) had, the ballad declares, been terribly crippled by a fall when she was barely five months old. At thirteen she was apparently a hopeless cripple; but, after reading a passage in the second chapter of St. Mark's gospel, she felt a flash of religious enthusiasm and belief sweeping over her, proclaimed her faith in the healing power of God, and immediately found herself strong and well. The ballad-writer says that "thousands hath seen her walk alone," and his statement is hardly exaggerated. In these days of faith-healing, auto-suggestive and otherwise, Miss Maillard's story should not seem in the slightest degree unusual; but in 1693 the thousands in London are said to have believed it the event of the century. The balladist puts his moralizing into five stanzas at the beginning, and for the remainder of his verses remembers that his function is that of a reporter. Stanzas 10 to 12 are pretty good. "Better fed than taught" is an apter descriptive phrase than one often meets in a ballad.[1]

The numerous pamphlets that were written on this cure — and all of them are later in date than the ballad — say nothing of a fall, but declare that Mary was born with a "disorder" in her left hip. One of them, *A Plain and True Relation of a Very Extraordinary Cure of Mariane Maillard*, was licensed at Stationers' Hall on December 23, 1693, and is preserved in the British Museum (1166. h. 6 [9]). During the following year (1694) at least two books on this subject were printed: *Light in Darkness, or, A Modest Enquiry Into, and humble improvement of Miracles, in General, upon occasion of this late Miraculous Cure of Mariane Maillard; Who was Prodigiously Lame for many Years, now Wonderfully restored by an immediate Power of God with her, on the 26th Day of November, 1693* (Harvard); and *A True Relation of the Wonderful Cure of Mary Maillard. . . . With the Affidavits and Certificates of the Girl, and several other Credible and Worthy Persons, who knew her both before and since her being Cured. To which is added, A Letter from Dr. Welwood to the Right Honourable the Lady Mayoress, upon that Subject* (British Museum and Harvard). The first is a 42-page sermon on miracles, in the course of which (pp. 15–23) the preacher cites Mary Maillard as a specific illustration. The second is an elaborate discussion of

---

[1] It is, however, a proverb, which appears, for example, in John Heywood's *Works* (1562), in J. Gruter's *Florilegium Ethicopoliticum* (1611), no. 56, and in Thomas Draxe's *Treasurie of Ancient Adagies*, 1616 (*Anglia*, XLII [1918], 377).

the case, in 48 pages; it was reprinted, with various additional documents, in 1730 under the title of *An Exact Relation of the Wonderful Cure of Mary Maillard*, (*Now Wife of the Rev^d Mr. Henry Briel*) (British Museum and Harvard). Still another reprint appeared as late as 1787 (British Museum).

Mary, the daughter of John and Charlotte (*née* Du Dognon) Maillard, was "born at *Coignac* in *Xaintoigne*, the 25th of *September*, 1680. Her Parents were drove from their native Country by the heat of the Persecution in *France*, a few years after her Birth; and they fled to *Lausanne* in *Switzerland*, and from thence passed through *Germany*, and, by way of *Holland*, came to *England* in the year 1689, and brought this Child, being Lame, along with them. They took a House near one Mrs. *Laulan*, a *French* Gentlewoman, who also had fled upon account of her Religion, and the Child going frequently to see her, this Lady took such a fancy to the Girl, as to take her home to wait on her." The 1730 edition, from which the preceding passage is quoted, has Mary Maillard (or Mrs. Briel) tell her own story (pp. 5–9):

> On the 26th of *November*, 1693, being *Sunday*, I went to the *French* Church in *Leicester-Fields*, and in the Street, as I came home in the Afternoon, the Boys called me opprobrious Names, reflecting upon my Lameness, and proceeded so far as to throw Dirt upon me; which very much affected me, and pierced my very Heart with grief. I went crying home to Mrs. *Laulan*, with whom I then lived, and told her I was very unhappy, in that God had not only laid the Affliction of Lameness upon me, but also in that I underwent the continual Uneasiness and Fatigue of being thus insulted by the Boys. . . . [Mrs. Laulan comforted her; and presently Mary, who was reading the second chapter of St. Mark, cried out:] Madam, these unbelieving *Jews* were very naught to Blaspheme against Christ, and not to believe, when they saw such things evidently before their Eyes; for my part, *If our Lord were here on Earth now, I would not do like them: I would run immediately to him, and I would firmly believe.* Upon which my Thigh-bone gave one snap, just as the Words were out of my Mouth, and I said, Madam, I am Cured. . . . [Filled with joy, Mary went to reveal her cure to her parents; then she went back with Mrs. Laulan, who] kept me a Fortnight; but Crouds came so thick to see me, that she was desirous I should be at my Father's House, where Multitudes of all Ages, and both Sexes, came to see me; and the House was so crouded, that I had hardly time to eat.

This account, the book tells us, "was taken from Mrs. *Briel's* own Mouth, *January 2d*, 17$\frac{29}{30}$," at which time she was living with her husband, a French minister, in Rose-Alley in Bishopsgate Street. Dozens of affidavits are included to prove the truth of her story.

The miraculous cure of Mrs. Briel did not long go unmatched. The *Athenian Mercury* for January 20, 1694, announced that John Dunton and John Harris would speedily publish "The True and Perfect Narrative, of the Miraculous Cure of Mrs. Savage's Crooked Hand"; and in its issue for February 13 appeared the following advertisement:

> *Yesterday was Published* A *Narrative* of the late Extraordinary Cure in an instant wrought upon Mrs. *Elizabeth Savage*, (Lame from her Birth) without the using of any

Natural Means, with the *Affidavits* which were made before the *Right Honourable the Lord Mayor*, and the *Certificates* of several Credible Persons who knew her both before and since this Cure: Enquired into with all its Circumstances by Noted *Divines* both of the Church of *England* and others, and by Eminent *Physicians* of the College, and many Persons of *Quality*, who have express'd their full satisfaction, with an *Appendix* attempting to prove that *Miracles are not ceas'd*. Printed for *John Dunton* at the *Raven*, and *John Harris* at the *Harrow* in the *Poultrey*. Price 6*d*."

For the tune of the ballad see the introduction to No. 22.

The Happy Damsel:
OR,

A Miracle of GOD's Mercy, signalized on Maria Anna Mollier, *living near St.* James's Westminster, *a poor lame Creature, who had been a Cripple from her Cradle, and on the* 26th *of* November, 1693. *she was perfectly cured by the Hand of Divine Providence, to the great amazement of all People.*

To the Tune of, *Summer-time.*

1   L Et unbelieving Men attend,
       unto this strange Relation here,
    Which as a naked truth I send
      to all the Land both far and near:

2   The Lord is good and gracious still,
      to we poor Mortals here below;
    To those who do obey his Will,
      he does his love and kindness show.

3   As we by sad experience find
      now in the World amongst us here;
    Yet were we faithfully inclin'd,
      strange Wonders daily would appear.

4   Alas it is through unbelief,
      that Miracles so long have ceas'd;
    And therefore now our pain and grief
      from Age to Age has been increas'd.

5　For God is merciful to all,
　　　that are in grief and sad distress;
　　If on his righteous Name they call,
　　　he will not leave them comfortless.

6　This Creature did sad Pains endure;
　　　at length, to God she made her moan,
　　Who sent her then a speedy Cure,
　　　down from his bright Celestial Throne.

7　The truth at large I will unfold,
　　　how by a Fall and fatal Stroke,
　　When she was hardly five Months old,
　　　her little Infant-bones was broke.

8　Her Thigh-bone clearly out of place,
　　　and likewise her poor Ancle too;
　　Crooked she was in woful case,
　　　the like of her you never knew.

9　Near thirteen Years this Grief she boar,
　　　as of a truth we understand;
　　At length God's Love she did implore,
　　　who heal'd her by a Mighty Hand.

10　*November*, six and twentieth day,
　　　this mighty Wonder strange was wrought:
　　Now as from Church she took her way,
　　　rude Children, better fed then taught,

11　Abus'd her as she pass'd along,
　　　because of her deformity:
　　As she suffer'd all this wrong,
　　　poor Soul, she wept most bitterly.

12　Her Mistress said, *Do not lament*
　　　in Tears, and make this pitious Moan;
　　But labour, labour for content,
　　　and put thy Trust in God alone.

13 The Bible then she took in hand,
    for to compose her grieved mind;
  Where she in *Mark* did understand,
    what cure the Palsie-man did find.

14 By Miracle, from Iesus then,
    his perfect Health he did receive;
  Yet Scribes and Pharisees were men
    that would not his great Works believe.

15 *O then,* reply'd this youthful Maid,
    my very Heart is fill'd with grief;
  I wonder they cou'd be, she said,
    such stubborn Men of unbelief.

16 *Would I had lived in those Days,*
    when he those mighty Wonders wrought,
  My Tongue should have set forth his Praise,
    tho' Scribes did set his Works at naught.

17 *Nay, gracious Lord, I do believe,*
    thou able art to cure me still,
  And I might soon my Limbs receive,
    if it were but thy blessed will.

18 These Words she had no sooner spoke,
    but Nerves and Bones did snap amain
  Thus God, who she did then invoke,
    in love her Limbs restor'd again.

19 Likewise this poor distressed Maid,
    who many Years this Grief endur'd,
  Did think she heard a Voice which said,
    Arise and walk, for thou art cur'd.

20 She then arose, and walk'd [1] upright,
    across the Room, then to and fro,
  Praising the Lord, as well she might,
    who did such dear Compassion show.

[1] *Text* walk.

21 Thousands hath seen her walk alone,
        both Young and Old, nay Rich and Poor,
    Who crys, the like was never known
        these many hunder'd Years before.

Printed for *I. Blare*, at the Looking-glass on *London-bridge*.

Additional Notes

ADDITIONAL NOTES

PAGE 7

Perhaps I should have remarked that Bartholin's account of Lazarus is reproduced in T.R.'s *The Amazement of Future Ages*, 1684, pp. 74–76, and that the British Museum broadside of 1815 also states that "in vol. II of the Eccentric Magazine, we have an entertaining account of a person of the name of JAMES PORO, who was born at Genoa, in the year 1686: he was publicly shewn in London, in 1714. This singular creature had an excrescence growing out of his side resembling a human being."

Martin Parker is frequently referred to in the successive issues of the almanac *Poor Robin*. For example, he appears in its "Roundheads' or Fanatics' Calendar" for May 31, 1663, January 6, 1664, May 27, 1668, May 29, 1669, May 30, 1670. *Poore Robin's As-tronomical Predictions*, 1665, pp. 23–34, has a scornful aside: "as *Martin Parker* well observes, those trees that blossome this month [June], are seldome bitten with the forst [*sic*]." In the almanac for 1681, A2, is this important reference (cf. my *Cavalier and Puritan*, p. 10): "*Martin Parker* an Asstrological Poet and a Tapster, who having in his time made many *Tiburn Dirges*, and could prognosticate thereby that the party was hanged, in one of his *Folio* Ballads thus concludes.

> *When Sun is gone,*
> *Then Night comes on.*"

PAGE 26

John Looks likewise often appears in the fanatics' calendar of *Poor Robin;* for example, in the issues for October 30, 1681, November 24, 1684, November 28, 1687, November 26, 1689. In *Merlinus Anonymus*, 1655, C6–C6ᵛ, "Raphael Desmus," or S. S. (probably Samuel Sheppard), predicts that "the more part of this year shall be spent in mirth, and some shall hunt for pleasures al *England* over though they take *Tyburn* in their way, many fine Sonnets, curious Canzons, and amarous Odes shal be penned this year by the two most accomplished Bards, *Murford*, and *Looks*." Nicholas Murford, a tavern-keeper, published his *Fragmenta Poetica* in 1650, and is attacked in Sheppard's *Faerie King*, fol. 80ᵛ (*ca.* 1650).

PAGE 36

An undated (about 1648) loyalist news-book, *Mercurius Insanus Insanissimus*, p. 28 (Bodleian, Malone 740), refers to the source of this ballad, — "a letter from *Brotherton* in *Yorkshire* as followeth":

ADDITIONAL NOTES

On Easter *day at* Brotherton, *it began to raigne wheat (that is the likelyest Grain* I *can compare it to) and every day since it hath raigned in more or less quantity; it fell at the first but in two places of the town, but now it lies scatered throughout, I have sent you here a sampler of it. But at the first faling it was of a fresher and more orient cullour (rather inclining to blood then Purple) at the first I made some question of the truth of it, but was confirmed upon the place by the whole* Towne; *and at that instant it raigned this upon my mans hat and handkerchif* [which he held in his hands] My Lady *Ramsden also gathered some of it herselfe (but newly falne]* which shee sent to Seriant *Green* [one *of the Iudges of the Sheriffs court, at guild Hall London.*]

This Letter was sent, with some of the Wheat to one Mr. Hurst, an Officer belonging to Woodstreet Cownter, who also keepeth the Fountaine Tavern in St. Anns Lane neere Aldersgate, where if any one be diffident or doubtfull of the truth, they may be satisfied either by Mr. Serjeant Greene, or Mr. Hurst. in the same letter was this following addition.

Vpon the warres breaking out betwixt the two Nations (some 8 yeares agoe) the like happened at Knottingley (the Towne on the other side the River, Fere briggs being between them) I will not tell you of Apparitions of men training upon a moore, not far from thence, called Barkstone moore, (because I saw them not but many credible persons do report it; these things fill all mens Heads with feares of a new bloodie VVarre, of which (without those sad presages) there are too many presumptions; God of his mercy protect us.

The brackets in the foregoing passage occur in the original, but I have corrected a few misprints.

PAGE 62

An undated broadside, "The Theatre of Gods Judgments . . . in 18 remarkable Examples" (British Museum, 816. m. 24 [88]), printed by C. Hussey at the Flower-de-luce in Little Britain, includes this item:

10. A woman in *Derbyshiere* having cosoned a boy of some money, was charged with it; but she stifly denyed it, and being after urged to confess the truth, she, (in a fearful manner) prayed God that if she had it, the earth might open and swallow her up quick, and immediately the earth opened and she sunk into it, and being afterward digged for, she was found nine foot deep in the earth, and that very money was found in her pocket.

PAGE 81

Stephen Batman, in *The Doome warning all men to the Iudgemente*, 1581, pp. 408–409, also tells the story of "the Citie of *Prage* in *Bohemia*" and "the towne Clarkes Wyfe called *Margaret*, of the age of fiftie and nine yeares." It had earlier been written up in a ballad, perhaps about 1555, of which Francis Douce owned three fragments (E. 35) that are now in the Bodleian. Of the Bohemians we read

That when they did no harme suppose,
[A w]onderfull great storme arose:
[Th]at they whiche in the Cittie weare,
[Du]rst not put out their heads for feare.

[238]

ADDITIONAL NOTES

In the tempest and earthquake, which lasted "an hower and a halfe," "ninteene houses fell sartaine, [six]e Parsones also there was slaine." A storm of hailstones, which did "waie three quarters of a pounde," "did continue halfe an hower," "thunder till nine did last," and then at midnight "it waxed light so fast" as if "it had been faire daie light."

> ¶Yet marke againe what I shall saie,
> A wonder greate doen in *Praga:*
> A woman that was graue and sage,
> Of nine and fiftie yeares of age:
> Whiche halfe a yeare sore . . .
> . . . .
> So that she was pricked with sodaine feare.
>
> ¶She beyng in this heauie plight,
> Was delyuered in that same night:
> Of three children straunge for to beholde,
> Whiche semed to be three yeares olde.
> Haueyng [th]eir full teeth in their iawe,
> . . . .
>
> . . . .
> . . . .
> Then after they had liued one daie,
> The first borne childe these wordes did saie:
> The daie appoincted whiche no man can shun,
> Then the seconde childe to speake begun.
>
> ¶The seconde child these wordes then said,
> Where shall we finde liuinge to burie the deade:
>   [Presumably six lines are missing.]
>
> These wordes once saied thei dyed straight waie,
> And not one worde thei more did saie:
> So then it waxed darke againe,
> Untill the mornyng this is plaine. . . .

The exact source of the Wood ballad was an eight-page pamphlet (preserved both in the Bodleian and in the British Museum), the impressive title of which, inexactly given on page 81, runs thus:

A Strange and True/ Relation/ Of a Wonderful and Terrible/ Earth-Quake,/ That hapned at HEREFORD on *Tuesday* last, being/ the First of this present *October*, 1661./ Whereby/ A Church-Steeple and many gallant Houses were thrown/ down to the ground, and several of the Inhabitants slain;/ with the terrible Thunder-Claps and violent Storm of/ great Hail-stones that then fell, which were about the big-/ness of an Egge, many Cattle being thereby utterly de-/stroyed as they were feeding in the Field./ Also,/ The prodigious and wonderful Apparitions that was seen in/ the Air, to the great amazement of all Spectators, who/ beheld two perfect Armes and Hands:/ In the Right-hand,/ being graspt a great broad Sword, and in

ADDITIONAL NOTES

the Left, a Bowl/ full of Blood, from whence they heard a most strange and/ loud Voice, to the wonderful astonishing of all present, the/ fright whereof causing divers Women to fall in Travel, a-/mongst whom the Clerks Wife, named *Margaret Pelmore,*/ fell in labour, and brought forth three Male-Children, who/ had all Teeth, and spake as soon as they were born, and/ presently after gave up the Ghost and died together, the/ like having never been known before in any Age!/ The Truth hereof is witnessed by/

Francis Smalman, and *Henry Cross,* Churchwardens. *Peter Philpot.* Constable.	*Nicholas Finch,* Gent. *James Tulley,* Gent. *George Cox,* *Robert Morris,* *Thomas Welford,* &c.

This pamphlet is adequately summarized in the ballad.

PAGE 101

The burning of the De Laun family is often referred to in the almanacs: as, in George Wharton's *Calendarium Carolinum,* 1664 (December 26); William Lilly's *Merlini Anglici Ephemeris,* 1667 (December 27); James Bowker's *Kalendarium Astronomical,* 1668 (December 26); Richard Saunders's *Apollo Anglicanus,* 1674 (December 25).

PAGE 107

John Drope's broadside is preserved also in one British Museum collection (1871. e. 9 [19]) in an issue dated 1666, and in another (the Bagford Ballads, C. 40. m. 11 [76]) in a revised edition of 1682.

PAGE 114

The woodcut of Tarlton also appears on a ballad in the Douce collection, II, 206ᵛ.

In *The Drummer of Tedworth* (1716), a book the full title of which is given below in the notes to page 172, we are misinformed that "our comick Poet" who wrote *The Drummer* was Sir Richard Steele.

The Kingdoms Intelligencer, April 20–27, 1663, as well as *Mercurius Publicus,* calls the drummer William Drury; both papers reprint his examination and that of Mompesson.

PAGE 139

A picture and a description of the monstrous Wiltshire twins appear also in Gerardus Blasius's *Fortunius Licetus de Monstris,* Amsterdam, 1665, p. 316. Pepys noted in his diary, November 11, 1664, that, as he and others were waiting in the Council Chamber at Whitehall, there "was a gentleman attending here that told us he saw the other day (and did bring the draught of it to Sir Francis Prigeon) of a monster born of an hostler's wife at Salisbury, two women children perfectly made, joyned at the lower part of their bellies, and every part perfect as two bodies, and only one payre of legs coming forth on one side from the middle where they were joined. It was alive 24 hours, and cried and did as all hopefull children do; but, being showed too much to people, was killed."

PAGE 162

Both this ballad and a 'small godly book' on Gabriel Harding are enumerated in William Thackeray's famous list (about 1690) of his stock in trade (preserved in the Bagford collection, C. 40. m. 10 [2]).

PAGE 168

Reference should also be made to *News from the Sessions House in the Old Bailey. Being An exact account of the Tryal, Conviction and Condemnation of . . . Francis Jackson, Walter Parkhurst, John Williams, John White,* 1674 (British Museum).

PAGE 172

The narrative of Edward Avon is also given (pp. 39–48) in *The Drummer Of Tedworth; Containing, The whole Story of that Dæmon, on which is founded, The new Comedy of the Drummer: Or, The Haunted House. With a particular Account of several Gentlemen of Fashion who went to see, and hear it; and of two Persons of Quality, sent on Purpose by King Charles II. To which is added, A large Relation of the Marborough-Ghost, seen frequently in the Day time. And Attested by the Reverend Mr. Joshua Sacheverell, Rector of St. Peter's-Marlborough. Father of Henry Sacheverell, D.D. Rector of St. Andrew's Holbourn* (1716). The anonymous author declares that his narrative "*was taken by* William Baily, *Esq; a Justice of Peace, in the Presence of* Christopher Lypyatt, *Esq; Mayor of* Marlborough, *Mr.* Rolf Baily, *Town Clerk, and Mr.* Joshua Sacheverell, *Rector of St.* Peter's Marlborough, *and Father of* Henry Sacheverell, D.D." He adds: "This being a most surprizing Event, and attested before Dr. *Sacheverell*'s Father, who, though a very *Low Churchman*, and Son of Mr. *Sacheverell*, a *Puritan* Minister of *Wincaunton* in *Somersetshire*, was an honest modest Man, and one whose Word was much more to be rely'd upon, than some Men's Oaths of *Abjuration*, &c. I have left the Story in the plain *Wiltshire* Style as I found it, but not with an Intention that any one of our modern Comick Poets should make use of it as an Incident in any future *Comedy.*"

A Thomas Goddard of Marlborough, by the way, is referred to in William Houlbrook's *The Loyal Black-smith And No Jesuite,* 2d ed., 1677, p. 45.

[241]

ADDITIONAL NOTES

PAGE 179

Another, and a very interesting, account of the Hennington ghost is given in a letter written on January 17, 1675, by one Fr. Morgan, of Kingsthorpe, to Robert Hooke. It is too long to reproduce here, but it may be read in *The Antiquarian Repertory*, IV (1809), 635–637.

PAGE 196

The title of the Leominster pamphlet was taken from the printed catalogue of the British Museum. I have since seen the pamphlet itself (another copy of which is in the Bodleian), and give its exact title below:

Strange News From/ Lemster in Herefordshire,/ Being a True/ Narrative/ Given Under several Persons Hands there, of/ a most Strange and Prodigious/ Opening of the Earth/ In Divers places thereabouts./ Also, a True Relation of several Won-/derful Sights, *viz.* A *Hand*, an *Arm* and *Shoulder*/ of the bigness of a Mans; And *Sadles* of Blood-Colour;/ which were seen to Arise out of the Earth and Ascend up to/ the Skyes./ Likewise, a Strange and Terrible Noise of Fighting,/ which was heard during this Miraculous Accident./ All Attested by several persons of Worth and/ Reputation; and Exhibited for Publick Information./ Licensed, *May* the *Third.*/ *London.*, Printed for *B. Harris*, 1679./

This *Strange News* makes no reference to Mrs. Griffithes.

PAGE 200

"The Theatre of Gods Judgments," referred to above in the additional note to page 62, states:

14. In *January*, 1677. One *John Duncalf*, of *Kings-Swinford* in *Stafford shire*, came to a Womans house to beg Victualls and drink, who freely gave it him; but while she stooped to draw him some Drink, he stole her Bible: being questioned about it, he stifly denied it, and wished that, if he stole the Bible, his Arms and Leggs might rot off, and accordingly they did in a little time after; and then he confessed the fact, and acknowledged that it was a Judgement of God upon him.

PAGE 215

It would be gratifying if our Dorothy Winterbottom happened to be the "Dirty Doll" who is listed in the fanatics' calendar of *Poor Robin* for November 26, 1672, November 22, 1674, November 1, 1676, May 7, 1677, May 10 and December 29, 1678.

PAGE 219

There are two copies of the pamphlet on Thomas Cox in the Bodleian (Ashmole G.12 [213] and Gough Middlesex 14 [16]).

ADDITIONAL NOTES

PAGE 225

The sad case of the "distressed gentlewoman" is closely paralleled by that of Sarah Bower, or Bowers, in 1693, as related in pamphlets by "Dr. M. D." and Richard Kirby (Bodleian, Gough Middlesex 14 [8] and [9]) and in a broadside called "Wonder of Wonders," 1694 (British Museum, 719. m. 17[17]).

PAGE 229

On Miss Maillard see also Richard Lapthorne's letter of December 22, 1693, printed in *Fifth Report of the Royal Commission on Historical Manuscripts*, app., pt. I, p. 384.

Indexes

INDEX OF TITLES, FIRST LINES, REFRAINS
AND TUNES

Titles, first lines, and refrains are printed in roman type, titles being distinguished by double and refrains by single quotation-marks. Tunes are printed in italics. An asterisk indicates that the ballad in question is merely referred to in the present volume.

INDEX OF TITLES, FIRST LINES, ETC.

INDEX OF TITLES, FIRST LINES, ETC.

INDEX OF TITLES, FIRST LINES, ETC.

INDEX OF NAMES AND SUBJECTS

References are to pages. A number in parentheses points to a stanza, an *n.* to a foot-note.

A., H., on a fasting girl, 36
A., W. *See* Avon (W.)
Aberdeen, Scotland, monstrous twins exhibited in, 9
adder, an, Mary Dudson swallows, a ballad, 132
Addison, Joseph, *The Drummer*, 115
Adlington, Lancashire, monstrous twins born in, 139
Albemarle, Duke of. *See* Monck
Allen, Sir Thomas, his daughter burned alive, 102
America, "prodigious" events in. *See* Brooklyn, Indiana, Manchester (Vermont), Maryland, Minneapolis, New York, Newbury, Peru, Tampico
Amsterdam, Italian twins exhibited at, 7 n.
Andersen, H. C., mentioned, 45
Andrews, Elizabeth, stationer, 106, 145
Andrews, John, stationer, 57
angel, an, appears to James Wise, 62; orders the Devil to kill Gabriel Harding, a ballad, 162, 241
Anne, Queen of James I, blazing stars and her death, 21
Anthony and the "Tedworth" demon, 116.
Antiquarian Repertory, The, cited, 242
Antwerp, Belgium, a proud lady of, killed by the Devil, 76
apparitions, at Barkston Moor, 42 (9), 238; in the air, Prague, Carlstadt, Hereford, 81 ff., 238 ff., various places, 38; in Germany, 21; Josephus on, 21. *See* ghost
Apulia, Italy, an earthquake at, miraculous preservation of a baby in, 38
Arber, Edward, *Transcript* of the Stationers' Registers, cited, 37 f., 107
Ashley, Staffordshire, wheat rains at, 210
Ashover, Derby, the prodigy of Dorothy Matley at, a ballad, 62, 238
Ashton, John, cited, 114 n., 162
Athenæum, The, cited, 37, 95
Athenian Mercury, The, cited, 230
Austria, prodigies in, 23 f. *See* Bohemia, Bregenz, Cracow, Prague
Averell, William, on wheat-showers, 210
Avon, Edward, the ghost of, appears, a ballad, 172, 241
Avon, Margaret, wife of a ghost, 173
Avon, William, son of a ghost, 172 ff.

B., A., gives birth to a child, a toad, and a serpent, ballads, 186, 191
Babb, Humphrey and Margaret, the rotting man steals a Bible from, 200, 242

INDEX OF NAMES AND SUBJECTS

INDEX OF NAMES AND SUBJECTS

INDEX OF NAMES AND SUBJECTS

INDEX OF NAMES AND SUBJECTS

INDEX OF NAMES AND SUBJECTS

INDEX OF NAMES AND SUBJECTS

INDEX OF NAMES AND SUBJECTS

INDEX OF NAMES AND SUBJECTS

INDEX OF NAMES AND SUBJECTS

INDEX OF NAMES AND SUBJECTS

INDEX OF NAMES AND SUBJECTS

INDEX OF NAMES AND SUBJECTS

INDEX OF NAMES AND SUBJECTS

INDEX OF NAMES AND SUBJECTS

INDEX OF NAMES AND SUBJECTS

INDEX OF NAMES AND SUBJECTS

INDEX OF NAMES AND SUBJECTS

INDEX OF NAMES AND SUBJECTS